HOW FINLAND SURVIVED STALIN

HOW FINLAND SURVIVED STALIN

From Winter War to Cold War, 1939–1950

KIMMO RENTOLA

Translated by
RICHARD ROBINSON

YALE UNIVERSITY PRESS
NEW HAVEN AND LONDON

Originally published as *Stalin ja Suomen kohtalo*, Otava, 2016. English language edition published by agreement with Kimmo Rentola and Elina Ahlbäck Literary Agency, Helsinki, Finland.

All reasonable efforts have been made to provide accurate sources for all images that appear in this book. Any discrepancies or omissions will be rectified in future editions.

For information about this and other Yale University Press publications, please contact:
U.S. Office: sales.press@yale.edu   yalebooks.com
Europe Office: sales@yaleup.co.uk   yalebooks.co.uk

Set in Adobe Caslon Pro by IDSUK (DataConnection) Ltd
Printed in Great Britain by TJ Books, Padstow, Cornwall

Library of Congress Control Number: 2023946539

ISBN 978-0-300-27361-8

A catalogue record for this book is available from the British Library.

10 9 8 7 6 5 4 3 2 1

Contents

Illustrations

Maps

Abbreviations

Archival and publication abbreviations can be found in the Bibliography

AK	Armia krajowa, Polish Home Army (1942–45)
Cominform	Information Office of the Communist Parties (1947–56)
Comintern	Communist International (1919–43)
EK	Etsivä keskuspoliisi, Detective Central Police (Finland, 1919–38)
GRU	Glavnoe razvedyvatel'noe upravlenie, Soviet military intelligence
GUGB	Glavnoe upravlenie gosudarstvennoi bezopasnosti, Soviet main administration for state security 1934–41
LVO	Leningrad Military District
MGB	Soviet Ministry of State Security 1946–53
MI6	British Intelligence Service (=SIS)
MVT	Soviet Ministry of Foreign Trade
NKGB	People's Commissariat for State Security 1943–46
NKID	People's Commissariat for Foreign Affairs
NKO	People's Commissariat for Defense

NKVD	People's Commissariat for Internal Affairs
OSS	Office of Strategic Services, US 1942–45
PCI	Partito comunista italiano, Italian Communist Party
RKKA	Red Army of Workers and Peasants
SAK	Central Trade Union of Finland (1930–69)
SDP	Social Democratic Party of Finland
SIS	British Secret Intelligence Service (MI6)
SKDL	Finnish People's Democratic Union (1944–89)
SKP	Communist Party of Finland
Smersh	Smert' shpionam, Soviet Military Counterintelligence 1943–46
SOE	Special Operations Executive, UK
UD	Foreign Ministry of Sweden
UM	Foreign Ministry of Finland
UN	United Nations
USSR	Union of Soviet Socialist Republics
Valpo	Valtiollinen poliisi, State Police (Finland, 1938–48)
VKP(b)	Soviet Communist Party (Bolsheviks)

Acknowledgments

In addition to those mentioned in the Finnish original, the author wishes to thank the following people, whose generous understanding and support have helped to bring about the book in English.

Professor Stephen Kotkin (now in Stanford) and Ambassador Sir Paul Lever (former chair of UK Joint Intelligence Committee) wrote supportive statements, which certainly helped in finding a publisher.

Ambassadors Mikko Hautala (now in Washington) and René Nyberg (formerly in Moscow) have actively promoted the book and instigated to publish it in English. My friend and colleague Dr Mikko Majander never refused to help.

Professor Geoffrey Roberts (Cork) has offered valuable advice, as have Patrick Salmon (Foreign and Commonwealth Office historian), the late Krister Wahlbäck (Stockholm) and Professor Peter Ruggenthaler (Graz). Dr Sergey Zhuravlyov (Russian Academy of Sciences) was seminal in obtaining Stalin's materials from the Russian Presidential Archives. Now this kind of cooperation is no longer possible. I miss in particular Dr Natalia Lebedeva, who found the Katyn massacre documents.

The Jenny and Antti Wihuri Foundation financed the translation. Dr Richard Robinson did the work skillfully, translating even our national poet better than earlier published attempts.

Yale University Press accepted the book in their program, and Julian Loose negotiated and made the deal. This book has mainly been taken care of by Frazer Martin and Lucy Buchan. The professional level in the publishing house seems astonishing.

My agent Elina Ahlbäck and her staff have efficiently and swiftly taken care of everything necessary.

My Finnish publisher Otava and in particular Dr Jarkko Vesikansa have helped in every way possible. Directors Marita Jalkanen of Kansan Arkisto (including the former Communist Party documents) and Pekka Lähteenkorva of President Kekkonen's archive gave generous permissions for the publication of photographs.

Luckily, there is family. Healthy advice is always abundantly available, as is the joy of following my grandchildren.

Kimmo Rentola, 31 August 2023

Introduction

In 2001 the former President of Finland, Mauno Koivisto, published a small book on the idea of Russia, a theme he had been pondering for decades. He had been a young front-line soldier in the war against the Soviet Union, then after the war a Social Democratic activist fighting hard against the Communists. From the early 1960s, he was among those Social Democratic leaders who saw the necessity to adapt his party to the conditions of growing Soviet influence, at the same time preserving the country's integrity and independence. Lastly, as the President of the Republic, he guided Finland through the collapse of the Soviet Union—at first very carefully, but when the time was ripe, he acted swiftly.

When his book was published in Russian, a Moscow journalist asked Koivisto, "Mr President, what, then, is the idea of Finland?" The answer was one word only, "Vyzhit'." To survive.

This book explores the basis of the survival of Finland, both during the Second World War and immediately after.

Following Russia's invasion of Ukraine, many analysts turned to the past to find historical precedents. The fate of Finland in the Second World War has loomed large in this regard. Indeed, while it is futile to expect history to neatly repeat itself, it cannot be denied that the Winter War, in particular, offers many similarities and plenty of food for thought. In the short but ferocious conflict between Finland and the Soviet Union in 1939–40, Moscow surely underestimated its neighbor's defensive capacity and will to survive.

It is an extraordinary fact that, among the capitals of the European nations participating in the Second World War, only three avoided foreign occupation: London, Moscow, and Helsinki. If the latter sticks out, it is for good reason: Finland was not only on the losing side of the Second World War, it was a small nation of 4 million, situated in the immediate vicinity of the Soviet Union, against which she had to wage two wars in five years. In spite of all this, once the fighting had ceased, Finland was able to hold on to its democratic government and capitalist economy. It developed "friendly" relations—at least on the surface—with Moscow. It did not turn into a "people's democracy," nor was it incorporated into the Soviet Union.

How was this possible? In order to answer the question, I seek to analyze events from the perspective of the Soviet leadership, that is to say, Stalin. My aim is to scrutinize in depth those occasions when Stalin was clearly the main decision maker and when the stakes for Finland were at their highest: when the fate of its social and economic system, its state sovereignty and the lives of its citizens all hung in the balance. The first of these occasions was the Winter War in 1939–40, when Stalin decided to attack and then, in an abrupt volte-face, to make peace. The second was the long journey to a separate peace treaty with Finland in 1944, marking the end of the Continuation War, 1941–44, when Finland allied with Nazi Germany to fight against the Soviets. The third occasion was the spring of 1948, when Stalin pondered whether or not Finland should be made a "people's democracy." Each of these three episodes ultimately concluded with Stalin settling for far less than he had originally intended to get. This book will examine what caused him to back down each time.

Despite the welcome rise of diverse research approaches to military history, the relevance of the field's traditional core area—power politics and international relations—remains undimmed. High politics is not reducible to the social. And it would be a mistake to be blinded by the immorality of the actors or the unpleasantness of their deeds. The historian needs to be guided by reason and to strive for analysis. "A successful revolution can be a tragedy. But tragedies can still be grand geopolitical projects."[1]

Finland: Background

A non-Finnish reader might need an overview of developments before and between the short periods examined in this book.

For six hundred years, beginning sometime in the thirteenth century, Finland was the eastern part of the Kingdom of Sweden. Fundamental Western institutions took hold in the region, such as the Roman Catholic (and later Lutheran) Church. In 1808–09, however, Sweden lost a war with Imperial Russia, and was forced to give up its eastern provinces. Finland became a Grand Duchy of the Russian Empire from 1809 to 1917. It was a separate state where Swedish laws still applied, and had an administration and later also a currency of its own. During the first decades, Swedish remained the official language, until 1863 when Finnish was also granted official status. Russian never became an official language, despite the empire's Russification efforts from the 1890s on. Finland established a unicameral parliamentary system in 1906, and the next year held its first democratic elections, in which both men and women had the right to vote and to get elected. It was the first country in Europe to introduce female suffrage.

Amidst the collapse of the Russian Empire, Finland declared independence on 6 December 1917. Three weeks later this was recognized by the new Bolshevik government in Petrograd. However, escalating tensions between "Reds" and "Whites" culminated in the

Finnish Civil War from January to May 1918.[2] With the help of Germany, the White army emerged victorious, and most leaders and many supporters of the defeated Reds sought refuge in Soviet Russia. The collapse of Germany in November 1918 helped create the conditions for a democracy, and in the elections of 1919 the Social Democrats again became the biggest party. The Communist Party, founded in Moscow by Finnish Reds, remained illegal in Finland until 1944. Official relations between Finland and Bolshevik Russia remained cool.

In 1930, Finland avoided becoming a right-wing authoritarian dictatorship, which was the typical outcome for the new states that had sprung up between Germany and Soviet Russia after the First World War. The kidnapping of the first President of the Republic as well as a failed coup attempt resulted in a loss of prestige and political support for the far-right Lapua movement. From 1937, the country was ruled by a center-left government consisting of Social Democrats and Agrarians. This government enjoyed the support of 75 percent of the electorate. At the same time, Finnish Red refugee communities were destroyed in the Stalinist terror.

These developments created the basic conditions for political actors during the first stage of the Second World War. For Finland, the most decisive issue was the secret division of spheres of interest in the non-aggression pact between Germany and the Soviet Union in August 1939. Finland was given to the Soviet sphere. This period is analyzed in detail in the first part of my book, which focuses on the Winter War.

After the Winter War, Finland's position was precarious. Germany's occupation of Denmark and Norway, and then the defeat of France, put paid to any hope of help from the West, which had seemed a real option during the Winter War. In summer 1940, three small Baltic republics, which had agreed to cede bases to the Red Army and Navy in 1939, were incorporated in the Soviet Union. It seemed fully possible that this would also be the fate of Finland. In

4

fact, secret preparations for this course of action had already begun in Moscow. When Foreign Minister Molotov visited Berlin in November 1940, Stalin instructed him to ask, first and foremost, whether the non-aggression pact between Germany and the Soviet Union was still in force as far as Finland was concerned. Areas had been divided as agreed, except for Finland. Hitler finally answered that "of course" the pact was in force, but Germany did not want any military disturbances in the Baltic Sea region. This response was enough to dissuade Stalin from taking care of Finland there and then.

At that time, Berlin was already considering and making preparations for an attack on the Soviet Union. Finland did not require much persuasion to participate in the offensive, at least to reclaim the territory that had been lost in the Winter War. No formal treaty or deal was signed, but practical cooperation was established through mostly verbal mutual understanding between the countries' militaries. Politically, Nazism was not particularly popular in Finland: the Social Democrats and many in the Swedish People's Party were opposed to it. Key leaders, like President Ryti and Marshal Mannerheim, remained essentially pro-Western. But Germany was, at this point, Finland's sole practical option.

Germany launched its offensive on 22 June 1941, and Finland followed suit a few days later. The Finnish Army was quickly able to conquer the areas lost in 1940, and much more besides, in Soviet Karelia. After these gains, the front was relatively quiet. But with Germany's defeat at Stalingrad in early 1943, it became clear that Finland was again on the losing side. The peace process between the Soviet Union began after the Tehran Conference of the Allies in late 1943. From the Finnish perspective, the main problem was timing: the peace had to be made while the Germans were too weak to enact any effective countermeasures, but the Soviets not yet strong enough to crush the Finnish defenses. How this exact set of circumstances came to pass is described in the second part of this book.

After the interim peace agreement was signed in September 1944, the Allied Control Commission arrived in Finland, directed by Andrei Zhdanov, one of Stalin's closest subordinates. The Communist Party became legal and even entered the government. In the elections of March 1945 the Communist-led bloc got a quarter of the seats and a coalition government of the "big three"—Communists, Social Democrats and Agrarians—was formed. For a time, it appeared inevitable that developments in Finland would proceed along the same lines as in Eastern Europe. It seems that the Soviets believed this, although they were aware that their power was more restricted, because Finland was not occupied, and the introduction of full control and the opening of a path to "people's democracy" was always too early for the Soviets, until it was too late.

With the onset of the Cold War, Stalin finally decided to take care of the Finnish question. His attempts to resolve it in spring 1948 form the theme of the third part of this book. In short, Finland—led by President J.K. Paasikivi—agreed to sign a restricted military treaty with the Soviet Union, which led to the Soviets dropping their offensive plans to facilitate the Communists' road to power. Indeed, the Finnish Communists were subsequently ousted from government after their severe election defeat. A Social Democratic government was formed, which was met by a hostile reception from the Soviets. To some extent, the atmosphere changed in 1950, after Stalin had given the go-ahead for the Korean War and a new Agrarian government had taken power in Finland. The underlying situation remained volatile, and the contrasting scenarios that the Soviets envisaged for Finland are outlined in brief in the book's fourth and final part.

Stalin made big decisions, but of course he was unable to determine their outcomes. History is full of unintended consequences: time and again, the best-laid plans have turned out very differently in practice. Often the result is something that no one involved had sought or wanted to achieve, and occasionally something that no one could even have imagined. As we will see, Soviet policies need to be analyzed in connection with the wider international situation and, in particular, with Britain, since it was a country that was constantly taken seriously by Moscow. Stalin was able to keep abreast of British thinking with the help of the Cambridge Five and other intelligence operations.

Stalin: Background

In Finland, it has been a tradition ever since the Second World War to believe—or at least to say—that our country was somehow a special case for Stalin. Having the opportunity to talk with Stalin on 13 June 1950, Prime Minister Urho Kekkonen claimed that the Finns had found out that "Mr Generalissimus Stalin has a recess in his heart of goodwill towards the Finns." Stalin's reply was courteous, but nowhere near as lofty. Faithful to his habits, he talked about concrete interests. According to him, the Finns were honest men, who accurately fulfilled their obligations. If this continued, every-thing would proceed smoothly.[3] In Stalin's eyes, the most important obligations to fulfill were the war reparations the country had been paying since 1944 and the military obligations agreed in 1948 to fight against any attack through Finnish territory against the Soviet Union.

Of course, Kekkonen "the Rascal"—to quote the appellation given by Communist leader Hertta Kuusinen—was aware that the Kremlin was not the place to speak the plain truth. The heart of the generalis-simus consisted of darker chambers and was ravaged by hidden demons. But it does seem possible that the Soviet leader had come to crave compliments of the sort expressed by the polite Prime Minister. Take the letter Stalin received from the Finnish Communist Party: he had marked sentences where he was thanked for his valuable advice. The better the Communists adhered to his words, the greater their forthcoming electoral success.[4]

Finland was certainly not a special case for Stalin before the Winter War, but not totally unknown either. He had visited the country twice when it was still a part of the Russian Empire. The first trip to a Bolshevik congress in Tampere in December 1905 later became seminal for the construction of the Stalin myth, because it was there that he met Lenin for the first time. As for Finland, he saw that it was a separate half-foreign state, with passports examined at the border with Russia, and with a separate currency. If anything was visible through train windows (it was the darkest month of the year), he would have seen forests and marshes in terrible weather and wondered how it was ever possible to build a state in these distant parts. In November 1917, Stalin visited the Social Democratic Party congress to encourage his Finnish comrades to take power just as the Bolsheviks had done. Afterwards, he offered harsh criticism of the Finns' hesitation and inconceivable timidity—ignoring any objective factors, such as the impact of a different political system. If experience in Baku in 1910 influenced Stalin's policy in Iran in 1946, as has been claimed,[5] it would be believable that the 1905 and 1917 Finnish experiences also left their imprint on him.

In power, Stalin continuously made decisions concerning Finland, but this neighbor was not in any way unique. It was one of the *limitrofy*, in the western border-country group with Estonia, Latvia, Lithuania, Poland and even Romania.[6] It was less common to see Finland in the Nordic (Scandinavian) group. However, there was one occasion when Finland did stick in Stalin's mind. In 1930, the Soviet Union's trade representative Suren Erzinkian defected in Helsinki, and tried to claim 5.2 million marks in bills of exchange from the bank accounts of the Soviet trade delegation. At that time, similar incidents frequently took place across Europe, and as a rule the court cases about money were won by the defector. Except in Finland, where the Helsinki Magistrates' Court ruled the money to be the property of the Soviet Union and found Erzinkian guilty of fraud. (It should be noted that there was no 'Finlandization' at that time,

Finland being as staunchly anti-Soviet as any of the *limitrofy*.) This strengthened the Russian stereotypical view that the Finns were so stubbornly law-abiding and honest that it verged on stupidity. The case was surely remembered by Stalin, since his close ally Anastas Mikoian submitted his resignation, because the Armenian defector had been his protégé and probably knew even Stalin himself. (The discharge was not granted, but for a period Mikoian did lose his responsibility for foreign trade.)[7]

The most significant decision concerning Finland by Stalin before the war was the repression of Finnish-related populations and, in particular, the almost total destruction of the Finnish Red refugees. This was called the Great Hate[8] by the survivors. Finnish institutions— military units, educational establishments and publications—were suppressed and, finally, any use of the Finnish language was prohibited. The specific details did not become known in Finland, but rumors abounded, as some refugees managed to return across the border. The overall picture could certainly be sensed in Finland, and it had an effect on the national mood, particularly impacting the left-wing mindset before and during the Winter War. There was nothing particularly anti-Finnish in these purges; the fate of minority nations was more or less similar, in particular close to the border areas. The repression was led and closely watched by Stalin. When a commission in 1935 proposed the removal of 5,000 families—Finns, Karelians, Ingrian Finns—away from the northwestern border areas, Stalin approved of the idea, but marked in the margin: "Why not more?"[9]

Sources

Extensive Soviet archival sources have been used, even a sizeable amount of intelligence materials. Because of the war in Ukraine, further archival research is now impossible. Extensive use of documents from Finnish, Swedish and British archives complement the picture.

This English translation is not fully identical to the Finnish original that was published in 2016. It has been updated to include source materials that have only recently become available, in particular documents from Stalin's files on Finland obtained from the Presidential Archives of Russia when cooperation was still possible.[10] New books and articles on the topic have also been taken into account.

I

The Winter War

1939–40

Early in the second week of the Winter War, on 8 December 1939, the Soviet torpedo boat *Razvedchik* ("Scout") struck a rock in Lake Ladoga under Finnish artillery fire.[1] If this was a portent of the calamity that would befall the invasion, then Stalin and his *razvedchiki* (intelligence officers) did not yet realize it. At first Moscow thought that the difficulties were technical in nature. A perplexed Marshal Voroshilov could only order the 9th Army "to speed up its advance" on Oulu to sever Finland's land connections to the west.[2]

At the front the Red Army's soldiers already knew that this was not a border incident or occupation, but a war.[3] The Finns were putting up a fierce resistance, not deceived by the puppet government ostensibly formed in the border town of Terijoki on 1 December 1939. This had been cobbled together from the few Red Finns in the Soviet Union to survive the purges, and was headed by the Communist International Secretary Otto Ville Kuusinen. When the seriousness of the difficulties, the scale of the losses and the problem of deserters dawned on Stalin,[4] he prescribed his usual first aid: new NKVD regiments. Seven of them were set up to control the rear, then he started to change the attacking forces' commanders.[5]

From the outbreak of war it was clear that the strategic intelligence of both sides had failed. The Finns knew about their opponent's preparations, but not their extent. They concluded that their eastern neighbor was trying to apply pressure: the Soviets had not issued any ultimatum, and they would hardly launch an attack in the dead of winter. Finnish leaders tended to rely on the support of the West and Sweden acting as a deterrent. Few believed the rumors that the secret part of the Molotov–Ribbentrop Pact, the mutual non-aggression agreement concluded between Germany and the Soviet Union on 23 August 1939, left Finland at the Soviets' mercy.[6]

On the Soviet side there was a failure to grasp that this conflict would not follow the precedent set by their occupation of eastern Poland in September. Then they had entered the country, which had already been invaded by Hitler from the west, with a great show of force: with tanks, airplanes and a million men. They encountered little resistance, however, so less would have sufficed. This was fresh in the memory when the Soviets were making plans to march on Finland in November. One sign of their complacency was the appointment of the greenhorn as the new NKVD intelligence *rezident* in Helsinki. Elisei Sinitsyn had only begun his foreign service earlier that year in Lwów.[7] Another was the strict order given to the Red Army's troops not to cross the Swedish border: they should salute the Swedes at the Tornio River, but they should not communicate further.[8] Only when Stalin's official 60th birthday—on 21 December 1939—came and went without a gift from the front did he inform the front-line commanders that "the war in Finland is a serious war, sharply different from our autumn raid [*pokhod*] on Poland."[9] Such an observation had certainly already been made at the front.

In Finland there prevailed the assumption that, upon the outbreak of war, the Communist refugees in Moscow would convince Stalin that the Finnish working class would side with the Red Army and rise up against their White oppressors. This was proved false on two counts.

First, it was shown that a puppet government was a regular feature of the Red Army's invasions, as it provided ideological justification for the military action. The Terijoki government, therefore, was formed regardless of whether or not the Finns would be politically inclined to support it.[10] Second, it became clear that the terror-stricken Comintern Finns were distant from Stalin and devoid of political influence: their leader, O.V. Kuusinen, was invited only to receive orders, not to help make them.[11]

Moscow's ideological authorities were in the dark about how things really stood in Finland. As Lev Mekhlis, chief of the Red Army's Political Directorate and one of Stalin's inner circle, confessed, it was imagined that "the workers and the peasants would greet us with flowers."[12] Yet it was not just ideological myopia that caused the Soviets to seriously misjudge the situation. Other explanations can now be found by examining the intelligence and security reports sent to Stalin by the NKVD (the People's Commissariat for Internal Affairs). This ministry was responsible for the majority of foreign intelligence and domestic surveillance, and its head, Lavrenti Beria, diligently ensured that the *Khozyain* (the Boss, that is to say Stalin) was kept up to date with its actions. In addition to these reports from the Lubyanka Building in Moscow, documents from both the Leningrad NKVD and the GRU military intelligence have now been published in Russia.[13] Together, these materials offer an opportunity to more accurately assess the information upon which Stalin made his decisions.

The Soviet Decision for War

On 28 September 1939, following the rapid collapse and partition of Poland, the Soviet Union and Germany agreed a new treaty of friendship. This modified the two powers' spheres of influence, and allowed Stalin to turn his attention to the northern countries that fell within the Soviet Union's delineated area.[14] The Western Powers, Britain and France, were still at war with Germany, but during the so-called Phoney War, instead of military action there was only anticipation of it. In the West it was believed that Germany could be demoralized by economic warfare, as in the First World War. Some hoped that the nations could then unite to direct their combined might against Bolshevism; it was precisely this scenario that Moscow feared.[15]

The three Baltic States and Finland did not constitute much of a security threat to the Soviet Union as long as the treaties with Germany held fast, but Stalin exploited his free rein over the border countries to shore them up for the future. He knew that circumstances would change, and Germany's surprisingly easy victory over Poland hardly reassured him otherwise. The Baltic States quickly agreed to cede military bases, but Finland, invited last to the negotiating table on 5 October, proved a harder nut to crack. Increasing the pressure, Stalin had to consider three major intelligence questions: what would Germany do, how would the Western Powers react, and what was the Finns' own capacity for defense?

As to the first, would Hitler keep his word and leave Finland's fate in the hands of the Soviets? In so doing, the Führer would betray the military ties established with Finland during the First World War, when over one thousand Finnish volunteers had fought for Germany. Known as the Jägers, they helped lead the White Army to victory over the Reds in the Finnish Civil War in 1918, and went on to form the backbone of independent Finland's military. Soviet intelligence had kept a mistrustful eye on these connections right up until August 1939 when Moscow made its pact with Germany.[16]

After obtaining Foreign Minister Ribbentrop's signature on the amended treaty in September, the Soviets saw in trade negotiations how the Germans were seeking close economic cooperation. Moscow always valued "deeds" like these more highly than "words," even if the Germans were unwilling to sell their best cannon.[17] Amongst those sent to Germany for procurement purposes was the young Dmitry Ustinov; decades later, during Leonid Brezhnev's rule, he would visit

Finland as Marshal and the Soviet Minister of Defense, trying (without success) to promote military cooperation between the two neighbors. The Brezhnev generation was first acquainted with Finland when they were tasked with organizing support for the regime's official stance before and during the Winter War. Their careers had only recently been rapidly advanced by Stalin's purges, which had left many high-ranking posts vacant. These fast-rising young men did not quite have blood on their hands, but plenty of it at their feet.

Stalin was comforted also by the intelligence reports about Germany. From secretly obtained British intelligence cables, the Soviets saw that Finland's head of military intelligence had been left "very disappointed" by Berlin's unwillingness to offer assistance.[18] In Helsinki, Soviet intelligence learned about a secret trip to Berlin by the former head of the secret police (*Etsivä keskuspoliisi*), Esko Riekki, and a couple of other Germanophile Finns. Riekki had never before heard his colleague Heinrich Himmler be so blunt, with the German commenting: "Stand firm if you want, but we will not help you."[19] Germany's frosty attitude was confirmed by the Japanese military attaché in Moscow, Colonel Doi, who was overheard by Soviet surveillance complaining to his Swedish colleague that he could not comprehend how the Germans could have given the Russians carte blanche in Finland.[20]

With the Germans keeping their side of the bargain, the more pressing question was what the Western Powers and Norway and Sweden would do. Monitoring the British secret cables from Helsinki, Soviet intelligence realized that neither Great Britain nor America had any advice to offer the troubled Finns. All Sweden had to offer was moral support.[21] Nonetheless, there was one cause for concern: notwithstanding the Phoney War against Germany, British intelligence circles seemed to believe that there was "a serious chance" of an Anglo-Soviet war breaking out within the next six months. This was despite the fact that the Foreign Office had instructed all embassies to refrain from anti-Soviet actions and to promote friendly rela-tions.[22] That they were publicly fostering concord but privately fore-casting war caught Stalin's paranoid eye. To at least assuage Sweden, his intelligence let leak that the Soviet Union's demands to Finland did not relate to the Åland Islands, the archipelago between the two Nordic countries.[23] The appearance of the Red Fleet in this strategic region would have threatened Stockholm and riled Germany, whose shipments of iron ore from northern Sweden sailed past the islands.

Finland itself was a minor concern for Stalin, who thought in terms of Great Powers more strongly than ever after the collapse of Poland. Moscow gleaned its most important information about Finland through London and the not-so-secret cables of the British diplomats. When Estonia agreed to Soviet military bases on its terri-tory, the British Legation in Helsinki reported on the mood in the Finnish government. The thought prevailed that, if the Soviets were to demand territorial concessions, "the Finnish would be unable to oppose them, because they are not in the sort of shape [*ne v sostoy-anii*] to be able to go to war with the Soviet Union." Ever the pessi-mist, the Finnish commander-in-chief, Marshal Mannerheim, confidentially informed His Majesty's Government of his personal view that Finland would have to give in to Soviet demands and surrender bases and island airfields. His top-secret assessment reached Stalin almost immediately after having been deciphered in London.[24] On the eve of negotiations, on 11 October, Finland had all men of serving age called up for duty. In the Leningrad Military District it was believed that the Finns deliberately dragged out the talks to gain time to mobilize.[25] That was not the case, but without this precaution the fate of Finland would surely have been different when the Red Army attacked.

Detailed intelligence on the outlook of the Finnish and Swedish armed forces was collected by monitoring their respective military attachés in Moscow. The Soviet information source was referred to as "our agent" in the reports,[26] although the verbatim quotations contained within are also redolent of eavesdropping. Given the circumstances, the attachés were rather loose-lipped, in particular Major Birger Vrang.[27] The Swede was a celebrity in Moscow diplomatic circles, for a recent Soviet spy movie had featured an actor bearing his likeness in the role of the main villain, a foreign military attaché. In the film his dastardly plans were dashed by a sharp-eyed boy.[28]

Discussing the Soviet threat with Vrang, the Finnish military attaché, Major Kaarlo Somerto, was in a confident mood. He and the Finnish headquarters did not believe British intelligence reports that there were thirty-three Red Army divisions on Finland's border, seven of which were in the inhospitable region between the Arctic Sea and Lake Ladoga. He thought there was no way that such a large force could be in that almost-roadless wilderness. (In fact, it turned out to be almost twice the size of British estimates.) Somerto was of the opinion that, when all was said and done, no attack would come, since it would fatally undermine the Soviet Union's much-publicized policy of peace. He informed Vrang that the Soviets were demanding the cession of a number of islands in the Gulf of Finland and a fairly small region on the Karelian Isthmus near Leningrad. Major Vrang responded that if just these parts of Finland were at stake, then Sweden would certainly not intervene.[29]

This comment caught the Soviets' ear. A mere major was not fully authorized to speak for the Swedish government, but he had been speaking freely in his position as military attaché, and Stalin valued the unguarded discourse gathered by his intelligence services more than any government announcement. For him, such details were nuggets of gold, and, in this case, time would show that the Swedish government would adopt the stance Vrang predicted. The Soviets also knew that Somerto expected as much, for they recorded his gloomy complaint: the Swedes repeatedly asserted that the Soviet

Union could not possibly attack Finland because it was a Nordic country, "but they never utter a word about help."[30]

The Soviets gleaned even more vital information from Vrang's discussion with one of Finland's most experienced intelligence officers, Colonel Aladár Paasonen, on 13 October 1939. Paasonen, himself a former military attaché to Moscow, arrived in the city on this occasion as an advisor to the Finnish negotiating team headed by J.K. Paasikivi,[31] and as Marshal Mannerheim's ear on the ground. He briefed Vrang on the Soviet Union's exact demands, detailing the territory that Finland would have to give up on the Karelian Isthmus and in the Gulf of Finland and speculating that the Soviets would also require a military base in Hanko, a seaside town at the southernmost tip of Finland. Strategically, the equally if not even more important Åland Islands were, in contrast, notably absent from the whole discussion.

Having outlined the stakes, Paasonen asked directly if Sweden would aid Finland should war break out. Vrang responded that Sweden would not go to war for those areas, which led Paasonen to declare that Finland was beaten, for without anti-aircraft artillery it was basically defenseless. The two officers then turned to their profession's favorite topic of conversation: speculating over what course a possible war would take. Presuming that a total of twenty-two Soviet divisions would attack (the deflated figure probably received from his Soviet agent),[32] Vrang reckoned that Finland could hold out for six months. Paasonen asserted that the Finnish Army would follow the same tactics that K.N. af Klercker and other Swedish generals used in 1808, when the Imperial Russian Army conquered Finland.[33] That is, they would slowly retreat westwards and northwards towards the land border with Sweden, fighting the whole way.

This was another nugget of gold for Stalin, and a new dimension was added to the Red Army's plan of attack in the latter half of October. Finland was to be cut in two at the latitude of Oulu, in order to sever land ties with Sweden, and this was presented as one of the attack's key aims,[34] which indicates that the idea came from the very top. A second indication of Stalin's personal involvement was the fact that the chief of the Red Army political administration, L.Z. Mekhlis, showed up in Suomussalmi to supervise preparations.[35] Mekhlis was the former editor of *Pravda*, and had distinguished himself in the occupation of eastern Poland by sending glowing reports ("many are crying with joy") of the Soviet soldiers' reception in Lwów.[36] He had also quietly undertaken the task of swiftly implementing the death penalty for those who had served in the Polish Army and for civilians who had committed "counterrevolutionary crimes."[37]

Stalin would reference the Finnish War of 1808–09 explicitly in a directive to his commanders after the first month of the Winter War. He stressed the need to learn from what happened then, when the Russians had been at risk of being encircled.[38]

The Soviet intelligence network in Finland was in a sorry state: experienced *razvedchiki* had been recalled during Stalin's Great Purge, and many of them executed.[39] The ban on recruiting Finns was in force, as Stalin sternly reminded the GRU when it was revealed that a radio operator working for them in Mongolia was actually a Finn, in spite of his clean and honest Russian surname of Voroshilov.[40] Between 1936 and 1938, Soviet intelligence in Helsinki did manage to obtain the summaries that Finland's Ministry of Foreign Affairs compiled from diplomatic reports. These had been disclosed by "a recently [*vnov'*] recruited source."[41] There is no information about who this might have been, and in the available intelligence documents from fall 1939 there is no longer any sign of such materials.[42]

Of the seasoned Soviet intelligence officers from Helsinki, Zoya Rybkina (Yartseva) survived the purges and was sent back as deputy *rezident* to re-establish contact with agents in the city.[43] The most active source was Cay Sundström, the Social Democrat Member of Parliament. The pro-Communist Sundström—agent name GRAF (The Count)—was widely known to be a parlor pink with suspicious connections. As such, he was not privy to sensitive information, nor did he have good relations with Finnish decision makers. When the Parliamentary Foreign Affairs Committee were discussing Soviet demands, Chairman Antti Hackzell exhorted him, a client of Moscow, to keep his mouth shut, as Sundström reported with irritation to his handlers at the NKVD. He also reported that Foreign Minister Eljas Erkko had declared that Finland did not need to make any concessions to the Soviets, as it had the support of England, the United States and Sweden.[44]

A more useful source was Hella Wuolijoki, writer, businesswoman and garrulous hostess of a political salon. She provided information about a "war cabinet" meeting on 16 October and the limit of possible Finnish concessions. The Finnish leadership were prepared to cede some of the islands in the Gulf of Finland and discuss the status of the Åland Islands, but they would not sign a military alliance nor permit any Red Army troops to set foot on the Finnish mainland.[45] This had the air of an offer about it. Perhaps the head of the Social Democrats, Väinö Tanner, was testing the water, aware as he was of Wuolijoki's Soviet contacts. Either way, it was not what Stalin was looking for. The Åland Islands were a tempting proposition, but any wrangling over them would be alarming for Sweden and Germany.

Well-versed in Helsinki gossip, Wuolijoki heard that Finnish leaders were fretting over a joke cracked by Stalin at the Moscow negotiations. When he heard that moving the border would require a significant parliamentary majority, Stalin quipped: "You'll get more than two-thirds, and then you'll have to add our votes, too." This caused the naïve Finns to speculate whether he was planning to interfere in their internal affairs. After the wars Finnish politicians would get used to the idea that the Soviets would try to exert their influence over the country's decision-making processes.

On the basis of her connections Wuolijoki tried to identify the diverging attitudes of the members of the war cabinet. Defense Minister Juho Niukkanen was hostile towards the Soviet Union, Foreign Minister Erkko was indifferent and Prime Minister A.K. Cajander was vacillating. Foreign Minister Tanner was the most level-headed, and he had urged that everything possible be done to find a peaceful solution. He was ready to make concessions, and even praised Stalin's personal role in the first round of negotiations.[46]

Upon the outbreak of war, Tanner became Moscow's *bête noire*, but in October his name was not yet soiled.[47] Colonel Paasonen's memoirs are probably accurate in their account of Stalin's favorable attitude towards Tanner in the negotiations. Beria's son has claimed that his father did not support a Communist puppet government in Finland, but rather proposed "working" the Social Democrats.[48] Even as the situation escalated, Stalin continued to receive relatively unprejudiced Soviet intelligence reports on Tanner's increasingly gloomy views. In the Social Democrats' parliamentary group he announced that the Finnish government would reject the Soviet terms and declared that "the situation is entirely critical." He denounced all talk of demobilization as irresponsible, arguing instead that "we must be prepared for even more."[49]

In addition, the NKVD and GRU intelligence officers provided eyewitness reports of how things were on the ground. They documented panic at the railway stations as people tried to flee the capital city, and repeatedly referenced the peaceful mindset, but dissatisfactory status, of the working class.[50] These accounts are steeped in ideological bias, something that is noticeably absent in the restrained commentary on the Social Democrats' attitudes. This suggests that the Soviets nurtured hopes of gaining influence, since the reports did not reflect the actual state of affairs in the SDP, but rather what the intelligence officers thought their superiors wanted to hear. It was always advisable to toe the line by adopting the tone expected by those at the top.

With military conflict on the horizon, neither the GRU nor the NKVD had permanent *rezidents* in Helsinki. These positions had to be hastily filled: the NKVD chose the aforementioned Elisei Sinitsyn (who adopted the name "Eliseyev" in Finland) and the GRU appointed the similarly inexperienced Colonel Ivan Smirnov. They both arrived in Finland only three weeks before the Soviet attack, and thus had insufficient time to re-establish networks or properly acquaint themselves with an unfamiliar country. In his memoirs Sinitsyn asserts that he warned Stalin about the Finns' weaponry, equipment and willingness to defend their country, but the actual reports of his that have been made public tell a different story. In these he stressed that the Finnish Army was in bad shape, that its rank and file were discontent, that the Finnish economy would be unable to support a military effort, and that there was a pervasive fear of war "in which they [the Finns] see their ruin." In the 1990s excerpts from Sinitsyn's reports were published by one of his successors, who rebuked them for being "utterly frivolous."[51]

Stalin did not make his decisions based solely on intelligence sources. Diplomatic reports of British attitudes also encouraged him to proceed with, rather than postpone, the attack. It is not clear, however, how much the Soviets knew about the internal position of the Northern Department of the Foreign Office. The British diplomats there doubted if "Finland's best course (i.e. from her own point of view)" was compatible with "the most useful service which she could render (i.e. to us)." The Finnish people were horrified by the threat of war and possible Soviet occupation, but for the British it opened up interesting prospects. Entering into war would consume Soviet oil, food and military equipment that could otherwise be sent to the Germans. Besides which, a Soviet invasion of Finland could still bring about a conflict with the Third Reich. As such, from the British perspective it was "desirable that the Finns should fight." For his part, Foreign Secretary Lord Halifax spread the idea that the Soviets might be bluffing. His assessment had an impact on the

*1 & 2. Soviet intelligence officer Elisei Sinitsyn (who adopted the name
"Eliseyev" in Finland) displays his poker face leaving Finland in 1939. When
he left in 1941, he was much bolder—brazenly taking a counter-photo.*

Finnish leadership, as did the outlandish schemes to assist Finland devised by the British Minister in Helsinki, Thomas Snow. One such diversionary tactic entailed tempting Japan to attack the Soviets along the Siberian Railway; this was rejected out of hand in London, as then China would have been left to the mercy of the Japanese, but the negative response took some time to reach Snow.[52]

These fantastic proposals may not have reached the Kremlin, but Winston Churchill's comment to Ambassador Ivan Maisky certainly did. The new First Lord of the Admiralty understood "well that the Soviet Union must be the master of the eastern coast of the Baltic Sea." If Estonia and Latvia were to lose their sovereignty, he was "very happy" that they would be incorporated into the Soviet system rather than the German one. Churchill declared that this was "historically normal," referencing the borders of Imperial Russia, and added that "Stalin is now playing the Great Game, and very successfully"; the British had no cause for complaint.[53] Maisky realized that the British government aimed "to avoid taking a stand against Russia." Sir Stafford Cripps—the future British ambassador to Moscow—explained to him that "the Finns, being awful provincials in politics, think that the 'moral support' of Great Britain is the anchor of salvation."[54] According to Churchill, the Soviet Union's demands on Finland were "fully natural and legitimate." Finland must not be allowed to impede rapprochement between Britain and the Soviet Union; the latter had "every reason to be a dominant power in the Baltic, and this is in the British interest." The stronger the Soviet hold on the area, Churchill informed Maisky, "the better for you and for us, and the worse for Germany." In the Great War, Russia had lost the east coast of the Baltic in spite of the fact it had allied with the West and helped save France in 1914. Now Moscow was due its compensation.[55]

To sum up, the British line on Finland was conflicted. On the one hand, they communicated their support to Helsinki and their skepticism of Moscow's sincerity; on the other, they almost incited the Soviets to take what was theirs, albeit while warning about the consequences of military action. This was not necessarily out of duplicity or double-entry bookkeeping, which Maisky saw as a quirk of the English,[56] but the emphasis of different geopolitical angles according to contact and context. Nonetheless, for Moscow the information from London made it clear that Finland's situation was hopeless.

In late November 1939 the Soviets orchestrated a false-flag attack on the border village of Mainila, using it as an excuse to renounce their non-aggression pact with Finland. This had been signed by Maisky in 1932 during his time as Soviet Envoy to Finland, and, with the prospect of war now looming on the horizon, he pondered what the British response might be. Lord Halifax told him that, although public opinion was strongly on the side of the Finns, His Majesty's Government had little interest in the matter. The Foreign Secretary was "shocked" by Maisky's supposition that the British were supporting Finland. The Under-Secretary of State for Foreign Affairs, R.A. "Rab" Butler, denied that his government was conducting a Machiavellian campaign in Finland. The British had discreetly advised the Finns to avoid being "unreasonable" in the face of Soviet demands, but the Finns were so "obstinate and inflexible" that the message did not get through. Butler felt that an improvement in British–Soviet relations was entirely possible; Halifax, for his part, proposed developing trade connections. Maisky's conclusion was withering: "Who will help them [the Finns]? The Swedes? The English? The Americans? Like hell they will! [*Cherta s dva!*] A racket in the newspapers, moral support, oohing and aahing—that, yes. Troops, aeroplanes, cannons, machine guns—that, no. Butler told me plainly yesterday: 'Should anything happen, we wouldn't be able to send a single warship to Finland.'"[57]

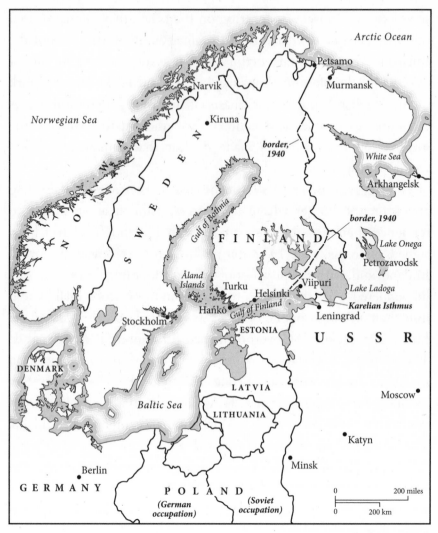

1. Northern Europe during the Winter War: November 1939–March 1940.

Ideology itself did not significantly impact the Soviets' decision to go to war, which was more founded on strategic calculations and intelligence-based predictions of the other Great Powers' actions. However, ideology did influence how the attack was politically framed and sugar-coated. As has been noted, the creation of the Terijoki government did not reflect any faith in the Finnish working

class accepting it. Rather, it was formed out of an ideological assessment of what the consequences might be if a major war broke out.
The First World War had flung the Bolsheviks into power in Russia
and led to a wave of revolutions across Europe. A new great war
would revive the possibility of this reoccurring, especially when
turmoil and upheaval had been such central themes in the recent
Spanish Civil War.[58]

On the anniversary of the October Revolution in 1939, there were
discussions in Moscow about how comparable their present situation
was to the years of the First World War. Or, more accurately, there
was a monologue on the topic in Moscow, given by Stalin to his
inner circle.[59] Since he had broached the matter, those who had been
in attendance dared to spread the word. They were inclined to think
that the Soviet Union's existence was the sort of factor that could
again make a wave of uprisings a possibility in the early stage of
the war. A single inevitable scenario was not assumed, but rather
a foreshadowing that the cost of a major war would be great
upheaval. Mekhlis explained to trusted writers that Germany had
done useful work by destabilizing British imperialism, "the implo-
sion [razrusheniye] [of which] will result in the widespread collapse
of imperialism—this is evident." The Soviet Union's main enemy
was "England, naturally." Vsevolod Vishnevsky, the author of An
Optimistic Tragedy, was present and taking notes. Discussing Finland,
Mekhlis vowed to get what the Soviets were looking for, "if not will-
ingly, then with blood."[60] Stalin seemed inclined to think that
Germany was weak. At the conclusion of the Friendship pact with
Germany on 28 September, he said to the German ambassador that
should Germany face a serious attack, the Soviet people would come
to their aid and "not allow Germany to be wiped off the face of the
earth."[61] Following this line of thought, Comintern Secretary General
Georgi Dimitrov speculated that anti-fascist and disillusioned sentiments would grow among Germany's masses and that liberation
movements would rise up in the occupied countries. Together these

would bring defeat for Hitler and destruction for Germany. O.V. Kuusinen knew that his "government" was connected with these ideas flying around: "The revolutionary perspective is now real, even though there is no reason to shout about it."[62]

There is no need to demonstrate how misguided this wishful thinking was: subsequent events speak for themselves. At the start of the war key actors in Moscow, on the basis of their ideological principles, underestimated both the West's and Germany's strength and resilience. They also overestimated the Soviet Union's revolutionary appeal, as though foreign countries and citizens had no clue what sort of state it had become since its revolutionary days.

Stalin had a voracious appetite for raw intelligence information, and not much interest in anyone's analysis besides his own. "Don't tell me your thoughts," he was said to have exclaimed to his intelligence officers, "state the facts and leave!"[63] He was always concerned about the trustworthiness of the human sources. His notes in the margins of the intelligence reports show that he demanded to know the agents' identities and those of the officers responsible for them. The reliability of a source is undoubtedly essential, but it is unwise to evaluate the information's validity based on this alone. Reliability and validity are usually first assessed and graded separately. If the trustworthiness of the source is the sole criterion, and if this is primarily dependent on one man's judgment, then blind spots will emerge and the potential jeopardy will be greater if events take a turn for the worse.

In late 1939, Stalin did not see that anything could go wrong. His intelligence and diplomatic reports all pointed to him attacking Finland. After the partition of Poland and the agreements with the Baltic States, Stalin could count on Germany remaining neutral. As for the West, Stalin knew that a Soviet invasion could well trigger calls to help the Finns, not least in France,[64] but in practice there was little those countries could do, especially if Sweden, as expected, refused to take sides. In any case the Western Powers would have no time to do anything, as Finland would be taken by surprise and rapidly collapse. Expecting a quick victory, Beria ordered camps be prepared for the imminent arrival of 26,500 prisoners of war. (The need for additional camp space was one of the factors pushing forward the process towards the Katyn massacres of the Poles in 1940.)[65] In order to heighten the surprise the Soviet source told the Finnish and Swedish military attachés on 29 November that Moscow's official line was now "no war, no peace."[66] Moscow's attack began early the next morning.

Soviet intelligence on Finland was ideologically colored, but it could not be blamed for failing to anticipate how steadfast the Finnish resistance would be. The Finns themselves did not foresee it. Information about Mannerheim's pessimistic outlook and about the confusion and lack of leadership in the government was fundamentally accurate, as were the reports detailing the Finnish authorities' doubts about the working class's willingness to defend the country. There was, however, one blind spot: it was impossible to observe, let alone report, the impact that Stalin's terror had had on Finnish left-wing opinion.

Even if Stalin had received better assessments about the fighting spirit of the Finns, he would hardly have paid them much attention. They were inconsequential compared to the big issues he was trying to solve. It would have been wise to remember Lenin's favorite quote from Napoleon: *On s'engage, et puis on voit*. Get involved, then you see.

The War

The manner in which the Soviets began the war on 30 November only served to fortify Finnish unity and resistance. A Great Power was attacking a small neighbor without any ultimatum or declaration of war. It had done so after a border provocation reminiscent of that which the Nazis had carried out in Poland, and it was now bombing civilian targets and workers' quarters. On top of everything else, it had tried to establish the puppet Terijoki government. The stakes were no longer distant islands and small border adjustments. This was about life and death and about the continued survival of an independent Finland. The government in Helsinki was now prepared to make concessions,[67] but the Soviet Union rejected the Finns' attempts to open contact lines by declaring that it was not at war with Finland. On the contrary, all issues had already been settled with the Kuusinen "government."

The puppet government was formed out of ideological necessity and the belief in a rapid victory, upon which the charade could be forced to become reality. In practice it turned out to be a terrible mistake. If the Soviet Union had attacked without a puppet government, invoking only concerns for the safety of Leningrad and the Gulf of Finland, like it had in the negotiations, then the situation would have been quite different, both internationally and within Finland itself.

Now the pessimist Mannerheim was raising his Marshal's baton to lead the Finnish forces, and the would-be appeaser Tanner was emerging as the most resolute political leader. The manual and agricultural laborers, used as they were to outdoor work in wintry conditions, were taking up arms to diligently do their duty for their country, proving loyal to the Center-Left government that they had voted into power. Even known Communists were spotted in their ranks. The Finnish military attaché to Moscow had predicted such national unity three weeks before the attack: "In our country the people will support the government, it won't be like in Poland, where different parties were pulling in different directions." His comment had, of course, been recorded by Soviet intelligence.[68]

The stubborn Finnish resistance deprived Stalin of what he needed the most: swift success. Instead, he was forced to wage a vicious war in awful conditions as an international outcast, condemned across the globe by democratic and undemocratic states alike (except by the

3. *The signing of the treaty between the Soviets and their puppet state, the Finnish Democratic Republic, in Moscow on 2 December 1939. Holding the pen is Molotov; behind him are, from right to left, O.V. Kuusinen, Stalin, Voroshilov and Andrei Zhdanov, who came to Finland in 1944 as the head of the Allied Control Commission.*

Nazis). Worst of all was his newly acquired reputation as an incompetent warlord. If the human sacrifice did not matter—Stalin later coolly remarked that his North Korean allies had no reason to complain, as they were losing "nothing, except for men"[69]—the loss of military prestige certainly stung.

Nor were the consequences on the home front negligible. Not even Stalin was immune to popular opinion, and rumors and hearsay were spreading fast. In the very first days of the war an eager young reporter from the railwaymen's newspaper *Gudok* ("The Whistle") managed to reach Terijoki, the conquered border town and supposed

4. Finnish soldiers heading to the front line at Summa, scene of some of the heaviest fighting in the Winter War, on 14 December 1939.

location of Kuusinen's government. After some looking around and inquiring, he rushed back to Leningrad to call his senior editors in Moscow: "There is no Finnish government in Terijoki, not a single one of Kuusinen's government ministers is to be found in Terijoki, nor have they ever even been there. Kuusinen's government only exists on paper, and our troops are suffering massive losses." As might be expected, the state security organs were abreast of this call, and the most momentous scoop in the newspaper's history went unpublished.[70] The fate of the young journalist is unknown.

Although the majority of Soviet citizens adhered to the official line, a surprising number expressed concern or outright dissenting opinions about the war. And someone was listening: *skorost' stuka prevyshaet skorost' zvuka*, a denunciation travels faster than the sound, as the Russian saying goes. The Spartak Moscow football star Aleksandr Starostin complained that his compatriots were such lousy politicians, as it was obvious to everyone that the Finns were no threat to Leningrad. Now the Soviets had lost friends of democracy across the world, and the popular front was no more. Helmut Liebknecht, the son of the founder of the German Communist Party living as an exile in Moscow, also thought that the invasion would lead to the Soviet Union's isolation. He believed that it would be justified to start a war for the purpose of world revolution, "but these are Hitler's methods."[71] The renowned geologist and ageing academic V.I. Vernadski initially supported Stalin's tactics, believing that the Terijoki government would prove appealing to the Finnish nation, but soon noted in his diary that the figure of Kuusinen "is well-known here, but apparently not well-liked."[72]

Discontent was most pronounced in Soviet Karelia, the western edge of which was supposed to form a part of Kuusinen's Finland, according to the agreement signed by him and Molotov. Finnish-speaking men in the region were conscripted into Kuusinen's army. Bumping into an acquaintance on a Petrozavodsk street, the Finnish-born Philharmonic musician Jalmari Honkanen exclaimed: "How have you not been forced into the devilish [chertovskuyu] Red Army yet?"[73]

But domestic dissent could still be dealt with, to paraphrase Brecht, through classical methods born out of knowledge of reality. Having failed to present the world with a *fait accompli*, Stalin's main concern remained the intentions of foreign powers. The Finns were fighting back, which gave foreign governments the opportunity to consider their options, all the while popular opinion put them under increasing pressure to act. Intelligence was, once again, crucial to the Soviets.

The Germans did not cause any alarm, even if they did allow (and Göring even encouraged) other nations to covertly sell arms to Finland.[74] Soviet intelligence monitored this uneasily,[75] but all their sources, including intercepted correspondence between the German Foreign Ministry and its embassy in Helsinki,[76] pointed to the fact that Germany was not going to interfere. As for Japan, the Soviets had obtained a telegram from the French Envoy to Tokyo that warned Paris and London not to rely on a Japanese flank attack against the Soviet Union's rear. The Japanese were in the thick of their war in China, and they were being threatened by the United States. The French ambassador to Washington made a similar assessment.[77]

The Americans were moved by the Finns' plight, but they lacked influence in these far-flung reaches of Europe, and their ideas were fanciful. At the US Embassy in Moscow, Charles Bohlen—bugged by the NKVD—outlined a compromise: Kuusinen should resign and Paasikivi take his place. This way the Soviets would save face by keeping the structure of their People's Government of Finland and the redrawn borders that came with it. The Finns, meanwhile, would get that which they most desired: peace.[78] Bohlen's suggestion was unrealistic and of little consequence to Stalin. The countries that counted were Britain, France and Sweden.

Britain and France had been mulling over possible anti-Soviet meas- ures for a couple of months, and the invasion of Finland was the impetus they needed to start sharpening their swords. Britain aban- doned the policy of avoiding direct confrontation with Russia, and began pursuing "more aggressive forms of anti-Soviet propaganda," particularly in the Balkans and the Middle East. These were initially designed by intelligence circles to target neutrals in these regions, to reassure them that they had not been left at the mercy of Soviet expansionism.[79] However, the British soon switched tactics and went on the offensive, targeting Soviet populations—those in the Caucasus in particular—with a whispering campaign and propaganda dissemi- nated "by underground means." On the second day of the Winter War, the Foreign Office urged its embassy in Ankara to establish close contacts with the Turkish military, since its General Staff had recently observed that there were opportunities to incite uprisings in the Caucasus. The British also planned to spread subversive propaganda among disaffected elements in Transcaucasia. It was decided that "for purposes of propaganda the Soviet Union should be regarded as an enemy country, and consequently handed over to Sir Campbell Stuart," editor of *The Times* and the head of a secret organization responsible for propaganda operations in enemy countries, known as EH, or Electra House, after the London building in which it was based. Prime Minister Neville Chamberlain approved this new anti-Soviet line on 12 January 1940.[80]

Stalin adopted a similar confrontational stance, and made no effort to hide it. On the day the Winter War broke out, he published an article in *Pravda* charging Britain and France explicitly with starting a major war. Germany had already called for peace, but the Western Powers rejected the idea. Stalin announced that the Soviet Union "openly" supported Germany's peace proposals.[81] So, he tied

5. *A British cartoon about the Winter War.*

6. *A French poster about the Winter War—"Finland defends itself valiantly against the Soviet invasion."*

himself to Hitler even more tightly than before, positioning himself against the West in the process.

Despite already being at war with Germany, London and Paris considered simultaneous military action against the Soviet Union. For a short period this seemed conceivable, but in spring 1940 it became apparent that they had overestimated their own might, while underestimating the strength and intentions of both Germany and the Soviet Union.

Thanks to thorough research on the West's strategies, it has long been known that the British had far more in mind in northern Europe than Finland's well-being. Above all, they wanted control of northern Sweden's iron-ore deposits, which were vital to the German war effort. There were political and logistical obstacles to Britain entering into outright war on the Finnish front, not least Sweden's unwillingness to allow troops to pass through its territory, for fear of German reprisals.[82]

Mannerheim's headquarters were twice visited by Brigadier C.G. Ling, sent at the behest of Sir Edmund Ironside, Chief of the Imperial General Staff. Mannerheim and Ling engaged in a lengthy discussion on 8 January 1940, in which the Finnish Marshal perhaps surprised Ling by believing that his army could hold out until May. While a fresh and large-scale Soviet attack was on the cards, for the sake of prestige, Finland could survive with additional military support of fighter planes, munitions, artillery and, more than anything else, 76.2mm anti-aircraft guns. To get these would be "famous," declared the old aristocrat in his rusty-but-comprehensible English, then "maybe the wonder will happen that we should be victorious—we must be." With regards to manpower, Mannerheim envisaged a foreign legion of 30,000 men, and referenced with a smile the Italian and German "non-intervention" in the Spanish Civil War.

However, the Marshal was reluctant to see regular British or French troops on Finnish soil, for fear that the Germans would take counter-measures and cut Allied supply lines through Sweden. Mannerheim wanted to avoid a situation in which Finland and Sweden were allied with the West against both Germany and the Soviet Union, since the Nordic countries would then be cornered by two hostile Great Powers. He exhorted the Allies to attack by other routes: "Do you think you will make a move in the Caucasus? With the army of General Weygand it should be easy." A worldly wise Imperial Russian cavalry general, Mannerheim realized "that the capture of Baku would be a deadly blow to Germany, as well as to Russia." Turning to the Arctic Circle, rather than the Allies attacking the Finnish nickel mine of Petsamo, Mannerheim recommended they invade Murmansk, or better still—and more distant—Arkhangelsk. "The English," he noted, "have always been good at such expeditions."[83]

As an immediate upshot of this discussion, the British Government Code and Cipher School (GC&CS) were given extremely useful cryptographic materials from Finnish radio intelligence officers, including a bullet-riddled Soviet code book. The exchange of valuable intelligence information is a good indicator of the level of relations between the states. These materials ended up in Finnish hands during the Red Army's attempt to cut Finland in the middle, as Beria was forced to inform Stalin, blaming his subordinates. In recent research the Winter War has even been seen as a decisive turning point for the West's ability to crack the Soviet Union's codes and encryption.[84]

Mannerheim's caution probably influenced London's timetable. Although the British had their eye on Sweden's iron-ore deposits, the expectation that the Finns could hold out until May informed their restrained plan of action in the north.[85] The French intentions were much more grandiose in scale, but, in retrospect, the number of weapons and troops they contemplated using seems to have been unrealistically high.[86]

As fate would have it, Stalin learned the details of the West's plans of assistance primarily from Soviet intelligence channels in Paris, not London. In January he was still receiving Foreign Office cipher cables to and from Helsinki and Stockholm. From these he gleaned that the Finns would get twelve Bristol Blenheims with which to bomb the railways and the cities of Leningrad and Moscow, but otherwise the British were offering only "limited measures" of help.[87] In February, however, the high-level intelligence stream from London was stymied, with important consequences, since the information from Paris made Allied intervention plans seem much more resolute and dangerous.

The British sources did not dry up; they were suppressed by Stalin himself. He became so suspicious of the intelligence emanating from London that Beria took the extreme measure of closing the entire NKVD *rezidentura* there and recalling its acting head—and last remaining officer—A.V. Gorski back to the Soviet Union. Gorski's career continued, so Moscow did not see him as culpable. Instead, the blame fell on the shoulders of the British agents themselves, who were suspected of providing disinformation. The most prestigious Soviet intelligence operation of all time, the Cambridge Five spy ring, was deemed too good to be true. By March, Moscow had come to view one of the five, Guy Burgess, as an agent of the British Secret Intelligence Service.[88]

Stalin was inherently mistrustful, but on this occasion he had good reason to suspect the British of disinformation: the Finnish war. Throughout fall 1939 the London *rezidentura* had reported the pessimism and defeatist attitudes of Mannerheim and his confidants, but now the Marshal's army was creating havoc in the Red Army. On the eve of the attack, Moscow had no cause to expect anything more than protests from London, but now the British were planning for large-scale military operations. Had Perfidious Albion (*'khitrii narod anglichanii'*)[89] been luring Stalin into a trap?

This sense of entrapment was intensified by Stalin's ill-fated attempt to cut Finland in two, which resulted in the Red Army's single worst catastrophe of the war. In the beginning, the Soviets were still full of confidence, so much so that Stalin's henchman Mekhlis almost got himself killed when his car convoy drove blindly into an ambush and he spent a long and frosty night lost in the forest as a result.[90] Worse was yet to come in early January 1940, when the Soviet 44th Rifle Division was routed by the Finns on a remote forest road. News of this only reached Stalin via Finnish news reports from the front line that were translated for him; the commanders of the Soviet 9th Army had fallen silent, having drawn "water into their mouths [*vody v rot*]."[91] On top of it all, Beria was forced to report that, in the chaos, the NKVD 3rd Rear Regiment's commander was shot by its political commissar while the commander was trying to stop troops from fleeing.[92] If an NKVD political commissar shot a commanding officer in order to escape from battle, who knew what could happen next?

7. *The results of Stalin's idea to cut Finland into two: dead soldiers and destroyed vehicles on the distant Raate road, 14 December 1939.*

On 13 January 1940, Beria informed Stalin of a meeting of the Allied Supreme War Council in which members had discussed how to assist Finland. According to intelligence from Paris, the British Minister of War, Leslie Hore-Belisha, had resigned because he was opposed to war with the Soviets. (In reality, he had resigned for other reasons, and had even been contemplating the idea of conquering Leningrad just like the other members.)[93] Stalin had sacked the Jewish Litvinov from the post of foreign minister in May 1939 to get closer to Germany, so he well understood what the departure of the British Liberal Jewish politician could portend: a new Munich agreement between the West and Germany.

The information from Paris was that the warmongers had prevailed in the war council. The most excitable were the fiercely anti-Soviet generals Weygand, Gamelin, Gort and Ironside, who were planning maneuvers in both the Caucasus and northern Europe. A Canadian division would be sent to the port and nickel mines of the northern Finnish town of Petsamo, to conduct operations from there against Murmansk and Arkhangelsk. "The main task will be the conquest of Leningrad," proclaimed the intelligence report, "according to the Allies, this should strike a powerful blow to the USSR." In the same blustering tone, it declared that 400 planes and 200 tanks had already been sent from the port of Bordeaux to Finland, along with 6,000 troops. It also outlined Allied plans to establish a national Russian government and mobilize all White emigrants at the immediate outset of the Western action.[94] Thanks to this report Stalin heard about Petsamo over a month before the Finns, whom the British kept in the dark. A memo from the British Joint Intelligence Committee instructed: "Inform Mannerheim of project at once but make no mention of Petsamo part of the plan."[95]

Later that same day, 13 January, Stalin was informed that French weapons, ammunition, engineering officers and fortification experts were also being sent to Finland. Most alarming was the information that General Weygand would travel to Syria and that plans were in place to launch air strikes against Baku, Batumi and Tuapse. Moreover, it was reported that Turkey would join in the assault on the Caucasus at a later date.[96] Beria took care to point out that this information, from emigrants and other sources, was as yet unconfirmed, but soon also the air attaché in London, I.I. Chernyi, sent a GRU report stating with certainty that air raids on Baku were imminent. He was invited to Moscow without delay, but was unable to substantiate his claim.[97] It is possible that the British were feeding him this information with the aim of unnerving the Soviets.[98]

And unnerved they were. They knew that it would be difficult for the West to intervene directly in Finland: it would be tricky for Allied troops to even get to the front, let alone function effectively without winter combat experience. Operations against Murmansk and Arkhangelsk were a threat, but not a first-rate one, as these northern ports did not yet have the same strategic significance that they would acquire in 1941. The threat to the Caucasus, however, was another matter, since the region produced 90 percent of Soviet crude oil and an even greater proportion of its petrol. If Baku's oilfields were devastated, it would prove fatal to the Soviet Union's war effort before too long, as well as to its commercial and strategic accords with Germany. In response, the Soviets began sending Red Army reinforcements to the Caucasus in the first half of January 1940; a steady flow of troops continued to arrive, soon tripling their military manpower there.[99] On 20 January the Red Army command also issued a new general order, permitting border troops and others to open fire on foreign aircraft entering Soviet airspace without first needing to gain permission from their superiors.

The Germans seized the opportunity to widen the chasm between the Soviets and the West, using several information channels to warn the Kremlin about French plans to attack Baku from Syria. Given Turkey's potential involvement, it became the focus of Soviet diplomatic efforts during the Winter War. Molotov pressed the Turkish ambassador for information about what went on behind the scenes during General Weygand's trip to Ankara and demanded to know what the Turkish Prime Minister had meant when he said that in times like these everyone conceals their aims.[100] Turkey recalled their ambassador, which did little to calm Moscow's nerves.

Soviet intelligence documents from Turkey were not available for this study. Moscow's reactions indicate, however, that Soviet leaders had some sense of what was brewing between Turkey and the West.

The British whispering campaign swelled into something bolder. Campbell Stuart and Rex Leeper, the Foreign Office's head of political intelligence, wanted information from the Turkish General Staff about the situation in the Caucasus and Central Asia, in order to "prepare the ground for action at a later date."[101] The Turkish Prime Minister agreed to the exchange of intelligence, as did the

Afghani government. When the British ambassador outlined his country's intentions to the Turkish foreign minister, Saracoğlu "brightened up and asked whether we had really got to this pitch with regard to Russia." He then showed on a map the regions of the Soviet Union inhabited by people of Turkish race, complaining that Georgians and Armenians formed a curtain between these areas and Turkey proper. The British ambassador acknowledged the curtain's existence in his report, but believed that there was "no reason why it sh[oul]d prove impenetrable once the Soviet frontier had been crossed." Still, it was clear that the realist Turks would not attack the Soviets on their own, even if doing so would help stir unrest in the Caucasus. With this latter goal in mind, the Turks introduced an Azeri emigrant at the British Embassy in Ankara, the former leader of Azerbaijan's Musavat Party and now a Turkish government official. He enquired as to whether the Allies "would seriously consider drawing up a scheme for armed revolt and general sabotage in Azerbaijan."[102]

Moscow intelligence would have been hard-pressed to miss the outlines of these schemes, and of other British ones involving Ukrainian nationalism,[103] since word had got out in emigrant circles, which were well-infiltrated by the Soviets. Given the nature of these channels, it is likely that the details were exaggerated and distorted by the time they reached Moscow. Besides which, the Soviet government had reason to be worried about popular unrest in their southern territories at that time, especially in Chechnya, Dagestan and Tajikistan.[104]

The Soviet Decision for Peace

Georgi Dimitrov, the Secretary General of the Communist International, ventured to keep a diary while moving in power circles in Moscow. He recorded what the Master said, including the very night that Stalin appeared to change his mind about the Winter War. This was at the Bolshoi Theater on 21 January 1940, after a

43

commemoration of the anniversary of Lenin's death, when Stalin gave an overview of the war to Politburo members. At first, his tone was brash, ideologically tinged and, from a Finnish perspective, very ominous:

> World revolution as a single act is stupidity [*glupost*]. It transpires at different times in different countries. The Red Army activities are also a matter of world revolution.
>
> It is clear now that Finland was prepared for a major war against us. They readied every village for that aim. Hangars for thousands of aircraft—whereas Finland had [only] several hundred of them.
>
> There are 150,000 Finnish *Schutzkorpists*—that's where the White Finns are strongest. We have killed [*izbihme*] 60,000; we shall have to kill the rest, too, and that will be the end of it. There should be nothing left but old people and children.
>
> We have no desire for Finland's territory. But Finland has to be a state that is friendly to the Soviet Union.[105]

There are many elements to unpick here. Having begun by taking a dig at his old rival Trotsky, Stalin presented his own theory of world revolution. It would advance piece by piece, one country at a time, and often with the help of the Red Army. Kuusinen's government was a part of this framework, and Stalin would continue to follow this piecemeal model after the war. As far back as 1925 when he adopted the thesis of socialism in one country, Stalin had come to the conclusion that the approaching revolutions in the West would be born from war and their success would depend on the Red Army's support. The failed coup d'état in Estonia in 1924 demonstrated to Stalin that the Red Army presence was fundamental to establishing new realities; without it "nothing serious could be accomplished," for things would never develop beyond ineffectual fuss and clamor. That is why it was necessary to be prepared: "If war starts, we can't sit with our arms crossed—we have to step forward, but step last." At which point the Red Army would throw its "decisive weight" into the mix and tip the scales.[106]

Dimitrov's notes show that Stalin himself was behind or at least allowing the assessment in Comintern circles that there was a revolutionary crisis brewing in Europe. This was explained in more detail in the instructions the Hungarian Communist Party received in Moscow at the turn of the year. According to these binding directives the time had come for the proletariat to go on the attack. The Soviet Union had "abandoned its expectant attitude. The wars in Poland and Finland. This indicates that a revolutionary crisis is to be expected. [...] The Soviet Union is nothing but an elite strike force and tool of the world's proletariat, which can help other states overthrow capitalism." The instructions thanked Stalin for his genius, since he had caused (with the August pact) war to erupt between England and Germany. It would weaken both of them, and ultimately allow the Soviet Union to claim an easy victory. In the fight against capitalism, the instructions promised that the West's proletariat could count on the Red Army's support. This should not be made public.[107]

Still, in summer 1940, Molotov seems to have tried to apply these ideas to the Baltic republics.[108] In practice, however, the Winter War killed Moscow's revolutionary dreams for Europe, at least for the time being. Soon after Stalin's monologue at the Bolshoi Theater, both the Western Powers and Germany proved themselves to be more resilient than the Kremlin had imagined, and it could not then discount the possibility that the rival sides would eventually find common ground. The boast in the instructions to the Hungarian Communists that Stalin had realized Lenin's dream of a shared border with Germany would also come to be seen in a new light. It was not so easy to export revolution that way, as had been believed.

In his monologue Stalin put the setbacks of the Winter War in an ideological context: the Soviets were not just fighting against Finland, but also against the familiar foes that had been lurking in the shadows ever since the Bolsheviks' rise to power. The White Finns and the civil guards (formerly the White Guards) were constant themes in Soviet propaganda. It was ideologically impossible to admit that the Finnish people were united in opposing the Red Army, with workers, smallholders and their children well represented at the front. The industrial city of Tampere had been a Red stronghold during the Finnish Civil War in 1918, but the sons of Red families went on to fight and beat the Soviets in the Battle of Tolvajärvi on 12 December 1939. This symbolic shift in allegiance drew praise from the Swedish labor leadership,[109] but none, of course, from Moscow.

Stalin's statement was informed by more than sheer ideology. Earlier that same day, 21 January, the author Hella Wuolijoki had met two Soviet intelligence officers in Stockholm: Andrei Graur and Boris Yartsev (né Rybkin). Although Wuolijoki was sent there by Foreign Minister Tanner to sound out the Soviets' openness to a peace deal, in NKVD books she was an agent (codename: POET) and treated like one, too, who was required to submit reports.

In her meeting, Wuolijoki informed the Soviets of Tanner's opinions: instead of full war, the Finnish government had expected an ultimatum from the Soviet Union. That would have forced the politicians and the people to make a choice. Without it, they could not agree to Moscow's demands, because contingents of Civil Guards would have opposed, which could have resulted in another civil war. Now the situation had been changed, as a large proportion of the Civil Guards had fallen at the front.[110] Although Tanner—at least in foreign affairs—could best be characterized as a cynical realist, it would be unwise to take these comments too literally. The Civil Guards' death toll had perhaps been exaggerated; Wuolijoki was adept at choosing her words according to her audience and situation. But this is what was reported to Stalin and presumably read by him prior to his reasonings at the Bolshoi Theater. He interpreted the message as a sign of weakness and responded in his monologue with the chilling threat of mass slaughter. He had already been given a heavily exaggerated total of the number of Finnish war dead (as he had the number of Finnish fortifications), but apparently the number was not yet sufficient.

Before the toast Stalin foretold what sort of Finland would be deemed acceptable in the eyes of the Soviet Union. In a way the thought would come true many years later, even if areas were scrabbled even then. In the end the Master raised his glass:

> To the fighters of the Red Army, which was undertrained, badly clothed, and badly shod, which we are now providing with [proper] clothing and boots, which is fighting for its somewhat tarnished honor, fighting for its glory!

Then the atmosphere suddenly changed. Deputy Defense Commissar Grigori Kulik brought bad news. Dimitrov did not specify what it was, only that it was unpleasant. In the manner of ancient rulers, Stalin directed his criticism at the messenger:

> You're lapsing into panic. I shall send you Chelpanov's book on the foundations of psychology.—The pagan Greek priests were intelligent people. When they would get bad news they went to the sauna, bathed, washed themselves clean and only then considered events and made decisions.
>
> The human being takes in through his organs various impressions and sensations—and every kind of shit. There are nerve centers inhibiting this. (But with Kulik those centers are weak!) You have to throw out all the garbage and make decisions on the basis of fundamental facts, not under the influence of momentary moods or terrifying, nonexistent things!

What was Kulik's news? It was hardly likely to be anything from the Finnish front: the Battle of Raate Road had been and gone, nor was the encirclement of Red Army troops at Lemetti, in spite of its scale, the sort of setback to cause such panic. Kulik received and delivered military intelligence reports from different countries, and he had apparently brought a report of the threat against Baku or the whole Caucasus. This can be inferred from the fact that, later that night when the conversation had turned to other matters, Stalin commented as if lost in thought:

> It is not we but the Turks who stand to lose. We are even glad that we shall be free of certain ties of friendship with Turkey.

Stalin, a former theology student, now readied himself to follow the Greek monks by weighing up the facts before making a decision. He found it hard going, and in the fortnight that followed he was observed to be both ill and despondent. Over the next twelve days he worked in his office on just a single occasion, 29 January.[111] His dark mood was reflected in a new wave of top-level executions. After more than a year since the last execution list, the military tribunal received one on 17 January containing 457 prominent prisoners, of whom 346 were to be put to death. Among them were the former Commissar of Internal Affairs, Nikolai Yezhov, and his two deputies, as well as the former Chief of Foreign Intelligence, M.A. Trilisser, and his two successors. There were also members of the cultural elite: the theater director Vsevolod Meyerhold, *Red Cavalry* author Isaac Babel and journalist Mikhail Koltsov, who would be immortalized that same year as "Karkov" in Ernest Hemingway's *For Whom the Bell Tolls*.[112]

Maisky's reports from London put further pressure on Stalin to resolve the Finnish question. In the first half of January the ambassador was still of the opinion that the British, being smarter than the French, would not launch a full-throttle intervention. However, he then noted the idea circulating in London that Germany and the Soviet Union had united as allies, and that the latter was the more vulnerable. Under the effusive deluge (*svistoplyaska*) of public opinion, support for intervention began to convert politicians. Churchill's volte-face on 20 January, marked by a commanding radio broadcast ("only Finland, superb, nay, sublime ... shows what free men can do"), was a decisive turning point for Moscow. In a long letter to Molotov, Maisky concluded that time was running out.[113] Informed by secret telegrams, V.P. Potemkin, as Deputy Commissar of Foreign Affairs, told an acquaintance that the Soviet Union ought to be ready for a major war. He added that Hitler could take part in the West's attack; the Nazi–Soviet pact was not to be trusted.[114]

Hella Wuolijoki's reports helped the Soviets weigh up the facts in relation to Helsinki. Before outlining details, however, she began by sending her regards to her old friend (and erstwhile lover), Trilisser. By morbid coincidence, he was on the execution list approved by Stalin, and was killed only a matter of days later, on 2 February. The intelligence information contained in Wuolijoki's reports made it clear that the Kuusinen government had not the slightest hope of winning popular support. The Helsinki government remained resolutely in power, but was ready to make reasonable concessions to obtain peace.[115]

Had there been time, Stalin would hardly have swallowed his pride by dealing with a stubborn government that refused to disappear even after it had been declared non-existent by Moscow. Not only that, it had undermined the reputation of the Soviet military in the eyes of the whole world. However, time was of the essence. On 28 January, Molotov sent a telegram to Stockholm, stating that, in principle, the Soviets had no objection to make contact with the Helsinki government. This U-turn surprised even the seasoned envoy to Sweden, Alexandra Kollontai.[116] The Kuusinen government was put on ice. Propaganda slogans were immediately softened. The Red Army political administration was now criticized for paying too much attention to international tasks and helping Finnish people against bosses and capitalism. The main slogan should again be to secure the northwestern border and Leningrad.[117]

On 29 January, Stalin commented internally that the British would be making a mistake if "they took the Russians to be as stupid [...] as bears whose heads work poorly."[118] Their heads had to work even harder when Under-Secretary of State "Rab" Butler told Maisky that he still did not know if the British could possibly refrain from action that the Soviets would call provocative. Butler noted that many in London believed the Soviet Union had a "cast-iron" agreement, if not a bloc, with Germany, the mortal enemy of Great Britain. "If only we knew for certain that you really do have a free hand, that you are pursuing your own independent policy, then many things would be otherwise."[119]

On 5 February the Allied Supreme War Council made precisely the sort of provocation that Butler had presaged: it was decided to send troops to Scandinavia. The main northern expeditionary force was to stay in Narvik, Norway, and in the vicinity of Sweden's ore fields; only 15,000 men were to advance into northern Finland. However, the strategic focal point was much further to the south. General Ironside thought that a significant military presence in Crimea would threaten the Soviets' oil production and help stoke unrest in Ukraine. Assessing the implications of hostilities with the Soviet Union on a global scale, the British Chiefs of Staff Committee considered that the key weakness of their would-be foe was reliance on Caucasian oil. Should the Soviets end up engaged in large-scale military action in other regions while still fighting in Finland, they would be faced with severe logistical difficulties. If these were then combined with the loss or sizeable reduction of their oil supply, the upshot might be "a general breakdown of the Russian military, industrial and agricultural systems." That would bring an end to the economic collaboration between Germany and the Soviet Union. The Soviets would defend Baku and Batumi with fighter planes and anti-aircraft artillery, "but the efficacy of these defenses, being Russian, is no doubt not so formidable as their numbers would suggest." Three squadrons of Bristol Blenheims (Mark IV "long noses") would certainly do the deed.[120]

The British saw signs that "popular discontent in Russia is spreading, particularly in Transcaucasia," in spite of the ruthlessness of the regime. Sir Orme Sargent of the Foreign Office demanded that the British Embassy in Ankara obtain Turkish intelligence, since "events are moving rapidly and it may shortly become a matter of even greater urgency than it is at present for us to be able to strike, if not directly, at any rate indirectly, at Soviet interests in the Caucasus."[121]

In response to the Allies' planned actions, the Soviets started preparations for a full-scale war on their southern border. The Soviet Air Force was ordered to send reinforcements without delay to three southern military districts (Odessa, the Caucasus and Central Asia) that had "especially important operational importance." Their goal was to turn defense into attack by bombing British-controlled oil fields in Mosul and Kirkuk in Iraq, the shores of the Bosphorus Strait in Turkey and even far-flung Alexandria in Egypt. The southern military districts were ordered to produce propaganda in English, French, Turkish, Farsi, Urdu and Pashto, the range of languages reflecting the countries the Soviets thought might attack. The most urgent task was, however, the strengthening of Baku air defenses; the order to do so was issued on 20 February.[122] The mere threat of military measures against Baku was enough to unsettle Stalin.

Another urgent measure for the Soviets was diplomatic. Molotov's lengthy written response to Maisky, which the latter then conveyed to Butler, was conciliatory, even humble in tone, given the disdain with which Soviet diplomacy[123] and propaganda[124] had treated the British over the past six months. Rejecting as "ridiculous" the idea that the Soviets would ally with Germany against the West, Molotov sought British mediation in the Finnish war. In order to highlight that the Soviets' primary concern was (now again, as in the negotiations before the war) Leningrad's security, he proposed that the Finno-Soviet border be redrawn in accordance with that established by Peter the Great in the Treaty of Nystad in 1721. This would appropriate far more Finnish territory than Moscow had demanded before the war, but it was still much preferable to the whole of Finland coming under Soviet control via a puppet government, which became the goal once the Red Army began its attack. In addition, the Soviets demanded Hanko and islands in the Gulf of Finland, but they were prepared to hand back Petsamo and its Canadian-owned nickel mines, which they had captured during the war. Such a concession was apparently intended to appease the British, and caused an astonished Butler to ask: "Are you thinking about our mediation?" His Majesty's Government declined to help.[125]

The Germans did not want the Western Powers at the Swedish ore fields any more than they wanted the Soviets, who were now uncomfortably close in northern Finland, so they began to get involved. High-ranking German officials hinted that Finland ought to accept the peace conditions currently offered, for in future they might not be so favorable. In mid-February, SS-Sturmbannführer Hans-Christian Daufeldt, in the upper echelons of the Sicherheitsdienst (intelligence agency of the SS), made a round trip of the four Nordic capitals. Moscow did what it could to keep the Germans from interfering. On 11 February, after months of haggling, the two countries signed a huge economic treaty. One consequence of this was that Finnish exports became far less economically important to Berlin, as the Soviets were offering Germany similar goods at a lower price.[126]

In spite of these efforts, there were signs that Moscow became more fearful of Germany, rather than less. Soviet intelligence observed that German troops were transferred to the east.[127] According to the later memoirs of the Baltic Fleet commander, the Red Fleet got an order at the end of February that warned of a possible attack, led by Germany and also involving Italy, Finland and Hungary.[128] Germany did not try to orchestrate anything of the sort. Maybe the list of countries originated from Wuolijoki, since she reported that Finnish businesses were trying to acquire war material from Germany, Italy and Hungary.[129] Could Soviet intelligence have caught wind of Hitler's order to make preparations for a military campaign to Norway, but have been unclear as to the operation's destination? In any case, if Moscow really did come increasingly to fear Germany just as it was nervously awaiting the Western Powers' next moves, then the tension must have been palpable.[130]

Soviet troops began a large new offensive on the Karelian Isthmus on 11 February, reinforced and regrouped under new commanders. Their dual aim was to force the Finns to accept harsh peace conditions and rehabilitate the badly damaged Soviet military reputation. Playing his part, the Soviet plant among the foreign military attachés in Moscow had informed the Swedish representative that the attack would only commence on 20 February, and that it would take place 600 kilometers further north than in reality.[131] The Soviets committed almost a million Red Army soldiers to the maneuver, which was 40 percent of the total manpower available at the time. It soon became apparent that Mannerheim's prediction of holding out until May had been too optimistic: his men were fighting hard, but they had to withdraw. Without immediate and robust assistance, they would soon be defeated. In fact, research on the level of military units has shown that they were on the verge of collapse.[132]

On 2 March, Britain and France informed Sweden and Norway of their intention to send reinforcements to help Finland. The two Nordic countries did not welcome this: wanting to avoid a world war and German boots on their soil, they refused the troops the right of passage. Mannerheim received word from Stockholm of Berlin's warning: if Sweden allowed Allied transit, Germany would be obliged to "join the game." Then, on 4 March, he received word from London that the French Prime Minister Daladier's last-minute promise—that 50,000 troops would arrive that same month—was grossly exaggerated. The real number would be far lower, and would only reach Finland by April, at the earliest. The Marshal concluded that Western assistance would be "too little and too late."[133] The

8. Vyborg cathedral destroyed in an air attack, 5 February 1940.

Finnish government deemed it better to accept Moscow's peace terms than officially to request Western aid. As Tanner put it, referring to the territory to be ceded, they decided to save the body by cutting off one limb.

NKVD intelligence from Stockholm made it abundantly clear that Finland's situation was desperate. In early March it was reported that the Finns would not last more than three weeks: they were lacking in heavy artillery and airplanes, and their soldiers were exhausted. Both Mannerheim and Tanner favored an immediate peace, as did the nation as a whole, but "there is no discernible revolutionary situation, not among the army nor the citizenry."[134]

Stalin, however, did not have three weeks to spare. The Red Army's advance was too slow; they urgently needed to get "out of the danger zone"[135] to avoid provoking an even greater international reaction. On 5 March, Molotov noted that "there is a great danger of foreign intervention."[136] Voroshilov was dispatched to Caucasia in order to strengthen the defenses there[137]—and thus pushed far from the Finnish front, where he needed to be able to wage war, here and now. All the while, NKVD intelligence from Paris was bombarding Moscow with alarming reports: the huge number of airplanes already sent (176 from France, 164 from Britain, 44 from the United States and 35 from Italy); the plans in place to deploy three divisions of troops in Finland itself, which Sweden would let through despite its apparent neutrality; the 20,000 snow camouflage suits and the same number of mountain rucksacks that the French Army's economic administration had already distributed; the exiled Poles forming first one, and then two, divisions to fight for the Finnish side.[138]

In this atmosphere of panic, danger and humiliation, Stalin committed an atrocity excessive even by his standards. He ordered the mass execution of 25,700 Polish officers and intelligentsia, previously captured or arrested in eastern Poland by the Soviets. The best-known killing field is Katyn Forest. Beria justified the killings by claiming that "Each of them is waiting for their freedom to get the opportunity to actively participate in the struggle against Soviet power."[139] With the threat of Western intervention in the Finnish war this assertion was not simply ideological lip service, but an expression of concrete anxiety. Stalin certainly remembered the precedent from the Russian Civil War, when freed Czech prisoners of war rebelled, formed a legion, and took over a section of the Trans-Siberian Railway. For a time, this was a mortal threat for the Bolsheviks.

The Finnish war was not directly mentioned in the Soviet leadership's decision to slaughter the Polish officers and adjacent personnel. Nonetheless, increasing the capacity of prison camps to hold the Finns had been raised on multiple occasions, most recently on 21 February. It was one of the underlying factors influencing Stalin's treatment of the Poles. And just before the decision to execute the

Poles, Stalin had to give up on any idea of massacring a similar group of Finns. The Poles now in his reach should never get the chance to become a similar thorn in his side. Once again, Poland had to live over the nationalist myth as "Christ among nations," forced to suffer so that other persecuted could find salvation.

The Moscow Peace Treaty was signed between the Soviet Union and Finland on 12 March and came into force the very next day. Peter the Great's border returned, Finland's easternmost regions were annexed. Alongside historical precedent, Soviet motivation for the new borderline was to ensure that Finland no longer had any territory on the shore of Lake Ladoga, thereby removing Finnish ships' right of passage along the Neva, that is, through Leningrad. In Stalin's eyes this was an intolerable right, and he had "indefinitely" suspended it at the end of September 1939. Additional peace terms included giving up islands in the Gulf of Finland and renting the coastal town of Hanko as a military base to the Soviets. Crucially, however, Finland's independence was preserved.

Whether or not independence would be preserved in the long term remained to be seen, for certain articles in the treaty suggested that Moscow had other ideas. The Soviet Union appropriated bigger part of Salla, in northeastern Finland; this made the country narrower at that latitude, and therefore easier to divide in two in the future, should the Soviets again want to sever its land ties with Sweden. To further facilitate this, the terms of the treaty obligated Finland to build a railway line right up to the eastern border. An additional purpose was to intimidate the Swedes.

Although the Soviets ultimately won the war, their victory was partial, bitter, and came at a terrible human and reputational cost. In the 1990s an official investigation in post-Soviet Russia determined that the most reliable estimate of Red Army losses (dead) was 126,875 soldiers. To put that into perspective, the Soviets lost far more soldiers in the 105 days of the Winter War than they did in ten years of fighting in Afghanistan. Fallen Finnish soldiers numbered 26,662, in proportion to population size by far the heavier death toll. In perhaps the Soviets' sole prevailing propaganda victory of the war; Molotov's inflated figures of the Finnish war losses have often been cited as facts.

On 14 March, the day after peace came into effect, NKVD intelligence from Paris reported to Moscow information that Mannerheim had received ten days earlier. Namely that there were serious problems with the Allies' planned assistance. Foreign Minister Lord Halifax had declared that it was impossible to send the one hundred bombers and 50,000 men the Finns had requested in March; at most they could dispatch 12,000, but not before April. And Sweden had categorically refused to grant the Allied troops right of passage.[140] By the time this information reached Moscow, Molotov's signature was already dry on the peace treaty.

Consequences

History carried plenty of weight with Stalin. Everything from the Byzantine monks to the Crimean War—"historically, the threat has always emanated from there"[141]—and foreign intervention in the Russian Civil War. In the background lurked three traditional enemies, Sweden, Turkey and Poland, the latter even when conquered and divided. And of course, their vanquisher, Peter the Great: he and Ivan the Terrible served as historical touchstones on those occasions when the Soviet leaders sought to justify their national security policies.[142] Even the revolutionary soldiers and sailors from Petrograd in 1917 were eulogized, albeit in hopelessly different circumstances. Stalin himself, in his monologue at the Bolshoi Theater, framed the Red Army's actions as being part of the world revolution, one that would take place by degrees rather than in one fell swoop.[143]

A historian should not complain about history being held in regard, but still, getting bogged down in historical analogies can make it difficult to understand the ways in which new situations are unique. On the other hand, there is no doubt that history *was* important. For everyone involved, the Winter War was a prime example of how history has functioned ever since the days of Thucydides: actions producing unintended consequences.

In early March 1940 the Finnish government had their moment on the traditional main stage of history. Had they officially asked for Western aid and/or had the West begun significant military operations against the Soviet Union, global events would have taken a very different course. This is food for thought for anyone contemplating the role of chance and timing in international relations and world history. However, the Finnish leaders opted for unadorned survival, since the struggle of their nation had made this choice possible. The constitutive myth of modern Finland is that this was a lone struggle against a Great Power; as we have seen, however, the country was not totally bereft of assistance. The threat from the West had decisive influence on Stalin, nor was material support from Sweden insignificant. "It was your war," Molotov complained to the Swedish envoy in September 1940.[144]

On the eve of the war, Stalin failed to appreciate the threat posed by the West, but after the first month of fighting Finland he had, conversely, started to overstate it. This initial underestimation, a result of the Soviets' arrogant attitude towards a small nation's geopolitical capacity, was duly corrected. By the summer of 1940, Helsinki ranked among the principal global locations for Soviet foreign intelligence,[145] a state of affairs that persisted right up to the end of the Soviet Union. The small capital city was blessed with a heavy presence of KGB officers.

Western intervention plans lost their impetus when Finland signed the Moscow Peace Treaty. In the north the British still aimed to capture the harbor of Narvik to gain control of iron ore, but on 9 April their plans were scuppered by the German surprise attack on Norway. In the south the threat to bomb Baku and other targets developed into a concrete plan: Operation Pike. At the turn of March the British Secret Intelligence Service organized two photo-reconnaissance flights over Baku. On the second occasion "Cloudy Joe," as the plane was known, drew anti-aircraft artillery fire. But around that time the Turkish government decided that the window of opportunity had already passed, and readopted a policy of restraint towards the Soviet Union.[146]

The Western Powers' intentions in the Caucasus and Central Asia require caveats. Firstly, they were quite far from undertaking a large-scale military operation. A Muslim uprising might have been brewing, but the Soviet Union could scarcely be seen as a hospitable setting for a campaign by any budding Lawrence of Arabia, even if the Chechens were as restless as ever. The rise of Ukrainian nationalism was a potential avenue to exploit, but a second Crimean War was hardly on the cards.

Secondly, why on earth would the West be shaping up for a conflict with the Soviet Union when it was already at war with Germany? The plan was based on a serious under-appreciation of the strength of the two dictatorships, with the Soviet Union viewed by the West as the new sick man of Europe. Possibly the Allies either hoped or assumed that Germany would at least remain favorably passive, if not outright turn its weapons on the Bolsheviks. On 8 March 1940, Britain's War Cabinet concluded that war against the Soviet Union was acceptable "if and only if it would bring about a quick victory over Germany." With the benefit of hindsight, it is difficult to see how this could possibly have been achieved. The flawed Western assessment of the balance of power was laid bare in May 1940, when France rapidly collapsed in the face of the German attack. Early 1940 marked the beginning of the end for the strategies of global imperialism pursued by Paris and London; their plan of action towards the Soviet Union was one of the last examples of such thinking. It soon became clear that the world had irreversibly changed,[147] as was proved definitively by the Suez Crisis of 1956.

Sweden's leading expert on the history of Finland, Krister Wahlbäck, laid out in his final work the long-term consequences of the Winter War for the arc of world history. Without this war and the West's plans for assistance, Germany would not have launched a surprise attack on Denmark and Norway. And without German occupation and Norway's five-year fight for liberation in association with the Allies, these countries would not have sought security from the West in spring 1948, when they were alarmed by Soviet actions and feared new surprises. From this began the process that led to the formation of NATO one year later. "Stalin had to pay a very high price for Vyborg and Karelia," Wahlbäck writes.[148]

The Winter War experience possibly contributed to Stalin's refusal to believe warnings from Churchill and others of an impending

9. *"Finland's cause is ours!"—a Swedish poster to recruit volunteers for the Winter War.*

10. *Swedish volunteers talking with Finnish canteen workers in Kemijärvi,*
February 1940.

11. *A Swedish volunteer soldier fighting in Lapland, 20 February 1940.*

German attack on the Soviet Union in 1941. He still harbored suspicions that he had been tricked, or even provoked, into foolish decisions during the Winter War, and he used intelligence reports to confirm his preconceptions, just as he had in the Finnish war. Most of the information he received was at least satisfactory, but mistrust prevented him from making full use of it. It is tricky to say to what extent more accurate details about the limitations of planned Western assistance would have influenced Stalin's decisions. His closure of the NKVD *rezidentura* in London had made facts much harder to come by, and the British were also spreading lies and feeding false information. In retrospect it is evident that Stalin realized he had lost a vital resource, for the *rezidentura* was rebuilt by fall 1940, and Gorski was sent back to re-establish contacts. An indication of the atmosphere of distrust that had surrounded the Cambridge Five at the beginning of the year was the new codename given to John Cairncross: KAREL, that is to say "Karelian."[149] Presumably this was an inadvertent reference to the area where most of the Winter War was waged.

Berlin and Moscow drew contrasting military conclusions from the Winter War. For the Germans, it confirmed their conviction that the Red Army was incapable of large-scale operations and its numerical superiority would not prove a decisive factor if it were up against a big, modern military.[150] For the Soviets, it led to a lengthy postmortem in April 1940: a four-day seminar in which the political and military leadership could offer fairly forthright criticisms, even if mentioning Stalin's miscalculations was, of course, taboo. On this occasion, at least, Stalin was willing to listen and learn. Ineffective use of intelligence was identified as one of the main reasons for the failure. Soviet agents had uncovered many enemy secrets, but their reports had been stamped *sovershenno sekretno* and kept under lock and key, so front-line commanders could not access them when it mattered. Voroshilov lost his position as Commissar of Defense and was replaced by Marshal Timoshenko; the act ratifying this transfer of authority gave inadequate use of intelligence information as a reason for the former's removal.[151] I.I. Chernyi, the air attaché in London who had raised the alarm about impending bombings in Baku, had his career cut short, and was later arrested.[152] I.I. Proskurov, the head of the GRU, was likewise dismissed, although his departure was postponed until July 1940, after France's capitulation and the Soviet incorporation of the Baltic States. When the Germans attacked a year later, Proskurov was arrested; he ended up being hastily shot, along with several other generals and one of the murderers of Tsar Nicholas II, at a small train station during the mass evacuation towards Kuibyshev.[153] Marshal Kulik, the bearer of bad news to Stalin at the Bolshoi Theater, also faced retribution. His wife, a known beauty who was said to have flirted with Stalin, was kidnapped in May 1940 and executed a month later. Her bloodline made her a "former person" from Tsarist times and, as such, as "unnatural" for a party member to feel attracted to.[154]

After the Winter War the position of military professionals was strengthened. Many of those who had risen through the ranks due to their political loyalty were transferred out of command roles. Stalin finally realized that his long-time "wingman" Voroshilov was "a good fellow, but he is no soldier." Mekhlis was similarly appraised, and demoted from his post as head of the Red Army's political directorate.[155] Evaluating the work of the Ministry of Defense, a commission led by Andrei Zhdanov confirmed that operational planning had been poor during the Winter War: besides shortcomings in intelligence, logistics and transport, the administration did not even have exact knowledge of troop numbers and positions.[156] On one occasion at his dacha, Stalin needled Voroshilov so mercilessly about the Winter War that, unable to take it anymore, the Marshal stood upright, red-faced, and smashed his plate to pieces shouting: "It was your own fault, you destroyed the military leadership!" Khrushchev, witnessing the outburst, had never seen anything like it.[157]

The authority of commanders was enhanced, titles of generals and admirals were reinstated and attempts made to improve planning and administration. Young officers were promoted, thousands of purged officers (such as Marshal Rokossovsky) recalled to service, new training programs were set up, the authority of unit commanders was confirmed at a tactical level and mechanization accelerated. While many of these proposals ended up as half-measures, without them the Red Army would have been even worse equipped to handle the German attack. In addition, they were thought to improve the efficiency of economic sectors vital to defense through, as usual, organizational reform.[158]

In a long discussion, Stalin blamed his intelligence officers for having presented the imminent air raid on Baku as a certain fact and for not having clearly distinguished between different driving forces of the Western governments. The primary cause of the failure, he surmised, was that the officers lacked a real spy's soul and were too gullible. This was a constant theme for him, and one he would return to just before his death, when he declared that a Communist who feared the grubbiness of intelligence should be thrown head-first down a well.[159] In the Winter War post-mortem, Stalin did not see excessive mistrust as being dangerous, quite the opposite:

> A spy's soul should be steeped in poison and gall; he should not believe anyone. If you were spies, you would know how these gentlemen in the West are criticizing one another: you don't have your knives sharpened, you have this vulnerability, you should know how they are exposing each other, disclosing one another's secrets. You ought to seize hold of this, select the best bits and bring them to your commanding officers' attention, but you are too pure-of-heart to do so.[160]

The Winter War decisively affected relations between Finland and the Soviet Union in both the short and the very long term. It undoubtedly made the Finnish government's decision to strengthen ties with Germany from August 1940 much more straightforward, as

Finnish public opinion was largely supportive, and it encouraged Finland to participate in the Germans' attack on the Soviet Union in summer 1941. This was reflected in the fact that the Finns referred to the new conflict as the "Summer War"; when summer was gone, it became the Continuation War.

At the last minute, the Finnish government decided to evacuate the whole population (over 400,000 persons) from the regions to be ceded. This was a surprise for the Soviets. On the second day of peace, on 15 March, the NKVD set up a new operative center for Vyborg. The task of the deputy head was assigned to L.L. Shvartsman, a notorious interrogator from the Moscow headquarters.[161] The apparent purpose was to bring the new inhabitants under control, but there was nobody left to be terrorized. It is not known who dared to report this to Stalin. Whenever Moscow was touting territorial gains, population growth was always stressed. On 1 August 1940, enumerating new areas annexed in less than a year (that is, after the Pact), Molotov mentioned the number of inhabitants in each of them, altogether 23 million, but former Finnish territories were not mentioned at all.[162] On one occasion Molotov was seen "painfully shaken" by the fact that the Soviets had found Vyborg completely empty. "Do they really take us for such barbarians?" he burst out.[163] A rhetorical question, for sure. For the Finns, the evacuation marked mutual solidarity, but Moscow surely tended to interpret it as an indication of relentless persistence and intention of the Finns to return.

The influence of the Winter War stretched well beyond 1944. The Finns gained a certain self-confidence for dealing with their overbearing neighbor. Having withstood the trials of war, why not withstand the ordeals of peace?

On the Soviet side the military leadership reached the conclusion that Finland's dogged defense was a peculiar anomaly,[164] an exception, and this assessment lasted a long time. More important was the political verdict. Paradoxically, the successful *modus vivendi* of

Soviet–Finnish relations after the Second World War was to a great extent based on the respect earned by the Finns in the Winter War. Seldom mentioned in mutual relations but always remembered, fierce warfare was a cornerstone of "friendship," as it was called.

For the rest of his long life, Molotov would remember the war that immortalized his name by making it synonymous with the innovative incendiary bottle. He thought it wise that Finland had not been subjugated by force and attached to the Soviet Union. He described the Finns as "very stubborn, very stubborn" people, who would have become a pestering wound in the Soviet body.[165]

When Stalin met Finnish representatives for the first time after the Second World War, in October 1945, he remembered what he had seen from the train window during his two trips to Finland in his younger days, once in November and once in December. He then turned to his experience of the Winter War, in typically diversionary fashion:

> You live the devil knows where [...] You live in bogs and forests, in spite of this you have built a state. You have fought for your state doggedly. Compare Finland to, say, Belgium. The Belgians consider the Finns to be half-backwoodsmen [*polukhutorskim*], not a cultured people. But the Finnish people developed their country and did not behave as the Belgians did in the war. The Belgians are held as one of the foremost cultured nations in Europe, but when war broke out, they surrendered. So I think that if Finns had been put in the Belgians' place, I feel that they would have combatted tenaciously against the German assailants.[166]

II
The Way to Peace
1944

On 12 November 1943, Soviet leaders received an intelligence report from Stockholm on the political situation in Finland, which had been on the German side in the war since 1941. The short report included two novelties. First, the opposition wing was growing in the Social Democratic Party and would soon achieve a majority in the nine-member party board responsible for day-to-day political activities. Only one more member was needed, and he was already wavering between the opposition and the hardliners around the party strongman Väinö Tanner, who thought it necessary to continue the war for the time being. As the party organization was strictly controlled by the Tannerites, the opposition planned to found a new socialist party to gather left-leaning elements in the SDP and outside it. The program of the new party would be "struggle for independent Finland with a pro-Soviet orientation."[1] Later on, opposition figures specified that they were striving for a similar type of government as the Beneš government-in-exile for Czechoslovakia; in foreign policy the model of Soviet–Czech relations would be adopted.[2]

This was big news. The largest party of Finland, the SDP, had served in coalition governments since 1937, guaranteeing working-class loyalty in the Winter War and on that basis even in the new war since June 1941 on the German side. Now the times were finally changing.

The second novelty of the report was at least as interesting in Stalin's eyes. Opposition figures believed that in the future they would receive Marshal Mannerheim's support, and his authority would be sufficient to keep the still strong pro-German contingent of the officer corps under control. As for senior politicians, the support of J.K. Paasikivi could be counted on.

There was an element of wishful thinking here, in particular as far as the strength and resoluteness of the opposition and the schedule for change were concerned. Wartime conditions and censorship made open political debate on issues like these practically impossible; even inside the SDP the campaign against Tanner had to remain clandestine (*nelegal'nuyu*). Still, this had potential, and Stalin certainly knew that even much slimmer potential than this could be turned into reality.

All this information was brought from Helsinki by three men[3] seeking financial support from the Swedish Social Democrats. The Swedish Finance Minister Ernst Wigforss perhaps gave favorable signals, but Prime Minister P.A. Hansson exercised his veto. The actual source for the Soviet report seems to have been Laurin Zilliacus, a key figure in the SDP opposition, with even some Western background and contacts. Instead of any direct contact with Soviet intelligence officers, he talked with the Slovenian-born journalist Augustine "Gusti" Stridsberg, who was a NKGB agent operating under the code name KLARA.[4]

Stalin acted swiftly. Only eight days later, on 20 November 1943, his envoy Aleksandra Kollontay told Erik Boheman, the top Swedish diplomat from the Foreign Ministry (*Utrikesdepartement*), that if the Finns wanted to talk about peace, the representatives of their government were welcome in Moscow. The Soviet Union had no intention of making Finland a province or limiting its independence and sovereignty, unless Finland by its own policy would force it to do so. Further, Kollontay had got an impression that the Kremlin considered Mannerheim's support important, otherwise the reconciliation would remain on flimsy grounds. To confirm the "impression," she brought to the very next meeting Stalin's guarantee that the Soviet Union would never make any demands on Mannerheim's person.[5] This promise was kept.

The promise (and conversely, the threat) probably had an effect on the old Marshal. In public appearances always outwardly calm, he was tormented by recurrent nightmares of invitations or more or less courteous journeys to Moscow to hold difficult talks with Stalin. How did the nightmares end? "Of course, as they always end—I was tortured."[6]

Stalin's abrupt volte-face was made less than a month after the three Allies' conference hosted by foreign ministers, where it was decided to demand the unconditional surrender of Germany and its satellites. A pre-meeting briefing from the People's Commissariat of Foreign Affairs stated that the Soviet government "views Finland as one of Hitler's principal allies and a most dangerous one," to which the principle of unconditional surrender should be applied. As a possible plan of action, Marshal Voroshilov outlined the occupation of Finland, all the way to the Åland Islands.[7] The commission on peace terms led by him prepared a 56-point document for the country's unconditional surrender (dated 15 October 1943). According to it, "a new power" would be necessary and the existing Finnish government demolished. For the time being, this paper remained shelved.

To prepare the "new" power, an old figure was needed. Following his misadventure in the Winter War, O.V. Kuusinen had been dispatched to head the new Karelian Soviet Republic. After the Battle of Stalingrad he had written—with the backing of Georgi Dimitrov, the Comintern head—an article advocating a separate peace for Finland, but Stalin had banned its publication.[8] However, in late summer 1943, Kuusinen was allowed to return to Moscow to work as

12. Finnish officers posing with a statue of Stalin in Soviet Karelia,
11 September 1941.

an editor for a new magazine focused on international issues: *Voina i rabochi klass* (later *Novoe vremya—The New Times*). He became a consultant for former Foreign Minister Litvinov's commission tasked with the post-war order. On the agenda for Finland were three points: the border, the Åland Islands, and the "the setting up of a new power [*sozdanie novoi vlasti*]" in the country.[9] Kuusinen penned a vicious pamphlet *Finland Without a Mask*, which was read out in Finnish on Soviet radio. Another figure of the 1939 puppet "government," Armas Äikiä, was already shrieking in Soviet radio propaganda to Finland, "Mannerheim has to surrender without conditions!"

Kuusinen was far from the optimal solution for Stalin. He was not the mastermind behind the Terijoki puppet government, but for the Finns he was its symbol, a detested traitor for most people. He was an emergency back-up, if it became necessary to resort to extreme solutions, like occupation and the establishment of a new power. Kuusinen was not immediately informed of Stalin's change of tack. On 30 November 1943, the fourth anniversary of the outbreak of the Winter War, he was permitted to hold a lecture in Moscow. Kuusinen supposed that excellent Russian cannons would again be needed as interpreters before the Helsinki "plutocrats" (a concept borrowed from the Nazis) would comprehend the Soviet demands. The outlook was good, for "Mannerheim's army" had lost, if not its entire capacity to fight, then at least its capacity to attack. When asked for details about the Marshal's attitude, Kuusinen deemed it widely known "that he is one of the most disgusting creatures [*merzavtsev*] over there. This he has been and will be until the end of his life."[10] Had the comrade putting the question a hunch that Moscow was now courting Mannerheim?

The Big Three in Tehran

Stalin's volte-face was an obvious reaction to the Stockholm intelligence report. The Winter War still fresh in his mind, and seeing that even leftist Social Democrats of the Peace Opposition vowed to fight for independence, Stalin deemed it wise to try the political road when it seemed to be available. The second motivating force was Sweden. If the Finns were forced to fight to the bitter end, Stockholm was concerned that the ultimate result would be a wave of refugees flooding across its borders. This would spoil Swedish–Soviet relations and create a festering wound between them, visible for the whole world to see.[11] At this point, the Allies were planning to persuade Sweden to take up arms against Germany. The Soviet Army's newspaper hoped that the current King of Sweden would act in the same spirit as the first Bernadotte on the throne, Jean Baptiste, as King Karl XIV Johan.[12] Only three years after the loss of the eastern half of the kingdom, he had introduced "the policy of 1812":

Finland would remain a part of the Russian Empire, and Sweden would get Norway instead.

Stalin wanted to get the Finnish issue moving before the Big Three conference in Tehran, where all three leaders were together for the first time. The main stumbling block there would be Poland, and to get that done Stalin needed to show moderation somewhere else. The terms for Finland's withdrawal from the war were shortly discussed on the last day of the conference, 1 December 1943, while Filipino waiters were still clearing away the remnants of a long lunch put on by the US President. Stalin, Churchill and Roosevelt were exhausted and in bad shape.[13]

As was his habit, Stalin had sought concrete benefits from the conference: a set date for the Western invasion of France, and Allied adherence to the 1941 boundaries of the Soviet Union. They were based on the secret protocol with Hitler in August 1939, but the pact was of course not mentionable in Tehran. It meant that the small Baltic republics, along with the eastern part of pre-war Poland, would be incorporated into the Soviet Union. Poland was the sticking point, because Britain had entered the war for the very reason of defending its sovereignty. On top of the border issue, there was the question of what form the Poles' government would take.

As for Finland, Stalin wanted the 1940 border established again. When Roosevelt opined that the Finns would abide by this, but they would still seek the return of Vyborg, Stalin flashed his yellow-tinged tiger eyes and cut the President short: "It is impossible."[14] He was not prepared to give the Finns an inch more than they had in 1941, when they joined the German attack on the Soviet Union to reclaim the land lost in the Winter War.

In other matters, he was more flexible. Finnish independence could be preserved, with Stalin noting that Moscow "had no intention of making Finland its province," unless the Finns' own actions made it necessary. So, the promise was qualified with a sizeable caveat. In May 1945 the Americans asked the Soviets if they would uphold the deals struck at the Yalta Conference, the second meeting of the big three in February 1945. "The Soviet Union always keeps its word," replied Stalin, before muttering an amendment that his interpreter, Valentin Berezhkov, neglected to translate. Roosevelt's interpreter, Charles Bohlen, interjected that there appeared to be more to the comment. The flustered Berezhkov responded: "Except in cases of extreme necessity."[15]

As for what form Finland's society should take, Stalin stated that the Finns could live as they please, provided they paid the reparations. In a tête-à-tête with Roosevelt in Tehran, Stalin sought historical justification for treating Finland differently from the three Baltic states, which "did not have autonomy before the Russian Revolution."[16] Most immediately, promising to preserve Finnish independence might have a positive influence on Sweden and encourage it to enter into the war against Germany, preferably in time for the landings in France.

Both promises and their provisos were significant. Stalin meant what he said, even if he was careful not to reveal all his thoughts. On the one hand, he promised Finland's independence and the preservation of its societal structure; on the other, he undercut this in the same breath by asserting (or granting) that he could make far harsher demands, and even appropriate the country into the Soviet Union. The old borders there also, but those of 1914 rather than of 1941. Allusions to Imperial Russia's borders and autonomy were no coincidence: at this time Stalin was keen to invoke the patriotism of the former empire. In fall 1943, around the anniversary of the October Revolution, the British ambassador noticed that portraits of Suvorov and other victorious military commanders had appeared on Stalin's desk. The pictures of Marx and Engels had been moved to a corner, and the ambassador asked why. "Well, they weren't Russians, after all," replied Stalin.[17]

In Tehran, Stalin said that it would "naturally" be better if Finland had an entirely anti-Nazi government. However, he was prepared to negotiate for peace "with [President] Ryti, too, or the Devil himself," i.e. with whomever the Finnish government chose to send. An evident lesson from the Winter War: do not have any dealings with other Finnish governments besides the one in power in Helsinki.

Stalin did not mention Mannerheim on the Devil's side. Still, his new policy did not signify unwavering acceptance of the Marshal, or of Finnish society in its current form. Rather, both were to be tolerated for the time being. Zhdanov's later instruction, that "the Marshal must be broken [*lomat*] gradually,"[18] undoubtedly came from Stalin himself. During the power struggles of the 1920s, this method had been the secret to Stalin's success. One member of the Politburo at the time, Nikolai Bukharin, who witnessed and experienced this first-hand, characterized Stalin as someone with a shrewd ability to manipulate situations in small, carefully measured doses.[19] Of course, crushing people little by little also revealed his sadistic streak.

Churchill needed to insist on getting the Soviet Union's exact conditions for peace with Finland spelled out in Tehran. The most important and specific was, firstly, a return to the borders established by the Moscow Peace Treaty at the conclusion of the Winter War. Stalin had just got word from Stockholm, where the initial inquiries were taking place, of the Finnish government's insistence that the boundaries be those of 1939. He branded that as unwillingness to negotiate, and even as a sign of belief in a German victory. Framing 1941 as the starting point for hostilities was a means of imbuing the Soviets with moral superiority and justifying their border claims. Then, Finland had sided with the Nazis in the latter's attack on the Soviet Union. Go back two years earlier, however, and in 1939 the Soviets had invaded Finland after striking a deal with the selfsame Nazis.

The Soviets' second demand was a strategic territorial exchange: they would cede Hanko, at the southernmost tip of Finland, in return for the permanent cession of Petsamo in the very north of the country. The narrow Hanko Peninsula gave the Soviets a commanding position in the Gulf of Finland when the lease period began in 1940, but its narrowness made it impractical for large-scale land operations, so much so that the Soviets had planned to substantially extend it.[20] Annexing Petsamo instead would give them control of its Canadian-owned nickel mine, while cutting off Finland's access to the Arctic Sea in the process. During the Winter War, the Soviets had seized the region and carried out a careful inspection of the mine, but then returned it to Finland to avoid irritating the British.[21] Now Stalin considered his position strong enough to claim it outright.

Another sign that Stalin's stance had hardened since the Winter War was his third requirement, the demand of indemnity for war damages. That should be paid in the form of paper, wood and other goods over a period of five to eight years. Next a self-evident claim: the German troops in northern Finland should be expelled, and all ties with Germany be cut. The fifth point was that Finland should "fulfil certain other conditions," including the "reorganization" of the Defense Forces, which in practice meant demobilization. Should the Finns not play ball, the Voroshilov commission's 56-point document contained plenty of additional demands.[22]

The Western Allies accepted Stalin's conditions with little protest, although Churchill did observe that, in relation to the war indemnity, those poor northerners hardly had anything more to give besides muskrat and ermine furs.[23] When the British Prime Minister invoked the Bolsheviks' former slogan—peace without land appropriation or other conditions—Stalin cracked a joke and was reminded to have already said that "I am moulding myself into a conservative." Churchill explicitly supported Stalin's border proposals, repeating his statement before the Winter War that Russia ought to have dominion over the Baltic Sea, and now also Baltic air space. Churchill had already instructed his own civil servants that Finland "should suffer in territory as a result of her execrable behaviour."[24] To paraphrase a recent study of the British leader, his greatness was matched by his meanness.[25] Churchill did not press Stalin on Petsamo with its Canadian-owned nickel mine. As for Roosevelt, he considered the swapping of Hanko for Petsamo a fair trade. Unlike before the Winter War, the Soviet Union was no longer offering its own territory, but was only prepared to exchange one part of Finland for another. The one solace for the Finns was that Stalin was still imposing conditions, rather than unconditional surrender.

Roosevelt was more amenable to the Soviets' propositions than Churchill, and the Soviet leadership wanted the United States to pressure Finland to swallow the conditions, but only from a distance: they did not want the Americans to assume the role of mediator. When former Foreign Minister Eljas Erkko visited the US Embassy in Stockholm with this in mind, the Soviet Embassy's Vladimir Semyonov sent a message: the Finns should not ask others to advocate on their behalf, but should engage in direct talks with Moscow.[26] According to a Russian researcher well-versed in counter-intelligence sources, Sweden's envoy to Moscow, Vilhelm Assarsson, kept his American colleagues so well informed of Finland's progress towards peace that he drew Stalin's ire. This led to the expulsion of Assarsson and military attaché Hans Nygren in mid-December. The diplomats could not guess the real reason for this.[27] Soviet aggressive intelligence and counter-intelligence operations against the United States— its ally in the war—was not yet known by outsiders. The vast scale of atomic bomb espionage—under the fitting code name ENORMOZ— only became clear to the Americans when it was too late.

The diplomats' expulsion was an over-reaction by the Soviets, insofar as the Americans were not paying much attention to Finland at the time.[28] In an informal discussion between Roosevelt and Stalin, the American President listed those "countries they [the Russians] could take over and control completely as their sphere—so completely that the United States could from this moment have no further policies with regard to them." They were Romania, Bulgaria, Bukovina, the eastern part of Poland, Lithuania, Estonia, Latvia and Finland.[29] The President wanted Stalin's assurance that the Soviets would not yet make public their planned seizure of Polish territory, since the

Poles were an important voting bloc in US elections. However, Roosevelt was not driven solely by immediate self-interest. Two months prior to Tehran, he had written to the Catholic Archbishop of New York on the topic, stating that there was "a good chance" that Stalin would demand Poland, the Baltic states, Bessarabia and Finland, "so better give them gracefully [...] What can we do about it?" He took comfort from the fact that, within ten or twenty years, this "European influence would make the Russians become less barbarian."[30] Stalin had no issue keeping Poland's territorial losses under wraps, but the President's generosity could well have aroused his suspicions. He used to look every gift horse in the mouth.

After Tehran, Deputy Foreign Minister Ivan Maisky—who was in charge of another commission on post-war conditions—wrote a lengthy memo on the Soviet Union's future national security requirements. These included mutual military aid agreements with Finland and Romania, as well as bases for Soviet land, sea and air forces in the two countries.[31] Maisky had personally heard Stalin make demands along such lines in December 1941, when the Soviet leader had spoken to the British Foreign Secretary, Anthony Eden, following Britain's declaration of war on Finland. Stalin had sought redrawn borders, Petsamo, a military alliance and bases on Finnish soil.[32] Maisky probably reasoned that if Stalin called for these with the Germans on Moscow's doorstep, then he would be certain to take them when the Soviets could glimpse Berlin on the horizon.

The military situation around Finland changed decisively in mid-January 1944, when Soviet troops broke through the Leningrad blockade and advanced to the Narva River, right by the Estonian border. Although the attack ground to a halt for many months, it was the first time in two and a half years that the Soviet Union had the opportunity to conduct large-scale military operations on the Karelian Isthmus. This was a seminal change shadowing the fate of Finland. The probable consequences were discussed in advance in a conference of Finnish military intelligence officers. Their chief, Colonel Aladár Paasonen, had the last word, observing that the predictable German loss of the Baltikum would create "an awkward situation," but the situation would still not become ungovernable. "The focus will turn to the south and we will be left aside."[33]

The British received an intelligence report detailing the damage that the collapse of the Siege of Leningrad did to the Germans' reputation in Helsinki. Their standing even fell among the Jägers, whose military training had taken place in Germany during the Great War. Finnish soldiers on leave now saw German defeat as inevitable and were hoping for peace, if the conditions were reasonable.[34] Feelings of insecurity and war-weariness were spreading. The security police overheard "strong expressions of defeatism," such as the gloomy prediction of a senior clerk at the large Kaukas paper and cellulose mills, that "the Russians are coming to occupy Finland." He did not think that the British would offer any salvation. A former cleaner voiced similar sentiments when she was accosted by a gentleman while delivering newspapers. He told her that newspaper distributors were not allowed to use the lift, causing the tired woman to snap: "the working class will no doubt use the lift, too, when the *ryssä* [a pejorative term for Russians] come here." Reported to the police, she regretted her excitable temperament, declaring that she had no interest in politics, voted for the Social Democrats, and certainly did not want "the *ryssä* here." The husband admired Germany. The couple were not known Communists. However, the security police did hear reports that workers in more left-wing circles were watching attentively to see if the Estonian front between Narva and Lake Peipus would hold, and to see when the West's invasion in France would begin.[35]

This section of the book will trace the various stages of the peace process between Finland and the Soviet Union, focusing on the latter's aims and conditions. Since the political side is the primary object, military operations will receive only a cursory glance, as will other themes well addressed elsewhere, like the decision-making in Finland and other countries, and the nature and development of Finnish society in wartime conditions. When the preliminary peace agreement was struck in September 1944 it was broadly based on the terms laid out in Tehran. Therefore, it would be tempting to imagine that the conditions remained largely unchanged for the whole nine months in between. However, this was not the case: the Soviets demanded Finland's capitulation in June 1944 during the heat of battle, in the midst of their large-scale assault. This section will unpick how the Soviet mindset towards Finnish peace developed: how it came to vacillate from one position to another, how the conditions were outlined and refined, and how Stalin came to make the decisions he did.

Contact

Messages between Moscow and Helsinki were transmitted through Swedish diplomats and the Soviet envoy to Stockholm, Alexandra Kollontay. The intermediaries tended to interpret and soften the wording of the dispatches, which served both to facilitate and cloud the decision-making process in Helsinki and Moscow. It was vital for Kollontay to report that she had fulfilled her instructions down to the letter, for Stalin and Molotov did not fully trust her, suspecting that she identified with the Scandinavians.[36]

A second channel of communication was suggested by Hella Wuolijoki, who was then in prison for treason, having been found guilty of assisting a Soviet parachutist. When Väinö Tanner and his wife, Linda, paid her a visit in jail, the author urged them to bypass Kollontay ("not fit to be used for such a purpose") and to use Madam Yartseva (Zoya Rybkina) as a go-between. Tanner recalled his incredulity about a "skirt conduit" when the matter at hand—peace—was so serious.[37] Wuolijoki's suggestion was most likely not based on anything more than her own past experiences with Soviet contacts in

Stockholm. Stalin prioritized, at this time, the official diplomatic channels; in these, too, a "skirt conduit"—Kollontay—was in a prominent position and in close proximity to Soviet intelligence, which was watching her every move. Her earlier code name in NKGB telegrams was KHOZYAIKA, but this was later changed to the slightly more fitting MISTRESS.[38]

In early February the banker Marcus Wallenberg traveled to Helsinki to initiate contact with the Finns. The Finnish security policeman watching his movements noted that in Wallenberg's "capers," as always, there was "a pretty trollop with her own important task."[39] Perhaps to draw the attention of observers away from the main purpose of the trip? Back in Stockholm, he complained, as if in jest, that Kollontay had encouraged him to take this mission, but then he found Russian bombers waiting for him. Helsinki was indeed bombed by the Soviets on the night of 6/7 February, the first of three heavy air raids that month. President Risto Ryti commented after the first: "There, you see, Moscow promises to talk to us while bombing us at the same time. We cannot show ourselves to be cowards." He went on to assert that the Finns could not agree to negotiate under the threat of air strikes.[40] Vladimir Erofeyev, then a young diplomat, has claimed in his memoirs that Kollontay, in her cable, expressly *recommended* bombing Helsinki during Wallenberg's visit, so that the banker would understand Finland's position.[41] If this is true, then life really had turned Kollontay, the former shining utopian, free-love visionary and friend of Finland, into a cold-hearted practitioner of Realpolitik.[42] When Wallenberg complained about the bombings, Kollontay laughed and said that Stalin and Molotov had just wanted to cheer the banker up with practical jokes.[43]

According to Wallenberg, Ryti, Prime Minister Edvin Linkomies and Foreign Minister Henrik Ramsay all wanted peace, and even close relations with the Soviets after the war. No one in the Finnish leadership believed that Germany would prevail, and moreover the Finns were no longer so dependent on Germans that they could not

13. *The Soviet Legation in Helsinki aflame during a Soviet bombing raid,*
7 February 1944.

risk opening the door to peace. In Wallenberg's assessment, they
could even rise up against the Germans, "although they will naturally
need a push." In Kollontay's telegram, there was no mention of the
Finnish leaders' hopes for Western intervention on their behalf.

As for the border, Wallenberg asserted that the main problem for
the Finns was the Saimaa Canal, an important export route; in
Finnish hands, it would serve to strengthen good relations in the
future. In her cable Kollontay invalidated this claim by bringing up
Wallenberg's long-established stake in the region's wood-processing
factories. The big capitalist and "the real King of Sweden" was, therefore, only looking out for his own interests. Wallenberg had also
informed her that the Finns feared the Soviets would demand a new
government and unconditional surrender once negotiations were
underway in Moscow. "That fear may be realized," Kollontay report-
edly replied, "if Finland does not withdraw from the war right now."[44]
Striking the balance between persuasion and intimidation was

integral to the peace process; the ability to achieve this was integral to Kollontay's success as a diplomat.

Wallenberg's account included a crucial concession from the Finns: the concern about the Saimaa Canal indicated readiness to accept the border of 1940, even if still trying to retain the waterway, and probably Vyborg along with it. This was bitter realism: the losing side in a war can hardly expect better borders than it had at the outset of the conflict. Since it is unlikely that Wallenberg had the gall to bring up an issue of this magnitude of his own accord, this probably came from Ryti. The President had already declared to Mannerheim: "Personally, I would take peace with the [1940] Moscow Treaty's terms, even with those borders, if such a peace were obtainable." The Marshal, for his part, had gone on to discuss this with Tanner, among others.[45]

These events formed the backdrop to J.K. Paasikivi's trip to Stockholm to inquire about the Soviets' peace terms. The former envoy to Moscow was the very person Kollontay wanted, as he had a good name in Stalin's books. During this initial peace probe, the inner circle of Finnish leaders referred to the Soviet diplomat under the code name MADONNA—as transparent as those used by Soviet intelligence for Kollontay, and as ill-fitting.[46]

On the morning of 13 February, Wallenberg went to meet Kollontay at the Grand Hotel in Saltsjöbaden, a quiet town just east of Stockholm on the coast. He informed her of Paasikivi's mindset in preparation for the Soviets' first direct contact with Finland since 1941. The banker asserted that, as long as there were no unreasonable new conditions, Paasikivi was ready to travel to Moscow for negotiations. Wallenberg himself made a suggestion concerning the Saimaa Canal: a secret protocol, whereby the Soviet Union would be prepared to reconsider the 1940 border in the future, should it cause serious harm to the Finnish economy.

According to Wallenberg, the German troops in northern Finland were of acute concern to Paasikivi. Would it be enough for Finland to pull out of the war, or would Finnish troops be expected to fight alongside the Red Army against the Germans? "The Finns," Wallenberg stated, "want to preserve their neutrality." The Finns had drawn up plans to cut General Dietl's lines of communication to the south and block his troops' departure, while preventing the arrival of new supplies or reinforcements in southern Finland. This would force the Germans to evacuate. Their boats "will, of course, be sunk, but this does not concern the Finns." So, it was believed that at least the Port of Kemi would stay in German hands for evacuation.

Paasikivi would also want to know if the sitting government in Helsinki would be acceptable. Not knowing that Stalin was prepared to sit at the table with the Devil himself, Wallenberg supposed that "Tanner will probably be removed, so that he would not disturb." He also outlined some wishes to the Soviets: efforts to make the Finnish government more left-wing would only delay the process, radio propaganda should be toned down and bombing campaigns post-poned. Should the peace process founder, Wallenberg promised that the number of Soviet air raids on Finland "could be doubled or tripled."

Before meeting Paasikivi, Kollontay checked with Moscow that she was permitted to talk to him, as well as what she was expected to say.[47] Molotov's answer, intended for Swedish (and Finnish) eyes, was reticent: "The Soviet government has no grounds to place much trust in Finland's current government, but if Finland demands [*nastaivayet*] it, the Soviet government is, in the interest of peace, amenable to negotiating with Finland's current government about bringing an end to hostilities." *If Finland demands?* It was not Molotov's habit to let Finland demand anything at all, but this was how Moscow skirted full responsibility for agreeing to sit down for talks, and it was also their regular practice to place the other side in the position of a supplicant.

Molotov decreed that the initial meeting would be an unofficial one. The Soviets needed to confirm that Paasikivi was acting with full governmental authority and to establish what kind of proposals the Finns had in mind. If it became clear that the Finns really wanted to withdraw from the war, Moscow would send further instructions and peace conditions.[48]

Wallenberg again showed up to prime Kollontay for the meeting. As for areas under consideration, the hot point was now Hanko, since Mannerheim wanted "to show at least one concession to his army and to his people." The banker was also keen to push to the fore his claim that Tanner had "in fact been edged out" and only had "a negligible bit part" in the Finnish government, but to demand his departure as a precondition to negotiations would only strengthen his position.[49]

As ever, Moscow kept its cards close to its chest, not even revealing exact terms to its own diplomat until the very last minute. At the same time, it assiduously extracted appraisals and suggestions from its Finnish opponents and the intermediaries. Thus it was able to establish whether there were concessions available without asking, offered up unprompted—such as Tanner's head. In Western and Nordic countries politicians and diplomats had more leeway to air their views and concerns, and Moscow used this to spot the cracks into which a wedge could be inserted. This being due to different political systems, the westerners could not do much about it.

Late in the evening of 16 February—the second night of sustained Soviet bombing in Helsinki—Wallenberg escorted Paasikivi to Kollontay's hotel room, with all the secrecy usually reserved for an illicit rendezvous. The diplomat observed that the Finn was "restless and nervous," as a first-time lover might be.

Paasikivi confirmed that the trickiest issue from the Finns' perspective was, in fact, Hanko. So not the state border, but a leased region. In 1940–41 it had caused a great deal of difficulty and created propaganda opportunities "for elements hostile to our friendship." Hanko would affect future neighbor relations. Kollontay cabled to

Moscow that her reaction to this was negative. Paasikivi mentioned the Saimaa Canal as an economic concern, but was less emphatic here.

Even the second concern came from Mannerheim: did Moscow intend to dictate the terms of demobilization for the Finnish Army? State sovereignty required self-determination, and a sovereign state also had the right to stay neutral. Would the Soviet Union force the Finns to fight against the Germans, and would some Finnish localities be occupied, as had been speculated in the Western press? *Pravda* and Stalin had not made any mention of this.

After the discussion lasting an hour and a half, Kollontay was left with the impression that the Finns were serious about wanting peace and that "the arrival of Paasikivi goes beyond merely sounding us out."[50] Paasikivi, in contrast, was disappointed by how few issues were discussed, and feared that Moscow's future demands would go further. He did not know that the lack of progress was due to the paucity of instructions from Molotov. Paasikivi's points of concern confirmed to Stalin that Mannerheim was crucial: if he was not on board, the conditions would not be accepted in Finland.

Late in the evening of 19 February, Kollontay presented to Paasikivi the preliminary peace conditions she had received from Moscow. She observed that his reaction was calm. Conditions were divided into two groups of three. To be accepted immediately were: (1) breaking off relations with Germany and the internment of German troops, with which the Soviet Union could assist; (2) the re-implementation of the 1940 Moscow Peace Treaty and the withdrawal of Finnish troops to that border; and (3) the immediate return of Soviet and Allied prisoners and forced laborers. The other group of terms were to be determined during negotiations in Moscow, and they consisted of: (4) the full or partial demobilization of the Finnish Army; (5) reparations for damages caused by Finnish acts of war and occupation; and (6) the issue of Petsamo.

The title of the conditions was *preliminary peace*. Paasikivi asked several times if the peace would later become final, and what form such a peace would take. Kollontay did not have any instructions, and Molotov's only response was that the difference between preliminary peace and peace was widely known, so no clarification was needed.

In Paasikivi's opinion, the German issue was difficult, but manageable. He accepted Molotov's argument: "If Finland wants to remain a neutral country, it should not tolerate a foreign power's military troops, rather they should at least be interned." There was no demand for Finland to go to war against the Germans, nor was it stated that matters could take such a turn. It was also significant that the Soviet Union did not merely accept the Finns' conception of their own neutrality, it went along with it.

Again, Paasikivi obstinately brought up Hanko as a separate issue: he claimed that it was an even greater source of unrest in Finland than the loss of Karelia, and made an earnest plea for the Soviets to reconsider. Molotov had Stalin's Tehran Declaration as his point of reference, so the answer came quickly: if Finland accepts the conditions without reservation, the Soviet Union could compromise on Hanko—for suitable compensation, of course.[51]

Paasikivi was informed of this during his third night-time conference with Kollontay on 21 February. According to her report, Paasikivi was extremely delighted, commenting that the news was "a huge relief and the Finnish people will be forever grateful to Marshal J. V. Stalin." In Paasikivi's own report it was Kollontay herself who was overjoyed. On the topic of demobilization, he said that, if the terms were presented as orders, it would hit Mannerheim the hardest (*otchen udarit*), which could make the process anything but straightforward. That was Kollontay's version, at least: in Paasikivi's account, he opined more obliquely that the matter was "sensitive, especially in relation to the army." As for the German troops in northern Finland, he asked: "If they simply leave and are no longer there, what then?" Kollontay replied that this was precisely what was not wanted; only internment would suffice. Paasikivi favored free passage of Germans, so "that you could beat them yourselves."[52]

In Moscow the conditions took shape little by little, and the final version only reached Stockholm after Paasikivi had departed. The delay was due to Britain's wishes, which were not originally incorporated because the Soviets gave their draft to the British only after Paasikivi had seen it. To conceal this, the Soviet ambassador to London, F.T. Gusev, decided, of his own accord, to refrain from mentioning this fact to the British. That way "the English would not come to know that we delivered the conditions to the Finns without waiting for their corrections." A rare example of an unsanctioned act by a Soviet diplomat, but Molotov did approve it afterwards.[53]

In order to increase the pressure on the Finns, Moscow had the conditions published. Finland's security police got wind of the reaction in left-wing circles, which found the Soviets' terms "less than comforting." The leftists yearned for peace, but the conditions failed to elicit a positive response, as they were wrapped in "veiled wording, composed with the deviousness of a true *ryssä*."[54] The war had taught the working man to search for hidden meanings in diplomatic language.

Although the conditions were considered reasonable in the British and the Swedish press, the People's Commissariat for Foreign Affairs viewed the response of the Western media to be entirely in Finland's interest. The Soviets were vexed by the view that Finland was at war through no fault of its own. According to a Soviet overview: (1) the press had been mobilized with the aim of saving Finland from final destruction (*ot okonchatel'nogo razgroma*) and with the purpose of preventing the Soviet Union from dictating terms that would destabilize the position of Britain or the United States in Finland; (2) the Americans had taken an interest in Finland's independence and its regional integrity (*tselostnosti*), which explained Washington's "patience" in maintaining political and diplomatic ties with Helsinki; (3) the sole purpose of the "symbolic war" Britain had declared on

Finland was to preserve its influence there and to continue to use the country as a buffer to stop Bolshevism from penetrating Europe. The newspapers' support of the Soviet Union's conditions was seen as a mere formality. The reactionary press was unable to conceal the Western Allies' hope, that "the Finnish question would not be solved by the Soviet Union alone, but also by England and the United States."[55]

The British began to outline how the Special Operations Executive (SOE), together with the Americans, would organize partisan actions against the Germans in Finland as soon as the country had withdrawn from the war. Some thought that the Soviet Union would agree to the operation, since the Western Powers would be better able to recruit Finns, while others believed that the Soviets could enlist their own partisans, "Finns with Communist leanings—and they do exist." The project was developed in the SOE's Stockholm office, which was also preparing intense sabotage operations in Norway.

The British did not believe that the Germans would leave voluntarily: the prospect of Petsamo nickel and Outokumpu copper was too tempting. As such, the British resolved that they would at least stop the enemy from using these resources. At the War Office the prevailing opinion was that the Finnish Army would turn its weapons on the Germans if ordered to by the government. In SOE circles, however, it was doubted whether the Finns would switch sides so easily: "They are not like the Italians, nor would turning on their former allies be at all compatible with the sense of honor found within the Finnish soldier." Nonetheless, among the Finns there were men unbound by any concept of honor, willing to become partisans on the promise of money or adventure. Led by British officers proficient in Finnish, their task would be "to harass remaining Germans in Finland, to cut off supply lines, to slit as many German throats as possible, and to carry out operations from Finland that target the removal of Germans from northern Norway." In the running to lead these Lapland throat-slitters was the former military attaché, "Shamus" Magill, who was "just the sort of tough chap" required.

Within the SOE, the belief was that Finland might allow Soviet troops into the north to help drive out the Germans, but probably not to prevent the Nazis from making their way between Hämeenlinna and Pori to evacuate through the southern ports. "Would they [the Finns] remain idle, if the hated Russians would be in the heart of the country?" The chief of intelligence judged the Finns to be so disciplined that they would even maintain a neutral position if that were to happen, "so long as the Russians conduct themselves civilly."[56]

Whether the Russians would want to fight in Finland against the Germans was another matter. If they did, British military intelligence assessed that the Soviets would first target Oulu and Tornio on the Baltic coast, then Sodankylä and Ivalo on the main road to the Arctic, but that they were unlikely to launch a big operation. The climate and the topography would remind the Soviets too much of the Winter War.[57] The far-sighted British saw that the partisans alone would not be enough to banish the Germans: that would require an army, whether Finnish or Soviet. In order to avoid the arrival of the Soviets on their soil, the Finns would pick the lesser of the two evils and themselves take military action against the Germans.[58]

The partisan project was aborted for a number of reasons: practical difficulties, terrible climate, relatively little advantage, predicted political problems with the Soviets—and, ultimately, the Finns' refusal to accept Moscow's conditions for peace. Some in the SOE had pre-empted this rejection: driving the Germans out might lead to Finland's occupation, "and, on top of that, the country would be turned into a battlefield [...] surely any Finn in such conditions would then consider it preferable to continue the war?"[59]

It is not known whether the British had a chance to present the partisan plan to the Soviets, or whether Moscow otherwise got wind of it. It is safe to assume that the Soviet leadership would not have received the proposal warmly. An SOE team sent to Poland ended up in a Red Army prison.[60] The project laid bare the dangers and threats that hung over the Finnish leaders when they made their decision. The overview on 16 February of the Head of Intelligence, Aladár Paasonen, to officers at military headquarters was interpreted as reflecting Mannerheim's attitudes. The main aim was perhaps to soften the officers up to the idea that they could end up fighting against the Germans. According to intelligence acquired by the British, Paasonen had a hunch that a fight between the Red Army and the Germans in Finland could result in a civil war among the Finns.[61] Soviet military plans were based on the presumption that the Germans would try to fight even in southern Finland.[62]

In Finland, Moscow's conditions were first debated in a meeting of the government's Foreign Affairs Committee, headed by the President, on 23 and 24 February. Paasikivi pressed for accepting the terms and entering into negotiations, arguing that no better offer was coming, but the ministers did not immediately agree. Soviet intelligence received a detailed report of this discussion.[63]

On 28 February, Stalin told the British ambassador Clark Kerr— referencing intelligence information—that he feared the sounding out of Paasikivi would not lead anywhere. If it did, he stated directly that the British government would not be needed in the negotiations nor even as a signatory to the peace agreement, adding that Britain could end its war with Finland through a separate document. His justification was that Finland and the Soviet Union had a great many specific bilateral questions to be settled between them, such as borders and reparations.[64] The British, however, insisted that they wanted to be involved in the composition of every article of the treaty and also wanted to sign it.

Stalin saw to it that the British were given correct, but meager, information, to keep them from getting intimately involved in developments. If the Soviets could squeeze more out of the Finns than had been agreed in Tehran, they would get the deal signed and the deed done. The West would not have a say, nor any particular interest. The Foreign Secretary, Anthony Eden, admitted to the Soviet ambassador that the British did not have any significant differences of opinion with Moscow concerning Finland. Unlike Poland, it would not prove a fractious issue.[65]

Stalin did not specify his intelligence sources. During the Soviets' discussions with Paasikivi another well-informed Finn arrived in Stockholm. Soviet intelligence aimed to recruit him, code-named TSILINDR, presumably "top hat" rather than "cylinder."[66] TSILINDR informed KLARA (her again) that the opinion in Finnish government circles was that the country had waged a separate war against the Soviets, so it could also make a separate peace. And "Tanner, who at one time was pro-German, is now demanding that the Germans leave Finland."[67]

While many details are shrouded in darkness, the available evidence points to TSILINDR having been Eero A. Wuori, the chairman of the Central Organization of Finnish Trade Unions (SAK). He left hastily for Stockholm on the invitation of the Swedish Trade Union Confederation (LO). The invitation was made at the request of Vladimir Semyonov at the Soviet Legation.[68] Semyonov would become a famous diplomat, and would lead the SALT negotiations for the Soviet Union in Helsinki in 1969. He is not thought of as an intelligence officer, but he does appear to have assisted with operations in Stockholm.

Wuori was in a different political league than the Swedish-speaking left wing of the Peace Opposition that the Soviet intelligence had earlier cultivated. He was one of the leading figures in the Social Democratic Party, a former close ally of Tanner and on good terms with Mannerheim. A big fish worth catching.

It is not known whether Wuori was taken in by Soviet subterfuge or whether he knew the lay of the land from the outset. No

14. Central Organization of Finnish Trade Unions head Eero A. Wuori (left) at a lunch to celebrate Marshal Mannerheim's seventy-fifth birthday. Also present was Adolf Hitler. Wuori later served as a Soviet intelligence source.

intelligence officer, KLARA was the stylish, cosmopolitan reporter Augustine Stridsberg, regularly to be found in Stockholm's Klara quarters, the favorite haunt of journalists. Having arrived in Sweden as a refugee in 1939, she had acquired citizenship through a sham marriage. Her recruitment by Soviet intelligence took place in the first half of the 1930s. She was an ideological Communist who was "completely devoted" to the Soviet cause, as the NKGB's new Stockholm chief V.F. Razin noted approvingly.[69] Stridsberg had a close-knit network of anti-Nazi contacts in refugee and diplomat circles, and she knew personally Sweden's foremost Social Democrats and journalists. She was the accredited correspondent of the *Toronto Star*, the Canadian newspaper for which Hemingway wrote; like him, Stridsberg had also undertaken journalistic work in Spain during the Spanish Civil War.

Her more important contacts were, however, her Soviet handlers in Stockholm: first Zoya Yartseva, and then Razin himself. Both kept an attentive eye on Helsinki, where Yartseva had served previously.[70] Evdokia Petrova, the Soviet intelligence captain who defected in Australia in 1954, claimed that KLARA, whom she had looked after briefly in Stockholm, was actually a double agent.[71] This is not impossible: the US Office of Strategic Services (OSS) undertook anti-Nazi espionage in Stockholm, and Vilho Tikander, its representative in the city, had a reputation as a parlor pink. However, there is no hard evidence to corroborate Petrova's assertion.

Razin asked Moscow for permission to recruit TSILINDR. The response was positive, but it is not clear what exactly happened next. Wuori came to Stockholm again less than a fortnight later to give information about the Finnish parliament's secret session, Finland's draft reply to the peace terms, and the contact made between the government and the Peace Opposition. He also outlined Tanner's opinions, stressing the desire for peace and anti-German mindset of the Social Democrats' leader.[72] This contradicted more ideological information that Moscow had received through Yrjö Leino's Communist network, which claimed that the Social Democrat opposition were operating "against Tanner on behalf of peace" and that they were under the influence of the Finnish Communist Party's newspapers. The latter claim was apparently based only on the fact that a Communist Party leaflet had been placed in the mailbox of J.W. Keto, a member of the Peace Opposition.[73]

The increasing need to assess and influence Finland's political life brought the NKGB political intelligence officer Elisei Sinitsyn (Eliseyev in the Nordic countries) to Stockholm in January. He had served in Helsinki before the Winter War and then during the interim peace in 1940–41, and he knew Wuori, even claiming in his memoirs that he had recruited the Finn at that time, under the code name MOSES. This could be boasting, for the Soviets now approached Wuori as a new target. He became MOSES in NKGB books: Wuori

means "mountain" and the original Moses received the ten command-
ments on Mount Sinai. The Bible was frequently used as a source for
code names. In any case, an intelligence officer who knew Finland
was badly needed in Stockholm, and there was no surplus of them.
Boris Yartsev was summoned back to Moscow after a prominent case
of espionage was exposed.[74] His wife Zoya soon followed. Andrei
Graur, who had been Wuolijoki's handler during the Winter War,
was currently in the running to be an official contact man in the
United States.[75] Razin, the intelligence chief in Stockholm, was an
experienced officer, but he had never served in Finland and had very
limited understanding of the country's political realities. Vivacious
young female journalists pleased his eye: first Mai Jarke in Stockholm,
and then, when he was transferred to Helsinki in 1945, a newswoman
was immediately found with strikingly similar looks.[76]

In order to influence developments in Helsinki, the Soviets took
a different approach from the one in 1940, when they had leant on
the far left. Now the focus was on ties with the Peace Opposition,
primarily with Social Democrats, but also with sympathetic bourgeois politicians. Paasikivi, of course, but others besides: this was the
moment when Urho Kekkonen of the Agrarians came under the
Soviet scan. Such names were seen as the backbone of the forthcoming "friendship-minded" government, of the kind that Stalin had
repeatedly required be in neighboring countries after the war. From
the pool of sympathetic politicians, "agents of influence" were
recruited for cultivation.

The requirements for changing the direction of the Finnish
government were different from those in many other countries
between Germany and the Soviet Union. Restoring democracy could
not be a clear target, since the Finnish government was voted in
through reasonably democratic elections, was broad-based, and still
enjoyed broad popular support. Democracy was not perfect, but it
was not absent here either. Nor could Moscow use the claim leveled
against Poland that a government-in-exile had lost touch with the

conditions of its people. Finland was not occupied, the government was in power, and the civil service functioned. There was no clean slate for the creation of a "new power," as if the old one had never existed; instead, it had to be built bit by bit inside the existing one, at least as long as Finland remained unoccupied.

Wuori and others like him were convinced to cooperate with the Soviets to serve the cause of peace by helping to disengage Finland from the war. They got some information from the Soviets, but it was fed in coordinated doses and for the purpose of influence. Not known for any shortage of self-esteem, politicians thought they could handle dealings with intelligence contacts, but more often than not they were alone and dependent on their own judgment. Their Soviet contacts, in contrast, were part of a hierarchical machine, in which information from different sources was compared before any decision was made on how to proceed; only then was information fed to the appropriate contacts. Be it the congenial female reporter or the unflinching diplomat with forthright opinions, both were following orders and accountable to their superiors.

Wuori's assessment maybe encouraged the Soviets to sound out Tanner. Semyonov supplied the Swedish Social Democrat Rickard Lindström with the information that the Soviet Union had no plans to conquer the Nordic lands, only the Balkans. He declared that the border issue "is not fixed, Vyborg could remain with Finland" and compensation would be given for the loss of Petsamo. He hoped that Mannerheim would visit Moscow. After dropping by Helsinki and chatting with Tanner, Lindström reported back to Semyonov that Finland was prepared to discuss all six terms, but it could not accept them without further discussion.[77] Now the Soviets knew precisely how to get the Finns to the negotiating table.

Mannerheim and the army leadership had, according to TSILINDR, perhaps the most comprehensive view of the situation. The Finnish Army was not in the service of the Nazis and its officers were usually not Nazis, especially General Erik Heinrichs. Defense Minister Rudolf Walden belonged to the "more decent crowd" in the government; he had a close relationship with Mannerheim, and he supported an agreement with the Soviets. Since the Finnish nation did not bear any hostility towards Germany, TSILINDR was of the opinion that the Finns would not turn their weapons on the Germans unless the latter did something to precipitate it.[78]

The Soviets tended to believe in information that was gathered covertly and via back channels. Maybe this influenced the Kremlin's decision to drop the demand to accept the conditions in advance, and to agree instead to discuss them with one or two authorized negotiators. Kollontay hoped that these would be Paasikivi and Walden, "or another person close to the Marshal." The old temptress insinuated that "Moscow's truly benevolent attitude will amaze the Finns." Erik Boheman, Sweden's State Secretary for Foreign Affairs, gave credence to this with his assertion for the Finns that Vyborg and the Saimaa Canal could be on the table.[79]

Giving up on preconditions was not a common tactic in Moscow's diplomatic toolkit. It was more likely to stick steadfastly to what had been uttered in the first place, at least in dealings with small states. The uncharacteristic pliancy indicates that Stalin was sincere in his desire to tempt the Finns—and Mannerheim in particular—to cross the Rubicon towards the third Rome, as Moscow had sometimes been known. In contrast to Caesar, however, the Finns did not have a single seer to forecast victory for them.

Still before the negotiations, Moscow received from Stockholm yet another intelligence report on Finnish left-wing Peace Opposition views. After describing the increasingly pro-peace opinion of the political and military leadership and the people in general, the source proceeded to current opinions of the left-most elements in the Peace Opposition. According to recent opinions, after the peace treaty the developments would inevitably take Finland the way of three small Baltic states. Swift succession of governments would give way "to post-war people's government which would raise the question of Finland's incorporation in the Soviet Union." The most probable source for this speculation was the journalist Atos Wirtanen, a Social Democratic member of the Diet, and the most probable location for loose and unrealistic talk was Gusti Stridsberg's salon.[80] There was, even later, some Finnish leftists who believed—on the basis of summer 1940—that this was what Moscow ultimately wanted, and that they better behave accordingly.[81] However, knowing what the incorporation of Finland could possibly involve, Stalin at this stage was searching to advance through political and military maneuvers. Reports like this could create in the Kremlin the impression that the government of Finland was losing ground and wavering. That might have contributed to Molotov's aggressive behavior in the Moscow talks.

Neither Mannerheim nor even Walden ended up leaving for Moscow: Paasikivi and the former Foreign Minister Carl Enckell traveled in their stead,[82] with Captain Georg Enckell as secretary, and as Mannerheim's ears. Carl's nephew, Georg, was the son of General Oscar Enckell, an experienced officer in Russian Imperial military intelligence. Georg was also a source for the OSS, the American intelligence agency, handing over to them the minutes that he recorded himself.[83] Staffan Söderblom, head of the political department at Sweden's Foreign Ministry, informed the Soviet Legation in Stockholm that in Finland there was hope for a meeting between Marshal Mannerheim and Marshal Stalin. According to Söderblom's understanding, the negotiations in Moscow would only be cursory, for the Finns would soon return home to report.[84] "In Finland" most likely meant "in Mikkeli," where the Finnish army headquarters were located, and Stalin undoubtedly understood this. The way to peace went through Mannerheim.

This impression was strengthened by the course of the negotiations. Finland's representatives were seeking clarifications, lacking a mandate to solve or even touch upon military matters. Moscow, for its part, had made preparations for such discussions on the previous evening by ordering General S.M. Shtemenko, chief of the Operations Directorate, to attend in a civilian suit. As he did not own such an item, a man looking like a magician was called to take his measurements, and the next morning a dark suit was ready and waiting.

The principal Soviet aim was to get Finland to sever ties with Germany. Thereafter the negotiations would undoubtedly proceed apace. Paasikivi and Enckell did not have the authority to discuss such an issue or even touch on military details, but only to seek clarity on the conditions. It was a shock for the Finns that there was no sign of the concessions that had been alluded to by Kollontay and the Swedes, to say nothing of Moscow's supposedly benevolent attitude. Molotov's interpretation of the terms could not have been more uncompromising, and he refused to yield on a single point.

Paasikivi touched upon military matters when he remonstrated that there was no hope of disarming the Germans because they were mostly in Soviet territory at the Litsa River, not far from Murmansk.[85] On this point there was friction between the Finnish negotiators,[86] also caused by the fact that Enckell did not have experience in Stalinist diplomacy, although he had served in Imperial Russia and conducted business with the Bolsheviks in the 1920s. Georg Enckell would later reveal that his uncle set out on the trip without any faith that it would prove fruitful.[87] As the Finns stayed overnight at a guesthouse (*osobnyak*) on Ostrovskiy pereulok, their arguments were eavesdropped on by the hosts. Enckell was the most enraged, but Paasikivi did not keep his cool either—second to nobody in that respect. Enckell opposed accepting the border straightaway; he agreed that demobilization was a natural part of the peace process and an economic necessity, but he also thought that the conditions had been written to humiliate. In his view, the document in general was suspicious, since "the Russians can't be trusted, you have to clarify everything with them." They should, he argued, tell Molotov that the terms were even more unjust and severe than in the peace of 1940. In Enckell's opinion it would be better to wait until September, when the situation at the front would be clearer and it would be easier to ascertain whether Germany or the Soviet Union would win.

Paasikivi, for his part, saw the obvious outcome of the war: the Germans' position was hopeless and there was no prospect of a compromise-based peace settlement, as the Soviets wanted to crush Germany. The conditions were harsh, but Finland would not get any better. The only point on which the two negotiators fully agreed was that the reparations were too high. They now knew that Moscow wanted $600 million paid over five years, but Paasikivi hoped the sum to be cut in half to $300 million.[88]

During the second session of talks, in the afternoon of 29 March, the two sides spent a long time wrangling over recent history, opening with the classic question: Who started ...? On the Winter War, Molotov had the gall to ask: "What caused the Finns to begin the war at that time?" Paasikivi responded: "We did not start that war," only for Molotov to note that, nonetheless, "the Finns turned out to be allies of Germany." Not wanting to break up the talks, Paasikivi did not state that during the Winter War the Soviet Union was a de facto ally of Germany, nor that it was Molotov who had signed the pact with Hitler that gave the backing to attack Finland. Instead, he argued that the Winter War failed to improve Leningrad's security in the slightest: without that war the city on the Neva River would have been better defended, since Finland would not have taken up with Germany in 1941 at the first opportunity. A pained Molotov at last complained that the Finns always plead naivety in international politics, "but if all neighbors would be so 'naïve,' life would become intolerable for us!"[89]

Negotiations terminated late in the evening that day, when Molotov presented the Finns with polished peace terms. These consisted of seven items, and included a couple of small concessions intended to placate the Finnish Army leadership. They were about the expulsion of the Germans and the demobilization of the Finns. The reparations, however, were still $600 million in kind over five years. Molotov claimed that the sum represented only half of the damages that, according to experts' estimates, had been caused by the Finnish Army in Soviet Karelia. Actually, it was based on calculations of Finland's volume of imports and its solvency, and on a careful examination of Finland's loans from and repayments to the United States during the First World War and even the Winter War. This time the reputation as a dutiful debtor worked to Finland's disadvantage.[90]

The amount and composition of the reparations caught the attention of the British. When Ambassador Gusev brought the conditions to the Foreign Office, "[Sir Orme] Sargent laughed and said that the Soviet Union will take all the forest from Finland and leave nothing for trade with England." The sum of $600 million was a hefty (*solidnaya*) one for a country like Finland.[91] A British government memo labeled the total excessive in relation to Finland's resources and urged the Soviets to take into account the British desire to continue receiving products from Finnish wood and paper industries. In addition, it reminded the Soviets that reparations could not be taken from British assets or receivables, and it demanded an agreement (with Britain and Canada) on compensation to the Mond Nickel Company, which had the mining concession in Petsamo.[92]

The trip to Moscow did not lead to actual peace negotiations, nor to a peace agreement, as Finland rejected the terms, primarily because it would have been exceedingly difficult to intern the Germans in the north. And Germany was in control of the Baltic Sea and still able to take countermeasures. Finland might end up in an insecure position at the Soviet Union's mercy; not a place of neutrality, but a theater of war. Peace on those terms would have shattered national unity, the very unity that had enabled the waging of war. Nor were the people quite ready to admit defeat.

Is This All?

The Soviet Union emphasized to both the British and the Finns that the seven conditions were a minimum. The British Permanent Under-Secretary for Foreign Affairs, Alexander Cadogan, noted in his diary that the Finns? would be fools if they did not accept, "although naturally no one can trust Joe to stick to his terms."[93] Finally agreeing to explain to Paasikivi why it was an armistice rather than a peace like in 1940, Molotov said: "The armistice allows for further terms to be levied during the peace-making process."[94] This was honest talk, but he declined to expand further, perhaps mindful of "Joe" Stalin's aphorism that a diplomat's words should not correspond to deeds, for an honest diplomat was as possible as dry water or an iron tree.[95]

Joe did not plan to stick to his terms. The Soviets indeed had additional conditions ready. In their papers, the seven terms were followed by items 8–12. They appear in the People's Commissariat of Foreign Affairs comparative memo, in which the Soviet Union's terms and the British comments on the first seven were presented alongside each other. The final points (8–12) have no comments, since they had not been shown to the British any more than to the Finns.

Item 8: the fortified islands of Suomenlinna in front of Helsinki to be leased to the Soviet Union as a military and naval base. These islands were first fortified in the mid-eighteenth century. This demand was inherited from the situation under the Russian Empire, when Suomenlinna (at that time Sveaborg) did not belong to Helsinki city or to Finland, but directly to the empire.

Item 9: a sea base on the Åland Islands for as long as the situation in the Baltic Sea region continued to be dangerous. The time limit was much more malleable than, for example, simply the termination of hostilities in Europe.

Item 10: the construction of railway lines to the military bases on Suomenlinna and the Åland Islands. And also to the base in Hanko, even though the Soviets were, in the same breath, promising to give it up. As for Åland, this was probably technically impossible at that time.

Item 11: Soviet consulates to be established in Rovaniemi, Vaasa and Turku. The choice of cities was based on the key locations for the German troop transfers through Finland in 1940.

Item 12: the final twist of the knife: the "correction [*ispravlenie*]" of the 1940 border, so that the Soviet Union would get the whole Saimaa Canal, the opening stretch of the rapids in the Vuoksi River, and the Saimaa lakeshore area (apparently the land between these two waterways in the region of Lappeenranta and Imatra). The aim was to get significant economic gains (from the area's wood-processing industry and the hydropower of the rapids) and to make the defense of Finland much more difficult.[96]

All twelve conditions and British comments to the first seven formed the basis of the draft peace treaty written in Moscow. Assumed signatories were the Soviet Union and Finland between the two of them, without Britain, despite the fact that it had declared war on Finland. However, British observations were taken into account.[97]

The starting point was the Moscow Peace Treaty of 1940, with the exception of the border, which now had Petsamo and the southern shore of Saimaa Lake transferred to the Soviet side. The latter change was presented as the border "straightening," although it added a kink to the straight line of 1940. British remarks about the reparations were ignored: the total was still $600 million, and the Soviets were prioritizing payment in forest industry products.

Several treaty articles aimed to weaken Finland's defensive capacity. The demobilization of the Finnish Army was to happen in two stages: first the size reduction by 50 percent, after which the peacetime numbers would be reached quite soon. The forfeiture of Saimaa's shoreline would have a substantial impact in this regard, as would the duty for Finland to destroy fortifications along the border, as well as sea bases on and around the Gulf of Finland, except in areas to be leased to the Soviet Union.

The selection of military bases was changed and extended in this draft. Suomenlinna and the islands in the Gulf of Finland were still on the list, but the Soviets had added new sites to be leased: Haapasaari, close to Kotka, and Porkkala Cape west of Helsinki, now mentioned for the first time. A military base on the Åland Islands was dropped, on the basis of three considerations. First, to avoid upsetting the Swedes. Second, the 1856 Treaty of Paris at the end of the Crimean War, was still in force, stipulating the islands' demilita-rization, and there were a number of signatories to contend with, not least Britain and France. Better to let the Finno-Soviet Agreement on the Åland Islands (11 October 1940) suffice for the time being. And third, the benefits of Porkkala as a base location. In conjunction with Estonia's Naissaar island, 47 kilometers due south, it gave the Soviets the option of closing off the Gulf of Finland with artillery fire. This was a military advantage Stalin had already noted in nego-tiations before the Winter War. At that time, according to his own announcement, he refrained from demanding these sites, since they were located too close to the two countries' capitals.[98] Now, however, it was precisely his intention to be able to put pressure on Helsinki and its Western connections, and to ensure that a swift intervention would be possible if needed. Suomenlinna was suitable for surveil-lance, but too cramped for the ground forces to take effective offen-sive positions. The Soviets had learnt their lesson from Hanko: they required a much larger military base, and control of the Helsinki–Turku railway line.

To change Finland's political situation, the draft agreement contained the demand to disband fascist and paramilitary organiza-tions, "such as the Civil Guards, Lotta Svärd, successors to the Lapua Movement and others." This was connected with the portrayal of the future political climate in Germany after the Tehran Conference, and was vital for foreign Communists interviewed by the Litvinov

Commission.[99] There is no evidence, however, that Moscow was planning to transform—radically and quickly—the societal structure of its neighbors at this stage, except for three Baltic republics, considered as parts of the USSR.

Reports about the Finnish parliament's secret session vote on Soviet terms made Moscow diplomats assess which were the worst political parties. The worst one, the pro-German but small Patriotic People's Movement (*Isänmaallinen kansanliike*) consisted of agents of Hitler and aimed to establish a complete fascist dictatorship. The second place was given to the Agrarian League, which was seen as representing the kulak class and at the current moment "supportive of the country's move towards fascism."[100] The real reason for the Agrarian vote against Soviet terms was the strong support enjoyed by the party among Karelians, who were destined to lose their homesteads once again.

On the basis of the British comments, articles were composed stating that German property should be confiscated and given over to the Allies. Finland was obliged to provide information about German finances and comply with Allied instructions about international agreements. Finally, it was decreed that the Allied Control Commission would come to Finland. Although the initiative here came from the British, these articles would later prove very useful to the Soviet Union. Moscow's suggestion was that the commission stay in Finland until the end of the war with Germany, but the British proposed it remain until the signing of a definitive peace treaty. As it turned out, that added two and a half years of service for the commission.

At the conclusion, Moscow's industrious officials drew up a document comparing the draft treaty with the Winter War peace agreement, to ensure that Finland would not escape with lesser demands in any of the conditions.[101]

The additional conditions reflected the priorities of military, intelligence and ideological interests, but they would not have got into the draft peace agreement without the blessing or rather an order from above. Rather than a scenario outlined by the diplomats, this was a list given from above, written to order, and sanctioned in the same vein as those shown to the Finns and the British. Nor were the extra conditions made at the preparatory stage and then sidelined, since both the draft and its comparison with the earlier treaty were further refined *after* Molotov's talks with the Finns. The evidence suggests that the extra terms were penned at the direct behest of Stalin and Molotov, but the occasion to present them did not materialize. Had the Finnish government cut ties with Germany and begun serious negotiations, these conditions would have been presented. After the war, Paasikivi often ranted that the most favorable peace was available during the spring of 1944, but it seems that this was not the case.

In April the American journalist John Scott, based in Stockholm, visited Finland for two weeks. Well received at the top level (by Ryti, Tanner, Paasikivi), he was also offered a tour of the countryside and the workers' quarters in Helsinki, as well as a chance to talk with Ingrian Finns evacuated to Finland from the Leningrad region. According to him, ordinary Finns thought that "Finland is an undefeated country in which wartime life is difficult but by no means intolerable." Paasikivi gave him a lecture lasting four and a half hours on his opinions and experience in recent talks in Moscow. The old man's general mood was pessimistic, but in the end he had something in mind in case Russia overran Finland. He stood up, shook a bony, freckled forefinger in the air and said:

> We will shoot from behind every stone and tree, we will go on shooting for fifty years. We are not Czechs. We are not Dutchmen. We will fight tooth and nail behind every rock and over the ice of every lake. I will not fight for long. I am old, but others will carry on.[102]

105

Scott had lived in the Soviet Union (mainly in Magnitogorsk) for nine years, until in 1941 he was given permission to return to the United States with his Russian wife and daughter.[103] According to a memoir written by the intelligence *rezident* in Stockholm, V.P. Roshchin (Razin), he made the visit to Helsinki on a request of the NKGB, and the results were excellent, because the Finns trusted him and were very frank. The Soviet conclusion, at least in Stockholm, was that Finland was in a completely hopeless position.[104] However, this was not that evident in Scott's report to American agencies.

Soviet intelligence in Stockholm sent at least one additional observer to Helsinki. On 9 May, Mai Jarke—a Swedish citizen and journalist—showed up in Helsinki. She was "dressed in a scarlet jacket, a reddish-brown hat, red shoes and black gloves on her hands. Her hair had been combed up, 'in washerwoman style'." She stayed in town until after midsummer in the empty central Helsinki apartment of Dr Laurin Zilliacus, a prominent figure in the Peace Opposition. As her boyfriend, Razin, was the Soviet intelligence chief in Stockholm, it seems that in addition to journalism, she was probing into the mood in Helsinki political and citizen circles. Jarke was observed at the offices of the Social Democrats on 26 June, after which she made haste back to Stockholm. Whatever information she had accumulated, her briefing in Stockholm happened fairly late, as events unfolded fast.[105]

Ordinary Finns remained waiting. Wishful thinking was widespread, but the general atmosphere was ominous. Such a feeling seeps surprisingly deeply into society, even if the precise shape and timing of the threat are unknown. One particularly sensitive group were the Estonians living in Finland, many of whom actively began to break away from official surveillance and/or headed off for Sweden.

Midway through May, a sentry on night watch in Helsinki was accosted by a drunk young artillery lieutenant, who urged him to watch "how a Finnish officer drinks wood polish." The guard was no greenhorn: his nose recognized the substance as cut brandy. Heedless of the sentry's accent, which revealed his Russian origin, the lieu-tenant started complaining that Finland was ill-prepared to ward off an attack, especially because of the lack of artillery and fighter planes. About the war, Finland does not "know anything. Different from civilian population in Germany! If he wanted, the *ryssä* could, natu-rally, make that sort of mark here, too. There would be no opposition to speak of from the Finns."[106]

Capitulation?

The Soviet Army launched its all-out attack on the Karelian Isthmus on 10 June 1944. The aim was to destroy Finland's main forces, advance to the Kymijoki River defensive line, and present a "tangible threat" to southern Finland's population centers. Looking at the map, Stalin assessed that Finland would stand down "when our troops reach Loimola station." The early stages of the assault were an unmitigated success, for the Soviets reached Vyborg in just ten days.[107]

During the preparations, three interconnected decisions were made by Moscow in April. The first was to seek a military resolution to the Finnish problem. As late as February the Soviet Union's plan of attack was centered on Germany's 20th Mountain Army in Lapland. A few days before Paasikivi and Enckell's trip to Moscow, the Soviet high command (Stavka) instructed that "operations on the Karelian Front were not being considered for the time being, not against the Finns nor against the Germans." When negotiations did not produce results, the high command began reconsidering. The focus of the attack was turned on Finnish forces: breaking through them would expose the Germans' flank and open the way to Finland's heartlands. Discussing the attack plans with General Shtemenko at the Kuntsevo dacha, Stalin said: "The Finns are no longer what they used to be. They are faltering in all respects and searching for peace." The initial decisions to attack were made in mid-April.[108]

The second decision was to ban contacts with the Finnish government. Tanner made a motion in mid-May that the Swedish Social Democratic editor Rickard Lindström contact Semyonov with a proposal: if it were guaranteed that Finland could keep Vyborg and the Saimaa Canal, then the Finns would be prepared to attack the German troops in their country. Kollontay suggested that they hear Tanner out, but Molotov's rejection was swift: no dealings [*ne imet' dela*] with the Finnish government. He stated that this decision could only be reversed at a meeting of all members of the Soviet government in Moscow, but that was unlikely in the near future as the majority of them were at the front lines. Kollontay told Boheman that she had received orders to pass on Molotov's rebuff "diplomatically and without hurting the Finns' feelings." Apparently she was instructed to adopt a pacifying tone, since she claimed that the Soviet government fully understood Finland's attitude and urged its leaders to wait for a more auspicious occasion. In the same vein the Soviet Embassy in Bern spread the rumor that the conditions could be considerably amended in the Finns' favor.[109]

This was reminiscent of the Winter War, when the Soviets refused to communicate with the government in Helsinki. However, on this occasion the Finnish leadership did not quite grasp what was going on. Molotov's response was approaching mockery, as if an outsider could not have any conception of how the Soviet government decided about war and peace. Stalin made the decisions, and he only seems to have made a single visit to the front during the entire war.[110] Unlike his successor, Stalin did not like to move among the rank and file.

The third decision was to insert Finland without reservations into the group of countries that would receive demands for unconditional surrender. When appeals were prepared, on the United States' initiative, to Germany's satellite states, Molotov proposed that Finland should be included, for it "is engaged in the war on the Germans' side and is Hitlerite Germany's satellite."[111] The protocol signed by the foreign ministers of the United Kingdom, United States and Soviet

Union in Moscow on 1 November 1943 does not describe Finland in such terms, which left open the interpretation that the demand of unconditional surrender did not apply to it.

The Western Powers used the concept of surrender more broadly than Moscow. It contained a sense of giving up, and was nowhere near as unconditional or uncompromising as "capitulation." Moscow began to consider the possibilities offered by the term's usage.[112] Ambassador Kerr hoped that "the conditions of surrender for Finland" would be formulated by a general commission.[113] A side issue, of course, was that semantics still enabled the Kremlin to shroud its possible demand of surrender in ambiguity. If the West would press the Soviets on why they had disregarded the Tehran Agreement, they could explain having used "surrender" in the same sense as the Western Powers.

Another, more substantial concern for the Soviets was the revival of American interest to Finland. The United States was officially a secondary party in discussions over Finland's future, as the two countries were not at war with each other. In May 1944, President Roosevelt commented to Ambassador William Averell Harriman, that he "didn't care whether the countries bordering Russia became communized."[114] American concern was, however, growing. Once he had reached Moscow, Harriman "unexpectedly" asked Vyshinsky on 7 June for news on Finland.[115] This surely startled those Soviets who knew what would take place on the Karelian Isthmus in a couple of days.

Through intelligence channels, Moscow received a memo detailing a Washington foreign relations brainstorming on policy towards Finland.[116] Officially there was no comment on the peace conditions for Finland, but after March the Inter-Divisional Committee on Finland, which included the renowned Soviet Union expert Charles E. Bohlen, did ponder solutions. Its memo was accepted by the Committee on Post-War Programs, one of the foremost groups in the State Department, led by Secretary of State Cordell Hull.[117]

According to the 'Treatment of Finland' memo the country was not at war of its own volition, but it had ended up on the losing side and was facing a period of transition, during which Soviet military and political interests would prevail. However, Finland's independence, form of governance and culture were worth preserving. The Americans' underlying aim was for an independent Finland that would have a good relationship with the Soviet Union.

In the preliminary version of the memo, it was even envisaged that the border could be that of the 1920 Treaty of Tartu, since the Soviet Union would no longer have to fear German aggression.[118] Then the committee consented more realistically to the border of the Winter War. Soviet annexation of Petsamo was also acceptable, but no more: it was necessary to protect the regional balance, in relation to the Åland Islands, for example. While the Soviets had the military might to compel Finland to accept a border of their choosing and the Americans did not have any direct stake in that part of the world, the United States was most definitely for securing peace in Europe. To this end, it was paramount to establish a border that safeguarded the fundamental interests of both neighbors.

For the Americans, more important than the exact demarcation of the border was Finland's societal structure. In contrast to Germany and its satellite states, it was not in the American interest to change the country's form of governance. Democracy would be upheld and strengthened, so long as the economic and military conditions for peace permitted. Even though the Soviet government's terms did not interfere with Finland's internal order, in his May Day greetings Stalin had urged the Finnish people to take matters into their own hands.[119] There were no signs, however, of anything akin to Kuusinen's puppet government from the Winter War. A majority of Finns wanted to keep hold of democracy, but reactionary and aggressive forces could exploit the pervasive fear of Russia in the country. The United States could make it easier for Finland's democratic forces to stay in control.

The Americans supported Finland's close relationship with Scandinavia, as long as it did not go against the United States' general international economic policy. Once again, however, Moscow's position was considered decisive. In order to avoid becoming a part of the Soviet Union, postwar Finland would have to cooperate closely with Moscow, not least by adopting a harmonious foreign policy. It would not undermine the United States' interests if Finland was able to maintain good relations with other peace-loving nations and engage in independent foreign trade, that is, forest industry exports, receiving foreign credits for that. For this to be possible, the colossal reparations Moscow wanted to impose on Finland would have to be limited. Since Finland was burdened with the loss of Vyborg and the resettlement of displaced Karelians, its economy should not be the target of excessive penalties.

The committee in Washington saw that attaching any American guarantee to the peace conditions would alleviate Finnish fears of the Soviet Union and help the transition out of the war. On the other hand, such a promise would run contrary to the general principles of the United States, and cause disquiet in Moscow. Thus, it would be best to help the country once peace had been made, by offering food aid and other assistance, and by assuring the Finns "that Finland's future security would be best ensured within the international security organization." This was a reference to the United Nations, which still lay in the future.

Although there was no mention of occupation in the Soviets' conditions, the Americans could not exclude that the Red Army operations could result in that. Shared interests of the Allies and European stability required dealing with the possible occupation of Finland as an issue for all the Allies and not for the Soviets alone. Declaring war on Finland would mean participating in the occupation, but this was not considered wise, for the Soviet Union's military and political interests would still be dominant.[120]

From the Kremlin's perspective, it was alarming that its great Western ally was interfering in earnest on the question of Finland. As the Soviet Army was steamrolling its way across the Karelian Isthmus, Harriman told Vyshinsky that President Roosevelt had decided to end the use of the term "unconditional surrender" in propaganda targeting Germany's satellites. Vyshinsky was a wily comrade, but even someone far dumber would have realized that the Americans were planning to scrap the whole demand.[121] The Soviets saw that the window to demand the surrender of Finland was closing. In order to preserve their free rein at this critical stage, the Soviet Union systematically ignored a constant stream of enquiries from the British regarding the peace conditions for Finland. When commanding his officials not to respond, Vyshinsky observed that "we are not accountable to the English on this question."[122]

With both Western Powers having highlighted their economic interests in Finland, Moscow composed a memo on 2 June that laid out how the Soviet Union would completely dominate Finland's economic future. The plan reflected the Marxist notion about the pivotal role of economy to society. Due to the ravages of war, the loss of territory and the reparations, Finland's volume of foreign trade would, according to Soviet calculations, shrink to 47 percent of its pre-war level. The Soviet Union aimed to assume a position of absolute dominance in such import sectors as oil products (thereby sidelining the United States), coal (superseding Great Britain), textile raw materials and fertilizers. As for Finnish exports, the majority of cellulose, paper and plywood would go to the Soviet Union, not to the West as before the war.[123] The prerequisite for achieving all this was the complete subordination of Finland and the control of both its domestic politics and foreign policy. The Soviets seemed to believe that the Finns would surrender.

The attack's political goal was to change the direction of the Finnish government and the internal situation in the country as a whole. The intelligence officer Elisei Sinitsyn said as much in conversation with the Swedish diplomat Sverker Åström in Stockholm on 12 June. He noted that it was difficult to find people who were both held in high regard among their own people and prepared to cooperate unreservedly with the Russians. Regardless of which, he underlined that national security necessitated an amenable, so-called "pro-friendship" government. This was unquestionably the case. Then again, Sinitsyn's apparent role was to appease, to shield the harsher aspects of the Soviets' actions from Swedish view and to slow down any measures, such as occupying the Åland Islands, that Sweden had planned in case of Finland's collapse. If the Red Army were already on the islands by that stage, Sweden could not do much.[124]

Sinitsyn's message was conveyed to Helsinki, where the convoluted and messy process of changing government was already underway. On 19 June, Erik Boheman, Sweden's Secretary of State for Foreign Affairs, brought to Kollontay the awaited announcement from Finland's envoy to Stockholm, G.A. Gripenberg: there would be a change of government that same day in Helsinki. Tanner and Linkomies would be removed, and "the task of the new government is to submit a request for peace to Moscow without delay." Mannerheim would not enter into the government, but he supported the change to create a connection for talks. Boheman stressed "that at hand is already a request for peace. His impression was that the morale of the Finnish leaders had quickly crumbled [*slomleny*]." They did not believe that the Germans could help. Their response to the cries for help had been "a total of 10 airplanes."[125] All this was based on Gripenberg's one-day trip to Helsinki to participate in bargaining over the new government (he succeeded in avoiding the position of the Foreign Minister).[126] Surely this and Boheman's impressions fed the assessment that chaos and panic had broken out in Helsinki—and weakness was never appreciated in the Kremlin.

On 20 June the Finnish Army had to take their bullet-torn and soot-smudged flag down from the medieval castle tower and retreat from Vyborg. The fall of this symbol of resistance made the threat of occupation immediate and accelerated the political process. Kollontay informed Moscow that a tense struggle had broken out in Helsinki over the composition of the new government. She brought the term "Tanner's clique" back into use, to describe those who "did not want to leave voluntarily," but instead strove to have only a couple of ministers removed in what would amount to a decorative change. A bigger upheaval, "the more or less radical solution to the crisis," would be the ascent to power of those in the Peace Opposition, such as Väinö Voionmaa and J.W. Keto. This would "at last strike with all its might against the current ruling clique." The delay was, however, unnerving: Nils Lindh, Russia-expert and head of department at Sweden's Ministry of Foreign Affairs, explained to the Soviet military attaché that Finland did not have suitable politicians: the old ones did not want to leave and the new lacked drive. Half-measures were useless, and those really able to make decisions sat behind bars or in concentration camps. This was quite a claim by a civil servant: the politicians imprisoned were the Socialist parliamentary group of six, members of the Finland–Soviet Union Peace and Friendship Society of 1940 (including its founder, the Communist Mauri Ryömä), and Communist Party members. Lindh suspected that the situation could not be resolved "without armed struggle."[127]

Around midday on 22 June, Boheman raised the topic with Kollontay again. Finland's envoy, Gripenberg, had told him early that morning a new government had been formed in Helsinki under the leadership of Foreign Minister Henrik Ramsay. Its intention was to request peace "under any conditions [*na lyubykh usloviyakh*]." In Gripenberg's diary entry, however, these words or something on a par with them cannot be found. That same morning the Swedish Communist newspaper *Ny Dag* had stated that Ramsay supported Hitler, and neither the British nor the Swedish thought that he signified a real shift. Boheman asked Kollontay whether the Finns ought to be instructed to change anew, or would this government suffice for the transition period until the peace deal. An urgent solution hardly had much significance, since "Boheman assumes that a demand of surrender is also possible from our side. But there cannot be more."[128]

Only an hour later, Boheman came back, bringing Gripenberg's announcement that Finland was ready to withdraw from the war on the German side and make peace. A delegation could be sent to Moscow with full governmental authorization. Boheman added that there was not, in fact, a new government in Helsinki, rather it would only be formed once Moscow had replied, to allow any Soviet wishes to be taken into account.[129] This was not the whole truth. What actually delayed the process in Helsinki was Mannerheim's reluctance to allow any change of government before the situation at the front had been brought under control. And all help from Germany was surely unavailable in case the Finns went to Moscow.[130] Having got wind of this knotty situation,[131] Boheman reassured Kollontay that the delay did not originate from German pressure in the slightest, but instead from Finland's domestic politics. There was a lack of signatories willing to put their names to the harsh peace treaty, and the desire to bring some semblance of stability to the front was proving inviting. The Germans had nothing more to give than verbal support, hence "Govorov's arguments are much more powerful." Artillery, that is, commanded by this general, now promoted to the rank of Marshal. The Finns had asked for military supplies from the Swedes, but the response had been unambiguous: stop talking, and bring the war to an end. According to Boheman, the Finns "will actually surrender themselves in your hands."[132]

Such was the message sent to Moscow for Stalin and Molotov to read. Chaos seemed to reign supreme in Helsinki, so Finland could probably be scared into capitulation. Sweden, as represented by Boheman, would swallow even the Soviet occupation of Finland rather calmly. These were the main novelties. The decision was presumably made in Stalin's office around midnight, once the Polish Communists had departed and before the military leadership arrived to discuss the huge attack just launched by the Red Army's Central Front.[133] In part, the decision was based on inaccurate information, polished by three intermediaries (Gripenberg, Boheman and Kollontay) in much the same direction at every step. The mood in Helsinki was certainly glum and helpless, but not as desperate as might be imagined from the Stockholm cables. The phrase "under any conditions" did not come from Helsinki, where the idea was the other way round: the Finns did not set any preconditions for swift negotiations. Neither did the Finns plan to throw themselves at the mercy of the Soviets. Naturally, the possibility of German help was downplayed and even hidden in the cables, to avoid irritating Moscow. As for Sweden, Boheman's cultivation of the term 'surrender' was reckless, and it is far from certain that his lenient views of the possible occupation of Finland would have prevailed in Sweden if tested by a wave of refugees and other consequences. Another senior national security expert and Helsinki hand, the Chief of Staff, General C.A. Ehrensvärd, asserted to Boheman that the occupation would lead to "a Red Soviet Finland. All the old wounds from 1918 will reopen, and the failed war and Russian agitation will take care of the rest."[134]

Moscow had prioritized the surrender option since April. The Stockholm cables were the immediate trigger, like Gavrilo Princip's bullets on 28 June 1914. Together with military successes, the cables created the momentum.

Early on 23 June, Kollontay brought to Boheman the Kremlin's shocking answer: both the President and the Foreign Minister would have to sign a statement "that Finland is ready to surrender [*kapitu-liruyet*] and ask for peace." However, in the original cable text in Molotov's handwriting the statement was demanded from the Prime Minister [*prem'yer*] and Foreign Minister.[135] It is not known who made the rare change and why. The simplest explanation would be that in Stockholm it was known that according to the Finnish constitution it was the President who had power over foreign policy. And from the Stockholm perspective, it was far from certain who would be the Prime Minister in Helsinki next day and after.

On 26 June, Marshal Voroshilov's commission delivered its 56-point document on Finland's unconditional surrender to the People's Commissariat of Foreign Affairs. It had been prepared in October 1943. In order to ensure surrender, it was suggested that the Red Army could occupy the whole or part of the country, and at least take control of the ports, the Åland Islands and the islands in the Gulf of Finland. The Finnish Army would be stripped of their weapons, as would the Civil Guards, whose members would also be interned. The Soviet Union would take charge of trials for war crimes, oversee the Finnish economy, and confiscate the banks' gold and currency reserves.[136]

This harsh document was not immediately needed. On the same 26 June, President Risto Ryti sent an official letter to Hitler, promising that Finland would not sign a peace deal with the Soviets without first getting German approval. Ryti was under intense pressure from the Minister of Foreign Affairs Ribbentrop, who had flown to Helsinki to secure Finland's continued support. To all intents and purposes, however, it was Mannerheim who had decided about this course of action. The matter was not taken before parliament, and no answer was given to the Soviet demand for surrender. Finland continued to fight with a desperate frenzy, and with German support.

In terms of Finland's resilience, it was pivotal that Tanner managed to keep the Social Democrats in government, even though he himself opposed the Ryti–Ribbentrop Agreement. The Social Democrat and future minister Veikko Helle would later admit that he and his brothers-in-arms had considered deserting their positions at the front if the party was removed from the government. One young infantryman, Mauno Koivisto, wrote to his worker father: "I'm trying my best to prevent our people falling into slavery." In 1982 he was elected President of Finland, the first Social Democrat in that office.[137]

In Swedish diplomatic circles it was the Finns who were scapegoated. Boheman went furthest, telling a British diplomat that "the best thing that Ryti could do would be to shoot himself." Now you could only hope for "the Soviet Union's rapid advance to Helsinki."[138] Another Swedish diplomat used a derisory saying to explain the decisions in Helsinki: "the Finns suffer from an incurable illness, namely stupidity." In his opinion, "the Finns are no politicians, it's a shame to say."[139] Reading the Swedish gentlemen's combination of condescending sympathy, frivolity ("a short occupation") and sense of superiority might bring to mind a poem created by seventeenth-century Finnish migrants in the forests of Swedish Värmland: *Don't you know the Swede's love? / How does he love?—like the spider / Loves that which he has trapped in his net!*[140] However, in this context that would be unfair. It is hard to conceive of how Finland could have withdrawn from the war in the manner it did without Sweden's mediation and, above all, its existence. Stalin was astonishingly respectful in his relations with Sweden. He took the country seriously, but he did not need to fear it. Unlike Finland, other Western neighbors of the Soviet Union did not have Sweden on the other side of them. They had Germany.

The Swedish military authorities that were oriented towards Finland disliked the diplomats' "ignorant and erroneous optimism." Foreign Minister Christian Günther got his share of criticism, too, for he had the nerve (*har mage*) to take a leave of absence "when Sweden's destiny was being decided, perhaps for generations to come." General C.A. Ehrensvärd concluded (to Finland's military attaché Colonel Martin Stewen) that the opportunity opened up by the First World War, for a new closeness between Sweden and Finland, had now passed. Each country had its own reason: Sweden's was its frailty (*orkeslöshet*), while Finland's was its real jingoism (*yverborenhet*) that was currently oriented towards Germany.[141] Ehrensvärd and his companions had volunteered for the White Guards in the Finnish Civil War,[142] but they had long since been in the service of Social Democratic governments in Sweden.

The Swedish government and Prime Minister Per Albin Hansson continued their careful policy and refused to allow representatives of the military leadership to travel to Finland to discuss solutions and persuade Mannerheim to change course. Nonetheless, the Ryti–Ribbentrop Agreement caused a great deal of astonishment within the Swedish government. The United States broke off diplomatic relations, but still declined to declare war on Finland.

What about Stalin's reaction? He realized immediately that he had blundered. He had finally pushed Finland into an unequivocal union with Germany and into continuing the war. In spring, when the Soviets were sounding out Paasikivi and Enckell, and when attempts at peace negotiations by Hungary had been disrupted by a German-supported coup of the Arrow Cross Party, Moscow analyzed (for the British) what might happen if Germany's satellites were offered no alternative other than unconditional surrender. This scenario could have the negative consequence of strengthening—rather than severing—these countries' relations with Germany, and thereby impede peace.[143] Ultimately, however, when the temptation grew too great, greed exceeded this wisdom.

Stalin realized that he had received misleading information from Stockholm. Suspicion fell on Helsinki: he complained to Harriman that "the Finns have deceived the Swedes, who themselves are honest, but have led others astray."[144] Himself an experienced swindler, he thought that he had been fooled on this occasion, although in Helsinki there had been no conscious effort to dupe him, but rather Hitler, to some extent. Kollontay would soon disclose that "those relevant" in the Kremlin were furious (*fâché*) and she had been ordered to refrain from taking any immediate action.[145]

The Soviet Union did not repeat the demand to surrender, but began to move back towards its former position. Vladimir Dekanozov, the deputy Foreign Minister, instructed his officials to compose a draft response to the new request from the British for Finland's peace conditions.[146] The Soviet Union's re-acceptance of a conditional peace became public on 3 July, when *Pravda* dismissed rumors of unconditional surrender as baseless speculation, claiming that they had been spread by the Germans to force Finland to continue the war.

After Vyborg the Red Army's offensive pushed on towards the Kymijoki River defensive line. The troops, however, were worn out and had scant prospects of reinforcements, since the Soviets launched their main attack against the Germans in Byelorussia (now Belarus) at the same time. Moreover, the West was advancing in France, so the attention turned to Central Europe. The Finns' fierce resistance brought the Soviet attack to a halt close to Vyborg in Tali and Ihantala, the biggest battle ever in northern Europe. At midnight on 11 July 1944, Stalin gave the order for the army to shift to defense on the Karelian Isthmus. The only politicians then present in his office were Molotov and, ominously, Zhdanov, along with three military men. The troops began to be transferred away a week later. The attack continued on the northern coast of Lake Ladoga, but Moscow went back to finalizing the peace conditions and Kollontay received instructions to begin sounding out the Finns from Stockholm again.

Interim Peace

In Stockholm, Kollontay got the ball rolling on 13 July 1944 when she told a Swedish diplomat that a negotiated peace was still possible, but swift action was needed: "If the Russians come to Helsinki, it is too late." The next day the Swedish envoy to Helsinki, Hans Beck-Friis, slipped in to meet her in room 118 at the Grand Hotel in Saltsjöbaden. The groundwork for contact had been laid by Eero A. Wuori and Nils Lindh from Sweden's Foreign Ministry, with help from Soviet intelligence. Kollontay did not warm to a Finnish government-in-exile, demanding instead that a new government be formed in Helsinki, one from which Tanner and Ryti must be excluded. Moscow sought a more radical transformation in the government than before, since Kollontay proposed four of the former Socialist parliamentary group of Six (*Kuutoset*) as ministers. Six MPs had established the group in early 1941 following their expulsion from the Social Democrats in fall 1940; in early 1942 they had received prison sentences for treasonous activity. In spite of this demand, Kollontay confirmed to Wallenberg that Mannerheim was still "acceptable," even though he was viewed with greater reservation than before.[147]

Mannerheim still signified certain guarantees: the army would follow his lead, the threat of a right-wing uprising would subside, and the pro-German camp would stay small. As Stalin himself observed, similar tactics would have worked in Hungary: "We would have accepted Horthy [the regent of Hungary], but the Germans took him." Hungarian generals had to agree again to the renewed 1920 borders of 'Rump Hungary' and the reparations. If they did not accept, they would be ousted and replaced by more amenable generals.[148]

Officials from the People's Commissariat of Foreign Affairs sent draft conditions to the British on 10 July 1944. Once again, the treaty was described as a preliminary peace. The Soviets stated that the reparations total was fixed, but they now promised to take into account the British desire for forest products. In practice, the Soviets abandoned their original plan to order payments in kind mainly in forest industry products and ordered about half of the value in metal industry products. With this Finland's post-war metal industry took shape and the possibility was opened up of earning hard currency by selling paper and other products to Britain. The Soviets also recommended that the British seek compensation for Petsamo nickel mines and industries from Finland, with which original contracts had been made—and thus not from the Soviets, who would claim those mines and industries.[149]

Finland's draft agreement was completed on 21 July 1944, when Voroshilov's commission sent it to Molotov. It was not passed on to the British. The uncompromising title was "Finland's terms of surrender," but it was a conditional peace, albeit a very severe one.

Finland would be allowed to keep "a suitable amount" of troops for disarming the Germans; the rest had to be demobilized and their weapons given up to the Soviet Union. The Civil Guards and their equivalents had to be stripped of their weapons and disbanded; their reorganization was forbidden, as was the service of Finns in foreign armies. Finland was to hand over the following locations to the Soviet Union as military bases: Kotka's fortified area and Haapasaari, Porkkala and Mäkiluoto island, as well as Hanko and Hankoniemi's fortified area. Soviet troops would occupy Helsinki and its fortified areas, the Åland Islands, Turku, Vaasa, Oulu and Tornio "as the need arises, until the war against Germany is terminated." Consulates were not needed and thus not mentioned in the Soviet terms. Outside of these areas, Finland would have to destroy its fortifications. War industry production had to be halted immediately. Those responsible for the war and those who had committed war crimes "whose names are on the lists produced by the USSR Government" had to be detained and handed over to the Soviet Union. Those who had acted for the cause of the United Nations had to be immediately set free. This meant pro-Soviet political forces. The reparations had been nudged up to $800 million, to be paid within five years and preferably in the form of goods from the wood-processing industry. In addition, there were a cluster of logistical articles to facilitate the operations of the Soviet Army and Navy against Germany. To oversee all these conditions, the Soviet government would appoint a control commission.

The biggest change in the conditions was the new border. The Soviets' territorial demands had noticeably increased from the spring, when they had had their eye on the region of Lappeenranta and Imatra. Now they wanted the border pushed back to the Kymi River and a slice of land from the Gulf of Finland to the level of Joensuu, about 300 kilometers in length and between 30 to 70 kilometers in width.[150] If the Soviets had reached the border of Peter the Great (1721) during the Winter War, now they were targeting the peace conditions of 1743 after the next Russo-Swedish War. The exception was the small town of Kouvola, which Finland would be allowed to keep. During the railway age Kouvola had become an important junction, akin to historic Verona, the fall of which would result in the capitulation of entire provinces.

In all, southern and eastern Kymenlaakso, South Saimaa and southern North Karelia would have been handed over to the Soviet Union. As well as resulting in much more difficult defense, these cessions would have had dire consequences for Finland's economy. Important ports, major roads, the biggest power plant and much of the wood-processing industry would have disappeared. There would have been around 250,000 additional people displaced, a 60 percent increase from the amount after the Winter War, insofar as smaller Finland would no longer have had the capacity to settle the evacuees.

Voroshilov's much-touted military reputation had been badly dented by the Winter War, but these terms were not about settling personal scores. His commission was also responsible for drawing up peace conditions for Germany, which was its principal focus. Stalin's brother-in-arms was in the leader's good books again: he went to the Tehran Conference as an "expert," and would next go on to head the Allied Control Commission in Hungary. Voroshilov was also in attendance when Finland's terms were finally presented to the British, and Molotov referenced him as the reason for taking Porkkala. When redrawing Finland's border, the Marshal and his commission were able to anticipate the direction in which Stalin's thoughts were moving, even if they could not be certain of his mindset in real time.[151] The proposed border looked as though someone had run a thick red pencil across the map, and officials then had to find the place names that the line happened to intersect.

The commission's proposal, therefore, was not final, nor had it received Stalin's blessing in advance. It was simply drawn up based on expectations of what the Boss wanted. Its incompleteness can be seen by the fact that Kotka and Haapasaari were listed as sites for military bases, even though the new border was supposed to be to their west. Moreover, regarding the reparations and their composition, the proposal made no mention of the fact that the People's Commissariat of Foreign Affairs had already prepared concessions for the British. Voroshilov's commission had the same fundamental idea that Kollontay had expressed: the conditions could not be less severe than those in the spring. The Finns had shed Soviet blood, and that required compensation.

Stalin ignored the big new demands, except for Porkkala and the release of UN political supporters. The most persistent remarks of the West were addressed by halving the amount of reparations to $300 million and by promising to pay $20 million to Petsamo's nickel company from it in compensation. With Mannerheim in mind, the stipulations about the expulsion of the Germans from Finland were diluted. The clause about disbanding organizations was rewritten so that the Civil Guards were not mentioned by name, which so upset O.V. Kuusinen that he launched an unsuccessful last-minute bid to reverse it.[152]

What was behind Stalin's moderation? Why did he drop some of the conditions perhaps dictated by himself only a little while earlier?

The West was advancing fast on Paris and Brussels, along with the rush to reach Berlin. The significance of this is undeniable, but in the Soviets' relations with the West there was another issue that was the most pressing. Not for the first time this was Poland. Stalin had promised to launch a relieving attack the moment Allied forces entered France. His surprise first strike came on the Finnish front, but on 22 June 1944 he unleashed the enormous main assault, named

Operation Bagration after the renowned Georgian general. (Having led Russian troops in the Finnish War of 1808–09 against Sweden, he was immortalized by the Finnish national poet Runeberg: "*Barclay, Kamensky, Bagration / Were known across Finland's nation / And intense battles were in store / When they came afore.*")[153] Operation Bagration destroyed the Germans' Army Group Center. After crossing the Soviet Union's former western border, the Red Army arrived at the River Bug on 17 July: for Stalin, that would be Poland's eastern boundary.

There was no Polish government that the Soviet Union would have accepted to take control of the conquered areas. Relations with Poland's government-in-exile had broken down in 1943, when, in the wake of the revelations about the Soviets' Katyn massacre, it declined to accept Moscow's version of events. Consequently, the Polish Committee of National Liberation (PKWN) was formed to conduct the affairs of state. Officially it was established on 22 July 1944 in Chelm, but in reality it came into being a day earlier, in Stalin's office. The Soviets had the same blueprint for the Terijoki government in 1939, down to the agreement on the new border signed immediately with the PKWN.

With Soviet troops approaching, the government-in-exile's Home Army (AK) launched uprisings against their Nazi German occupiers, first in Vilnius and then in Lwów (now Lviv). The Red Army disarmed the Poles; the AK's commanders and officers were arrested and taken away. When the vanguard of the Red Army reached the Vistula River, on 1 August 1944, the Warsaw Uprising began. This AK-organized insurrection was large and initially successful, but its chances of success were scuppered when the Soviet advance halted. The Red Army had run out of steam, and neither did Stalin want to enable, or even allow, the West to help. After two months of fighting, the Germans were able to quash the rebellion. Hitler ordered that the city be razed to the ground and all residents killed, but this diktat was not fully realized.[154]

This affected Finland in two distinct ways. As would be expected, Moscow's relations with the British deteriorated sharply. The Americans, too, voiced their concerns: Harriman reported that since early July the events had taken an unsettling turn, Moscow did not care about Western interests and was becoming "a world bully."[155] In this chilly climate, Stalin needed to show restraint and make concessions elsewhere. Finland was a useful chip for that. In addition, for as long as Warsaw's fierce resistance continued, Stalin would have found it hard to justify sending more troops in Finland's direction. Maintaining a good reputation was probably never one of his top priorities, but it did sometimes have to be taken into account, as in September when he finally agreed to allow airdrop aid to the beleaguered Poles in Warsaw. Refusing to help Warsaw while simultaneously attacking Helsinki would only have diminished Stalin's international standing further.

As the Polish situation would surely continue to demand a hard-headed approach, there was no need to make Finland a second bone of contention. Instead, the Soviets could take what had been agreed upon in Tehran, plus a little more besides. A redrawn Finnish border would not be accepted without a fight, although it would be less of an issue for the British than the Americans. Foreign Secretary Eden would probably acquiesce, since in January 1944 he considered the Soviets' territorial claims entirely reasonable, stressing that the borders would be significantly more advantageous for Finland than they were in the days of the Russian Empire.[156] The Americans, on the other hand, wanted the Soviets to adhere to the 1940 border, and were prepared to dig their heels in.[157] Stalin knew this.

Secondly, Moscow would need more manpower to break Finland. This was visible from the Battle of Ilomantsi, where the Finns triumphed against the Soviet onslaught, destroying two Red Army divisions in early August. On 14 August 1944, after warning the Finns not to make a big deal out of the victory, since Ilomantsi was not comparable to the Soviets' Karelian offensive in June, a Soviet diplomat welcomed initiatives to talks. Addressing Helsinki through Swedish diplomatic channels, he declared that Finland's new government did not meet Moscow's expectations, but as it embodied the Marshal's mindset he would not say anything further. "The Soviet Union looks upon things realistically," the diplomat stated, "and its attitude towards Finland and its new government is determined solely by the facts." He also noted that Moscow would welcome a delegation: "As things stand, the Soviet Union's peace terms are very reasonable, and it has no desire to destroy Finland's national independence."[158]

The government of Finland was changed on 1 August. The domestic desire to achieve peace, the pressure from Sweden and the West, and Kollontay's messages—the most important being the official announcement that the Finns were not required to surrender—led to Ryti's resignation. Mannerheim was chosen as President of the Republic and Antti Hackzell, director general and former envoy to Moscow, became Prime Minister. The new government did not represent a move in the direction of the Peace Opposition; on the contrary, it was an attempt to keep the right wing as involved as possible.[159]

Mannerheim proceeded with caution. On 17 August he informed Field Marshal Keitel that he did not consider himself bound by his predecessor's letter to Hitler. Then on 24 August he got the diplomatic process moving in Stockholm. At this point General C.A. Ehrensvärd was moved to write of Kollontay in his diary that "this cynical old hag does indeed have a weakness for Finland somewhere deep inside her."[160] The Finns went through the process of cutting ties with Germany before agreeing a ceasefire with the Soviet Union on 4 September. Their delegation, led by Hackzell, left for Moscow on 7 September. In its assessment of the negotiators, Soviet intelligence highlighted Hackzell's status as a trusted hand for capitalists. In Soviet books, it was men of this sort who had the real power. Oskar Enckell was viewed as a general who was popular with his officers; it is not known what this appraisal was based on, as the general was a former Russian Imperial officer who had, at one time, been bitterly

15. Marshal Mannerheim visiting the front in 1941.

rejected by the Jägers. War Minister Rudolf Walden was confirmed to be Mannerheim's right-hand man and a great industrialist from whom Russian Jews had once bought paper for their newspapers.[161]

The Finnish delegation had to wait over a week in Moscow. The Soviets were also engaged in negotiations with Romania, and Finland's conditions had to be formally accepted by those Allies that had declared war on Finland. In addition, the Soviets perhaps wanted to see how things looked on 15 September, which was the deadline for the Germans' departure from Finland. And what was better than to let the Finns stew a little? If Soviet eavesdropping on the delegation was not the reason for the delay, they did nevertheless take full advantage of the opportunity.[162]

After Hackzell's salutary visit to Molotov on 8 September, the Finns spent the time discussing the impending negotiations among themselves. They went through those conditions they were aware of, and debated tactics: what to say, how to respond to particular issues.

16. *The first meeting between Soviet and Finnish soldiers on armistice day at
the Saimaa Canal, 4 September 1944.*

17. *A heavy mortar being packed away on armistice day at Ihantala,
4 September 1944.*

Soviet officials compiled a list of the matters that concerned the delegation: Would there be a big peace conference on Finland's conditions? Would the British help? Would the Americans get involved? What would the Russians demand in reparations? And what would be the British attitude to this? Hackzell, familiar with Finland's exports and industries, believed that reparations could still be settled on a maximum of $250 million, but that this would still have a deleterious impact on the country's standard of living. The Finns were very aware of the sum of $600 million that had been tabled in the spring. Upon reading this intelligence report, Stalin and Molotov no doubt took particular notice of the Finns' hopes for Western involvement.

Neither General Heinrichs nor any other Finn in Moscow believed that the Germans would be able to leave northern Finland by the deadline, even if they wanted to. In Walden's assessment, if the Soviets came to help to expel the Germans, then their stream (*potok*) of troops would branch out, unimpeded, across the whole of Finland. General Oskar Enckell speculated, surprisingly, that the possible fight of the Finns and the Russians together against the Germans might increase the Red Army's popularity. Hackzell disagreed, because there was "too much antipathy towards the Russians" in Finland, in fact hate (*nenavist*). As proof he saw Walden's gestures at the exhibition of Soviet war booty. The War Minister had been impassively surveying German weapons, tanks and a general's uniform, but when he came to a Finnish uniform he fell silent and clenched his fist.

Hackzell felt the situation to be almost at an impasse. The Finns did not want Soviet troops on their soil, but the expulsion of the Germans on their own would come at the cost of a heavy death toll and perhaps even a civil war, as there were plenty of Germanophiles among the officers. If the attempted removal was unsuccessful, then it would spell ruin (*k gibeli*) for Finland, as it would if the country continued to side with the Germans. Hackzell bemoaned that Finland had placed too much trust in Germany; no one had wanted to analyze the balance of power between the Great Powers.

When the Soviets' negotiations with Romania got underway, the Finns scrutinized the peace conditions that came to light. Moscow was demanding only $300 million in reparations, even though Romania had oil. Moreover, this loser was getting back a large chunk of territory, Transylvania, taken from another German ally, Hungary. The Finns suspected that Romania was receiving favorable treatment because its government had veered sharply in a pro-Soviet direction. Hackzell considered it unlikely that the Communists or Socialists (i.e. anyone left of the SDP) would enter the government in Finland, since they had such a low level of support – in general (and honest) elections half a year later, Communists and Socialists allied with them received almost a quarter of the votes.

Once the week was up, Hackzell said that he was tired of waiting and would return home for the time being, as he had plenty of work to do there. Soon, at 6.30 p.m. the Chief of Protocol of the People's Commissariat of Foreign Affairs, G.I. Fomin, showed up at the hotel and announced that negotiations would begin that same evening. Less than an hour later Hackzell had a stroke, from which he would never recover.

The first session of negotiations commenced in the guesthouse of the People's Commissariat of Foreign Affairs on Spiridonovka Street on 14 September 1944 at 11 p.m. Molotov led the Soviet Union's delegation, the British were represented by their ambassador, and the Finns' spokesman was General Walden, who requested that a plane be sent to Helsinki to pick up a new delegation head to replace Hackzell.[163] The Finns were given a draft on the preliminary peace agreement, containing twenty-three articles. This was the first time that they saw the condition about Porkkala being leased as a military base. The area should be cleared of residents within ten days of signing the treaty.

The British had accepted Porkkala out of pragmatism. The Soviets seemed to be interfering in the situation in Greece, and the British did not want to give them any pretext to claim that the British were doing the same in Moscow's sphere of interest.[164] When Foreign

Minister Eden was justifying his decision to the War Cabinet, he acknowledged that Boheman, from Sweden's Ministry of Foreign Affairs, had been greatly depressed by the prospect of the Soviets being stationed at Porkkala. However, Eden dismissed such a

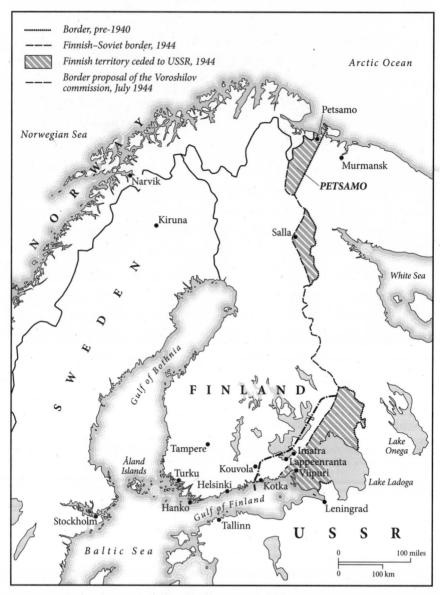

2. *Finland: territorial changes in 1944.*

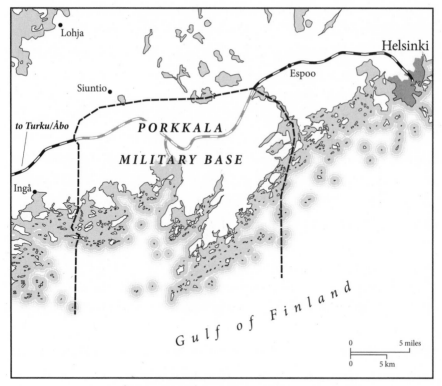

3. *The Soviet military base in Porkkala, 1944–56.*

reaction as exaggerated: Porkkala was not an important trade route like Hanko, and the Soviets had to be reassured that their Baltic Fleet could no longer be blocked off at the eastern end of the Gulf of Finland. He also downplayed the threat to Helsinki: the capital could just as easily be destroyed by air raids. Other potentially important factors, such as the large size of the base and its significance for the Red Army ground troops, went unmentioned in his speech.[165]

In the negotiating room, the Finns' shock at the Porkkala revelation was such a blow that they paid little attention to the fact that the reparations had been halved to $300 million and the payment period extended to six years. Not only that, but, unlike in Romania's case, Finland was neither obliged to declare war on Germany nor to subordinate its troops to Allied command.

133

In the evening of 15 September 1944 a plane left Moscow to pick up the new head of the Finnish delegation, Foreign Minister Carl Enckell. To avoid any possible German action, the plane followed the main road from Vyborg to Helsinki sticking close to the ground, at a height of 300–700 meters. When the Finnish leadership got hold of the draft treaty and saw that an area of 380.5 square kilometers of Porkkala, including the coastal railroad, were to be leased to the Soviets, Mannerheim exclaimed: "Lord Jesus! Not this as well!" He suggested trying to change the base's location from Porkkala to Hanko, the very place that he had seen it was necessary to retain in the spring.[166] When it became clear that Hanko no longer sufficed, in desperation the Finns even floated the idea of the Åland Islands, but they did not even have a chance to make the proposition to the Soviets. This did not stop Stockholm from getting wind of the idea a little while later; as might be expected, the Swedes were not best pleased.[167]

One particular detail of the negotiations is worth noting, namely that Molotov became furious with Carl Enckell at nightfall on 18 September, when the Finnish Foreign Minister remarked that the treaty would have to be approved in parliament. Molotov vented his spleen against Finland's bloodthirsty, criminal government, telling the Finns to head back home if they would not put pen to paper. The consequence would be Soviet occupation, something for which Moscow had already prepared, as he lied.[168]

The Finnish parliament did end up approving the preliminary peace treaty early in the morning on 19 September. It was signed in Moscow at 12.30 p.m. Zhdanov was the signatory representing both the Soviet Union and Great Britain, and he would go on to become Chairman of the Allied Control Commission in Finland. His political standing and abilities were substantially greater than that of Marshal Voroshilov, who had taken the role in Hungary, or Vyshinsky, the former show-trial prosecutor who had been dispatched to oversee the commission in Romania. In the eyes of the commission's British representative, Zhdanov still appeared to be mediocre for such a

18. Glad to be alive, Finnish soldiers enjoy a sauna at Vuosalmi after the armistice was signed in September 1944.

strong position, despite a certain unworldliness about him, even spirituality reminiscent of a dignitary in the Catholic Church.[169]

The control commission's eleven-man vanguard flew from Leningrad to Malmi airfield in Helsinki two days later. Among that group the qualities of unworldliness and spirituality were presumably in short supply.

Reflections

The preliminary peace treaty was viewed as severe in Finland, although people were of course relieved that the war was over. The Finns were unaware of the far harsher conditions that Moscow had initially drawn up in March and April 1944, and then again in June and July. Stalin's policy was not set in stone, he simply aimed to take what could be taken (plus a little extra) in any given situation. On the basis of the material outlined above, it is difficult to see how Finland could have got a better deal in March, let alone at Midsummer, although delaying it did come at a substantial human cost.

How did Stalin feel about his accomplishments in Finland in 1944? There is no source material that sheds a direct light on this. He had been scrabbling after more, but was ultimately satisfied with what he got, given the availability of resources and how the situation developed. The best guess is that even with this result, he saw Finland coming under his control. This was also the Western interpretation, and no doubt Soviet intelligence was able to get this information, perhaps even documents about it. In the Soviet view, from this point on Finland had to be dealt with care, one step at a time and as the situation demanded, but the grip would not loosen any longer.

19. The first officers of the Allied (Soviet) Control Commission arriving at Helsinki airport, 23 September 1944.

That Finland survived without political or societal collapse, and without occupation, rests on three factors above all. First, *geography*. As seen from Moscow towards Germany, Finland was an island and aside at that. If Stalin could have sent his tanks through this country to Berlin, he would have done so. The mere fact of Sweden's existence had an impact, as did, to a lesser extent, the actions of its government.

The second element, *timing*. For the Soviets, the crucial factors were the western advance in France and the heated situation in Poland. The Finns had known that their best hope was to try to hold out until Germany was too weak to inflict harsh reprisals against Finnish withdrawal. However, it would be an overstatement to see the timing as a product of cool deliberation. The Finns were in an emergency, desperate and helpless, arbitrating between conflicting opinions and scraping together dwindling resources. This tumultuous process yielded the moderately fortuitous timing.

Third, a combination of *the nation, the soldiers and the Winter War*. Finland's society was far from perfect and there were shortcomings in its democracy, but the majority of the nation felt that their country was worth defending. As the Florentine historian Guicciardini memorably put it, "God loves the republics," even if he himself served the Pope.[170] Contrary to Stalin's evaluation in spring 1944, the Finns were not all that different from "before," that is to say from the time of the Winter War. After meeting the Prime Minister of Poland's government-in-exile at the start of the Warsaw Uprising, Stalin complained—jokingly—to Foreign Secretary Eden that the Pole was so dogged and obstinate that he must be of Finnish extraction.[171] The experience of the Winter War Finns still weighed heavily on Stalin's mind.

With regards to timing, it was advantageous that peacetime began to prevail, for most of Finland, nine months before the Second World War came to a close in Europe. This gave the Finns nine whole months to address, at least temporarily, the big post-war issues; as it happened, many of these short-term solutions proved to be rather enduring. The most important were the general elections and the formation of a new government while the Allies were still allies and all accepted the process.

From the perspective of Finland's future, the most critical factor was that the core of the country became neither a battlefield nor a site of occupation. In this respect, Finland was almost unique in Europe. The state and other institutions were preserved, and there was a continuity almost on a par with Sweden. Churchill bemoaned that all that was left on continental Europe were "a litter of broken states" or "helpless nations."[172] Finland was not among their number.

How Finland made peace had one unintended consequence in Soviet Karelia. In August 1944 the vigilant, calumny-minded part of leadership in these areas came up with the idea of expelling Karelians and Finns from Soviet Karelia. Chechens, Crimean Tatars and many other nationalities had been exiled, accused of cooperating with the enemy. This initiative in Karelia was driven by powerful forces, but it was rejected at the highest level in Moscow. It was not Stalin's style to show compassion in such matters unless there were firm political grounds for doing so, which suggests that he was wary of provoking the Finns at that time. There is little doubt that Moscow's new relationship with Finland would have become extremely strained if the Karelians had been expelled. The Winter War relieved the Finnish language from the ban in the Soviet Union, and perhaps the outcome of the Continuation War in 1944 kept the Soviet Karelians in their homeland. As in 1940, even this time the Finnish Karelians were evacuated to Finland and the areas were ceded without the people, empty. Had they been left under Soviet rule, the consequences would have been destructive for the mutual relations.

Finland's dearth of civilian casualties was another consequence of the way in which peace was reached. When a foreign historian is informed of the total number of Finnish soldiers killed in the war (a little under 100,000) and asked to guess the civilian death toll, the estimates are invariably in six figures. The correct answer—2,000—is difficult to believe, as it is so exceptionally low. Of the countries that went to war, only Australia's death ratio between civilian and military casualties is comparable.[173]

Every loss is a tragedy to a person's nearest and dearest, and lots of young Finnish men lost their lives. But it is more natural, if it is appropriate to use that word here, that wars result in the death of soldiers. Due to scant civilian losses, the Finnish nation did not experience the same lingering bitterness and distress that occurred in countries where murder, rape, robbery and destruction had been wrought by occupiers or warring armies. In Eastern Europe the wake of devastation left by the Red Army undermined, for a long time, the legitimacy of the people's democracies that came after the war. Even the pro-Soviet Czechs branded the Red Army "the anti-Bolshevism league," but Soviet conduct was even more wanton in Germany and other countries on the Axis's side [174] In Finland it was the displaced Karelians who felt the most sorrowful yearning, if not bitterness, but the loss of their native region was a mild fate compared to what, say, the Poles or Estonians suffered.

At the conclusion of the Finnish classic war novel *The Unknown Soldier* (*Tuntematon sotilas*, published in 1954), Vanhala, the blithe private, sums up the war in sportscast style: "The Union of Soviet Socialist Republics won, but persistent little Finland crossed the line a respectable second." This sentiment reflects the nation's emotional state. Such a mild level of resentment also enabled a foreign policy of avoiding directly opposing the Soviet Union, which was seen as unavoidable in the post-war years. As a sign of this, note the (ironic) use of the official name of the neighbor instead of the pejorative *ryssä*. It may seem odd to search in the war for the origins of this policy, pursued first by Paasikivi and then by Kekkonen. But there are roots: the small civilian death toll, and Finland's resilience and success in waging war. It gave the Finns sufficient self-confidence and earned them necessary Soviet respect.

In his comparison of the German and Finnish wartime leadership, the German researcher Michael Jonas has observed that the self-destructive instinct which took hold in Hitler's bunker as defeat loomed was absent from the Finns. The central factor in the Finnish mentality was the preservation of the state and the people, without any desire to drift into a spiral of self-destruction. The Finns' criterion for making foreign policy was *der auf solidem politischen Realismus gründeten Staatsräson*—national interest grounded in firm political realism—as Jonas puts it.[175] This is a bit exaggerated, since everybody's actions in this field contain irrational and emotional elements. The leadership of a small state usually ends up suppressing such notions out of necessity. Compared to Hitler, Mannerheim and Tanner were cool and level-headed indeed. As for Mannerheim's contribution, during the trade negotiations in the spring of 1946, when the old Marshal was no longer the President of the Republic, Stalin asked about his health. He then added that "Finland stood in a debt of gratitude to Mannerheim. Thanks to him, the country had not been occupied."[176]

There was perhaps one group of Finnish civil servants who were most consumed by the feeling that the world was ending: those until September 1944 tasked with repressing Communist activities. At the end of June all remaining suspects were rounded up, the last death sentences were enacted in early September, and even after that some Communists were killed while being detained.[177]

The Finnish qualities that fed into their sheer instinct for survival were touched upon during an in-depth discussion on 5 February 1945 between Zhdanov and F.M. Shepherd, the British representative on the control commission. This was apparently the only one they had. According to his own notes, Zhdanov had observed in Estonia in 1940 that "each nation is born with its own mentality, with its own devils."[178] Now the Russian and the British representative were ruminating on Finnish quirks: they agreed that the Finns were painfully slow in all actions, immersed in their own affairs and ignorant of global goings-on. They had no conception of Germany's dark side, indeed, you could say that a deliberate blindness prevailed. Zhdanov speculated that there was German-style militarism in Finland, to which Shepherd remarked that, on the contrary, being stuck between Sweden and Russia for hundreds of years had made the nation a military one. The Russian granted that there might be some truth in that. Then, in rather a paternalistic fashion, both he and Shepherd noted that the Finns had, all the same, made good progress towards democracy.[179]

III
The Coup Threat
1948

O n the eve of Christmas 1947, Stalin decided to take care of
Finland's geopolitical alignment. Europe was being divided
between East and West at the start of the Cold War, and Finland's
position was still uncertain. In contrast to Western countries,
Finland's Communists had not been forced out of government; the
coalition of the left-wing Finnish People's Democratic League
(SKDL), the Agrarian League and the Social Democrats was
creaking, but still in power. In terms of foreign policy, the country
had bowed to pressure from Moscow and reluctantly ruled itself out
of the Marshall Plan, but it had simultaneously avoided attaching
itself to the Soviet Union's camp.

Stalin himself had come up with the idea of two camps—the
imperialist and the socialist—and to that one now needed to adapt.[1]
Once Finland had signed the Paris Peace Treaty on 10 February
1947, Moscow's primary aim for the country was to make it a part of
the Soviet Union's security zone via a military treaty or alliance. It
had struck or renewed such agreements with the other "small countries" in Eastern Europe. Earlier treaties were made against Germany,
but now Moscow aimed to define the potential aggressor in more
general terms so that the treaties could be used against any Western

interference.[2] President J.K. Paasikivi had, however, spent the whole fall obstructing the Soviets' plan for Finland.[3] In the opinion of the Soviet envoy to Helsinki, A.N. Abramov, of all the Finnish politicians it was precisely the President who was "the strongest and most intelligent enemy [*vrag*] of all" and a perpetual brake on Moscow's progressive measures.[4]

Now the Finnish question had to be resolved. The haste was necessitated by the situation in Germany. When things heated up in Germany, the temperature of Finland's relationship with the Soviet Union also began to rise. This was the case long after the fall of the Third Reich, at least until the early 1970s.

In mid-December 1947, the foreign ministers of the four victorious powers ended up at an impasse in London about Germany's peace agreement. A solution was visible in the distance but always gliding out of reach like a mirage. In Western occupation zones a new currency was introduced, the Deutsche Mark. It could be seen—and was seen—as a significant step towards a separate western Germany. The British Foreign Ministry memo that appeared on Stalin's desk contained potential guarantees that three Western Powers could offer West Germany in case of Soviet aggression.[5] Stalin had earlier received intelligence information about the West's intentions to incorporate western Germany into the European economy and the Marshall Plan. Legislation for the US aid program would arrive in Congress over Christmas, and the West's plans would soon be buttressed by a huge supply of American dollars. To top it off, the United States had announced that western zones would no longer send reparations to the Soviet Union. This forced Moscow to curb its immediate compensation claims in the eastern zone, to stop the region's economy from collapsing. This and other countermeasures were dealt with in Stalin's office on 3 January 1948.[6]

Neither Finland's neutrality nor its Nordic identity were enough to prevent it from having to pick sides. The division of Europe in two was a dichotomy: Moscow was not prepared to recognize a third option, seeing any attempt to find a middle ground as camouflage. The plans for a Scandinavian defense union initiated by Sweden were seen in Moscow as influenced and incited by the United States and Britain. In reality, Washington disliked the idea just as much as Moscow. The Soviets interpreted the notion of Nordic identity as an attempt by Sweden to pull Finland further from their clutches. In a similar vein, they took Finland's endeavors to stay out of the Great Power conflicts—this was the motive used by Paasikivi in declining to participate in the Marshall aid—to be a maneuver by the President to undermine Soviet friendship and clear a path for Western influence.[7]

In the tense post-war atmosphere, Stalin did not consider a Nordic and neutral identity to be an acceptable option for Finland. In a two-camp world, each country would have to show its colors.

This chapter will examine how the Soviet leadership—ultimately, Stalin—tried to get Finland to reveal its hand at the start of the Cold War. What did the Soviets try, what means did they employ, what was enough for them and why? Traditionally, Finnish research has tended to revolve around the contemporary conception that there was a Communist coup plot in the works. This notion will be scrutinized here in relation to Moscow's policy both in Finland and in Europe more broadly. The actions of the Finns as well as those of Sweden and the Western Powers will be analyzed in terms of how they relate to the Kremlin's decision-making

Setting the Stage

On 5 January 1948, Stalin and Zhdanov watched—but did not like—the opera *The Great Friendship* by V. Muradeli in the Bolshoi Theater.[8] After being exposed to jazz, atonal music and errors in the nationalities question, the politburo seven proceeded to Stalin's office for a briefing of the new Soviet envoy to Finland. This was lieutenant General G.M. Savonenkov, former vice-chairman of the control commission in Helsinki. The nights before and after this short discussion were dedicated to the German question.[9] Since the West was setting up its own Germany, it was urgent for Moscow to secure agreements with the former Nazi allies that were now under the Soviets' sphere of influence: Romania, Hungary and Finland.

Trickiest of the three was Finland, for it was not inevitable that the country's leadership would accept a military treaty. In Romania and Hungary, where the Communists' power was secure, the leaders' options were limited to thanking Moscow for the agreement, enquiring how they should interpret its wording and asking when they ought to sign it.[10] In Finland, however, the Communists had just suffered losses in the municipal election, the coalition government was still standing but on the brink of collapse, and President Paasikivi could not be forced to request a military agreement.

Halfway through January, at a Yugoslavian dinner at Stalin's dacha, Zhdanov bemoaned the Soviets' failure to occupy Finland when they had the chance. Then everything would be simpler. Molotov responded: "Ah, Finland—it's small potatoes." (On another occasion he noted: "Poland—a big thing!") Stalin himself commented that it would have been worthwhile to occupy Finland. Moscow had paid too much attention to the Americans, they would not have lifted a finger.[11] These thoughts alone can hardly explain the Soviet leadership's actions in 1944, but they reflect well the mood that prevailed in January 1948.

All three of the Soviet Union's main foreign-policy agencies (or "lines," as the saying went)—diplomacy, intelligence, and the party—were deployed to advocate for the military agreement in Helsinki.

In the diplomatic channel, the envoy in Helsinki was changed. G.M. Savonenkov was a military man, ordered to appear always in his general's uniform to remind people of the control commission, which had departed from Finland in October 1947. He received precise instructions from the Politburo upon his appointment:

Cde [Comrade] Savonenkov's primary task is to ensure Finland's turn in the direction of rapprochement with the Soviet Union [*obespechit' povorot Finlyandii v storonu sblizheniya s SSSR*].

Cde Savonenkov must lay the ground for Paasikivi's arrival in Moscow in the near future, for which he has to make understood the prevailing discontent in the Soviet Union towards the political situation in Finland, especially the unsatisfactory progress of the war criminals' court cases, and also in relation to Finland's general political line, to bring about Paasikivi's initiative of the improvement of Soviet–Finnish relations, in connection to which it must be stated that, without Paasikivi meeting in person with representatives of the Sov[iet] Gov[ernment] in Moscow, getting out of the impasse that has arisen would hardly seem possible.

Cde Savonenkov must use all available means of exerting pressure toward achieving the above-mentioned main task, such as: the peace treaty, the articles of which oblige Finland to take action against fascist elements and war criminals; and also economic measures, for example a trade agreement, the use of former German assets in Finland, and others.

All possible support must be given to Finland's democratic circles (the SKDL) to strengthen their influence in Finland's state machinery, paying special attention to helping the people's democrats while they prepare for the next parliamentary elections in summer 1948.[12]

By war criminals the Soviets did not mean wartime leaders. Rather they were referring to the long-awaited hearings of those who had concealed weapons caches across Finland right after the Continuation War, and those groups like the thirty-eight men whom the Soviet Union demanded should be handed over as their citizens. These men were branded "traitors" for having served in either the German or Finnish Army; the majority of them were Estonians, which made the matter morally sensitive.[13]

The main issue was listed at the very top of the instructions. Finland's position was adjudged to have slipped so far from the Soviet Union that a full U-turn, a turning point, was necessary. This was what *povorot* signified: the word was often used about a change in direction at a state level, one that was unambiguous but more moderate than a revolution or coup. One tool for redirecting Finland was the military agreement, but this was not mentioned in Savonenkov's written orders. There is no doubt that he received oral instructions on the matter, just as it was surely impressed upon him that it was ill-advised for an envoy to blab about it.[14] The issue would be taken care of by more competent comrades in Moscow.

Stalin wanted an agreement with Paasikivi. That was the best way of making it appear legitimate to both Finnish and foreign eyes. But when Paasikivi met with the new Soviet envoy, he did not swallow the procedure offered by Savonenkov. Rather, he identified it as a similar ruse to the one Hitler had pulled on Emil Hácha, the President of Czechoslovakia, in 1939. It is possible that the President's wariness was heightened by the news that the Americans were publishing a collection of German documents, entitled *Nazi–Soviet Relations*, which made public for the first time the secret protocol of the Molotov–Ribbentrop Pact, along with other inflammatory material.[15] Paasikivi rejected the idea of traveling to Moscow, invoking his age (seventy-seven) and the restlessness that such a trip would cause among the public. (Seven and a half years later he was not too old to go and receive the Porkkala base when the Soviets decided to return it.) Savonenkov wound up at a disadvantage in the discussion, since he was prohibited from citing an invitation from Moscow, but had to try to persuade Paasikivi to take the initiative. Fumbling, he ended up lying unconvincingly that he had not spoken to Stalin or Molotov, nor had he been ordered to propose the trip. In fairness, his instructions called for a tricky balancing act: to win round Paasikivi, he had to be ingratiating and "chummy" (as the

20. *President J.K. Paasikivi played a vital role in spring 1948. Seven years later he traveled to Moscow to receive the Porkkala military base after the Soviets returned it. He is pictured here (left) with Voroshilov at a reception in the Finnish Embassy, September 1955.*

President put it), but to effectively apply pressure he would also have needed to use rougher language. Ultimately, the combination proved too demanding for him.[16]

Savonenkov's appointment was a one-off scare tactic. As a soldier he had been able to obey and carry out Moscow's instructions, orders and assignments to the letter, but he was not cut out to be a political operative, being altogether too stiff. His official title was Lieutenant-General of the Intendant Service, that is, he was not a fighting soldier, but rather his responsibility was for soldiers' uniforms, food and drink. When he was replaced after three years, the Deputy Minister of Foreign Affairs, Valerian Zorin, explained to Stalin that a stronger and more experienced diplomatic representative was required in Finland.[17]

Just as in fall 1939, Soviet diplomats sought to ascertain Sweden's attitude. The Soviet Union's envoy to Stockholm enquired of Foreign Minister Östen Undén whether Sweden's foreign policy was changing. The Soviet diplomat made no mention of his own country's preparations, nor of its own policy shift that was already underway.[18]

Moscow's second channel, intelligence, made use of its contacts among Finland's political elite. A "councilor" arrived from Moscow to handle them; Mikhail Kotov introduced him to the Finns respectfully, but muttered his name so that it was not caught by Finnish ears. The identity of this high-ranking officer is now clear: he was Aleksandr Mikhailovich Sakharovsky, head of the foreign intelligence department for Scandinavia. In his official CV, now published, a special assignment in Finland in 1947–48 is mentioned, and this is backed up by a card in the Finnish Foreign Ministry's register for one *Sakharovski, Alexandre, councilor*, who received a stamp in his diplomatic passport in January 1948 authorizing multiple trips to the country. A certain self-assertion is reflected by the fact that his passport was under his real name.[19]

Sakharovsky was abroad for the second time; his operative baptism had been as a chief mate on a ship in the Adriatic Sea in 1940. He had been recruited into the profession in February 1939; due to the Great Purge there were plenty of vacant positions at that time. Until then he had been employed at shipyards in Leningrad and in the Red Army. He got a feel for Finland during the war while serving as head of intelligence, amongst other roles, in the regional administration of the People's Commissariat for Internal Affairs in Leningrad. His CV highlights his activity against "German usurpers," but neglects to note that there was also another enemy, the Finns. A promotion after the war took him to Moscow. Sakharovsky was considered handsome and demanding, and was known for avoiding cliques. His main deficiencies were held to be his scant education and his complete lack of Western experience. Perhaps this made him wary of making mistakes. Upon his arrival in Helsinki he was a thirty-eight-year-old lieutenant-colonel.[20]

It is unknown how long Sakharovsky spent in Helsinki, although it is reported that he visited on multiple occasions (*neodnokratno*). His permit allowed trips until the beginning of August.[21] You may wonder if leadership alone gave any additional competence to operate in a foreign country, but, on the other hand, it was a matter of inspection. The chief needed to see with his own eyes that the registered "agents" in the location had not been invented, but that they were real contacts and prominent individuals. The assignment in Finland was seen as a success, for, upon his return, Sakharovsky was promoted to deputy chief of the intelligence department for Europe. In this role he worked with the Greek Communists on damage-limitation measures at their defeat in the civil war, before he was appointed to Romania to advise on the construction of a people's democracy. Such was the dark side of many Soviet intelligence officers politely presented as friends in Finland: many of them were responsible for harsh acts and even for deaths elsewhere.

According to a contested memoir, a similar, if cruder, high-level intelligence operation was being carried out in Prague at the same time as in Helsinki. In the Czech capital, preparations were also being made for a political change of direction, with Molotov giving instructions in Moscow.[22]

In Helsinki, Sakharovsky probably met all the top-level political contacts the Soviet intelligence had. For a possible meeting with Prime Minister Mauno Pekkala, however, there is no source. It is probable that he had already been taken care of in November in Moscow, when the Soviets pressed hard to obtain an initiative for a military pact. He certainly needed a reminder of his role, however, for under pressure he turned to alcohol and frequently went missing, leaving issues at a standstill.

The Foreign Minister Reinhold Svento was certainly contacted. In a memo to the President, Svento deemed a military treaty almost unavoidable, as Moscow had already raised the matter back in November. He asserted that Finland's aim should instead be to establish an agreement that was clearly distinct from those signed in Eastern Europe, so that the country would be its own special case, *sui generis*. Discussing the matter later with the President, Svento claimed that the memo did not really reflect his views; he was, in fact, a "pacifist" and a pessimist when it came to small states dabbling with military issues. The best thing would be to declare Finland's permanent neutrality, but the minister admitted that this was unrealistic.[23]

The Finnish envoy to London, Eero A. Wuori, was more open about his contact when he spoke to the President on a short trip back from Britain. A high-ranking Soviet had inquired whether a friendship agreement could be approved and how Paasikivi and Foreign Minister Carl Enckell saw this. The Soviet suggested that it might be a good idea for Enckell to give up his ministerial role and instead take the post of Finnish envoy to Moscow. Wuori was much less forthcoming about his side of the conversation, but he opined to the President that the Soviets' purpose was "to isolate us from the rest of the world and to get us, in front of the whole world, to tie ourselves to the Eastern Bloc."[24]

There was a shared feature in both Svento's and Wuori's conduct. On the one hand they were incited to act by Soviet contacts, but on the other they made their own assessments and addendums that were unlikely to have been sanctioned by Moscow. This was the ambivalent position of the "agents of influence," as they were later called.

Although the Deputy Speaker of the Diet, Urho Kekkonen, neglected to mention it to the President, he, too, seems to have been on Sakharovsky's meeting list.[25] It is known that he met a high-ranking Soviet, and the timing and topics of conversation were the same as with Wuori. The hypothesis that it was Sakharovsky is supported by an event eight years later. In spring 1956, after Kekkonen's victory in the presidential elections, his *éminence grise*

Kustaa Vilkuna met a certain intelligence officer in Moscow: "this one fellow," in other words someone he had previously met. If this "fellow" was Sakharovsky, then a meeting in January 1948 would explain why he and Kekkonen were already familiar with each other. In spring 1956, Sakharovsky was promoted to head of the First Chief Directorate (foreign intelligence) of the KGB, holding that position until 1971, longer than anyone else.[26]

So, we have found a new actor in the post-war history of Finland by piecing together the evidence (not bountiful, but already tenable). Although the source situation has drastically improved, it is still often necessary to study the political operations of Soviet intelligence as one would address antiquity or the early Middle Ages, by making deductions based on slender circumstantial evidence.

Both Savonenkov's instructions and the high-level influence or intelligence operation indicate that Moscow's primary goal was a military treaty, preferably with Paasikivi himself. The agreement would be driven through on a tight schedule. It was far from certain, however, that Moscow would be able to bend the President to its will, for he had stalled with such resilience up to this point. Should he continue to do so, the Soviets required a plan B, one that touched on the fourth paragraph of the envoy's instructions: changing Finland's direction from within.

The back-up plan rested on the Communists. This channel was operated by the international department of the Soviet Communist Party central committee.[27] At the turn of the year, the leaders of the Finnish Communist Party (SKP)—husband and wife Yrjö Leino and Hertta Kuusinen, plus party secretary Ville Pessi—were called to Moscow at short notice. There, at Barvikha Sanatorium, they were given directives in reorientation by Stalin's subordinates, first Zhdanov alone and then, to drive home the point, in tandem with Malenkov. In her letter to a Finnish writer (by then, her lover), Hertta Kuusinen described her feelings upon a later return to the sanatorium: "Five years ago I lived in this same place for ten gruel-ling days. I can barely remember anything besides the oppressive, noiseless walks in the snowy forest."[28]

The Communists were informed that a defense alliance was imminent. They were ordered to launch a vigorous political offen-sive, with the aim of electoral victory and a parliamentary majority (101 seats) for the political factions controlled by or close to them. In practice, this goal required a crushing blow against right-wing Social Democracy so that the remnants of the SDP would be forced to join the Communist-led bloc. As Hertta Kuusinen saw it, the defense pact campaign would create favorable conditions for this. On their own and at the pace up to then, the Finnish Communists would reach a majority only after one hundred years, she said in Moscow.[29] Zhdanov and Malenkov blamed the Finnish Communists' lack of success on excessively moderate policies. It naturally went unmen-tioned that the SKP had adopted this line after the war on the advice of Zhdanov, who, for his part, was acting under orders from Stalin. Neither of them would take the blame, but the perpetual question of *kto vinoven?* ("whose fault?") still required an answer. The role of scapegoat fell on Interior Minister Yrjö Leino, who, on top of his moderation, was also suspected of nationalism. He was the target to whom Zhdanov and Malenkov dictated their "Satanic chapters."[30]

A shadow had already been cast over Leino two years earlier, in November 1945, when he took a hunting trip to an elk forest with Urho Kekkonen, Mauno Pekkala and two Finnish-speaking British intelligence officers, Rex Bosley and Colonel James Magill. The main activity was not hunting, but rather a whisky-soaked discussion on the trial for their responsibilities during the war of former leaders of Finland. Leino's lenient attitude surprised the British, who were more or less in line with Moscow's approach to the matter.[31] The boozy trip reached Soviet ears and influenced Zhdanov's report to Stalin. The chairman of the control commission needed to shift the blame from himself, so he sharply criticized Leino for his strange conduct of the trial.[32] The affair no doubt stuck in Stalin's mind, but the Soviets did not lose trust in Leino at that moment. The intelligence line, in particular, kept faith in him, and with its support he was able to oust his Communist Party rival Aimo Aaltonen from the position of deputy head of the State Police (Valpo).

In January 1948, however, Moscow decreed that Leino should be removed from the government and from the party leadership. Only the latter order was fulfilled immediately, but only in part, since the minister was needed in many meetings and his removal from the party's core was kept secret. For fear of provoking a political crisis, the SKP did not dare pull him out of the Finnish government, despite a clear decision of the Soviet Communist Party, as Savonenkov remarked.[33]

Yrjö Leino was the first foreign Communist Party leader that Moscow ordered to be sidelined as it began disciplining its own at the outbreak of the Cold War, but he would not be the last. Next in line were Tito in Yugoslavia and Gomulka in Poland. Even Bulgaria's Georgi Dimitrov only narrowly avoided removal, despite being a long-time confidant of Stalin.

An abrupt turn was easiest for Moscow to pull off in those countries where the political line could be dictated, or "given" as it was said. It was harder when the beliefs and opinions of supporters and rank-and-file party members carried some weight. Although national Communism was now banned, in Finnish conditions it could not be simply removed immediately. This was demonstrated by the publication (for May Day) of *Suuri linja* by Raoul Palmgren, subtitled "national studies," an ambitious attempt to seize the mainstream cultural history of Finland. Palmgren was the leading Communist cultural writer and a former protégé of Hertta Kuusinen and Leino. In a speech in mid-March at the Academic Socialist Society, he compared the fatherland to his other hobby, women, concluding that the fatherland does not make decisions blindly like a mistress, but "on the basis of much more business-like viewpoints." At least, he added, the fatherland did not venerate its abuser as a wonderful lover.[34] Improper insinuations? Certainly, if Moscow ever cast its malevolent gaze over this.

The difficulty of changing direction is demonstrated by the SKP leaders' decision to hide from its activists the newly assigned target of 101 parliamentary seats. Party members did not believe it possible, and the leadership itself knew it to be unrealistic. Extraordinary measures were required. Zhdanov and his companions cited Hungary as an example, where the opponents had been scared and subdued with arrests and charges of conspiring with foreign powers. This was not purely a Hungarian affair, for Soviet officers had taken part in the questioning of the accused, using their trademark methods of interrogation. Stalin followed the situation closely, and gave personal permission for the highest-profile arrests (like that of Prime Minister Ferenc Nagy), justifying his decisions on the basis of information that had been procured by Soviet intelligence.[35]

Hungary's template was developed for Finland. The Communist-led security police Valpo, the SKP leaders, and a small circle of Soviet intelligence officers made preparations for politically motivated arrests, which it was believed would lead to a political about-turn. Valpo concocted a right-wing plot as a pretext for the arrests. Top targets were the Social Democratic leaders Unto Varjonen and Väinö Leskinen, since Zhdanov had designated the right-wing Social Democracy as the primary enemy of the working class in Finland. This was not, then, going to be a classic revolution, in which the external pretender overthrows the government, as the Bolsheviks did to the Kerensky government in 1917. Instead, it was an attempt by an already-powerful section of the government to push through a decisive shift in the balance of power, one that would be sealed in carefully controlled elections.

Given the actions of the Soviet Ministry of State Security's representatives in Eastern Europe[36] and the arrests and purges that

Sakharovsky later helped orchestrate in Romania,[37] it might seem possible that he was in Finland not only to exert influence on prominent Finns, but also to oversee the detention operation and the instruction of the SKP and Valpo for this purpose. There is, however, a more likely candidate for the role: Councilor Aleksandr Fyodorov, who arrived in Helsinki in Sakharovsky's wake.

Nicknamed "Iron Tooth" by Finnish officials, Fyodorov was a former colonel in the control commission, officially the deputy head of internal inspection, but secretly the second-in-command of the Finnish branch of the iron-fisted Soviet military counter-intelligence Smersh ("death to spies"). On the night before 21 April 1945 he had led the arrests of twenty "dangerous war criminals" who came to be known as Leino's prisoners.[38] Then, the Finns were wary of even mentioning Fyodorov by name (for Leino he was simply "lt.col. F."),[39] but in 1948 his bite was no longer what it used to be. The diplomat had become chubby and did not seem so dangerous in civilian clothes, especially as he kept such a low profile that many in Helsinki did not even realize he was the same man from the control commission. But he knew Valpo well and knew how to organize arrests.

Leino's prisoners, almost all of them emigrants, were seized on the Communist Interior Minister's fourth day in office in 1945. It was not revealed to the Finns that the arrest of these "White Guards" who had assisted Finnish or German intelligence was done "in accordance with Comrade Stalin's instructions." As the orders came from the very top, Smersh's operatives in Helsinki acted as if in panic. Such was their rush that they did not even keep track of whether or not they had detained the right men. Who cared?—even those arrested in error would confess.[40] Smersh sent its initial interrogation findings directly to Stalin.[41] His directive appears to have been comprised of two parts: 1) a general order to hunt and detain Soviet emigrés who had taken part in military and intelligence activity; and 2) immediate permission for the Smersh group in Helsinki to arrest those who appeared on a prepared list. No one involved in these acts was too insignificant for Stalin. He had himself been in a hopeless situation when the First World War broke out, exiled in the northern Siberian city of Turukhansk, and a decade later, he was mightier than the last Emperor of Russia.

The leader of the Smersh branch in Helsinki was a surprisingly high-level official, no less than Smersh deputy head, Major-General Sergey Kozhevnikov. His career had advanced at a wild pace, similar to that of the notorious V.S. Abakumov, who had rapidly risen to be the chief of Smersh. In contrast to his colleagues in Eastern Europe, Kozhevnikov did not really show himself to the Finns, nor did he hang around long, returning to the Soviet Union for good in summer 1946.[42]

Abakumov had suggested the arrest of White Guard agents "through [*cherez*] the Finnish police" on 10 April 1945. This was before the government had even been appointed, but two days after Leino, on Zhdanov's instruction, had proposed that the Communists fill the post of interior minister. (Prior to Zhdanov's redirection, the Communists had been pushing for Leino to have the ministerial post of agriculture.) Apparently, the order to operate through the domestic police force came from Stalin, since it was emphasized in the implementation report. Leino's name was not mentioned.[43] Elsewhere in the Soviet Union's sphere of influence, it was typical for Smersh operatives themselves to take whomever they wanted, not only emigrés, but also foreign nationals and political opponents of the local Communists. The famous disappearance of Swedish diplomat Raoul Wallenberg in Budapest in 1945 was the direct work of Smersh.[44] The arrest of Leino's prisoners in 1945 remained the one and only such Smersh operation in Finland.

The political idea of the pattern sketched out for Finland in 1948 resembled the one in Prague. Deputy Foreign Minister Zorin was sent there from Moscow in February to persuade the Czechoslovak

Communists to abandon compromises and to attack. They were to stop showing so much respect for the constitution and the President, and give up the belief that everything would run smoothly through a parliamentary system. The Communist Party leader Klement Gottwald asked for Red Army exercises in the vicinity of the border to help ratchet up the pressure, but this was ruled out because Moscow did not want to show its hand. When Gottwald accosted President Beneš to demand a hard government line, the latter's response was: "And if I do not accept?" Gottwald threatened a general strike and the appearance of a workers' militia on the streets, before adding: "And then the Soviet Union is here!" Beneš folded and let it be known that he could not do anything against the threat of invasion. With that, the transfer of power was clear.[45] Foreign Minister Jan Masaryk's probable defenestration in March and the arrests in April brought the other parties into line, and in May a new constitution and controlled elections confirmed the new direction in Czechoslovakia.[46]

Moscow's orders to Pessi and Hertta Kuusinen were based on analogous thinking, but Helsinki was no Prague. Pessi could not threaten the President nor bluff about a Soviet invasion with any conviction. Leino would have been able to do the deed, but he no longer wanted to.[47] Nor would Paasikivi have surrendered quite so meekly: "We are not the Czechs," he habitually reassured himself and others. Besides which, the Communists' power in Finland was smaller; the two other big parties in the coalition government, the Social Democrats and the Agrarian League, were capable of resistance. As for the military, it was not at all under Communist command. This differed decisively from the situation in Czechoslovakia, where "there was no organized power that could be leant on," as President Beneš complained just before his death.[48] Neither would Moscow be able to arrange any extra precautionary measures in Helsinki like it had in Prague, where 400 Soviet intelligence and security service officials posing as civilians were dispatched.

For Stalin's part, relying on the SKP was a back-up plan. First, he wanted to see Paasikivi's cards. At the moment of truth, would the President dare to say no?

Going on the Offensive

In the end Stalin himself had to take the initiative, in the form of a letter to Paasikivi on 22 February 1948. Two weeks earlier, Molotov had announced to the Bulgarians that, provided the Hungarian agreement was ready, "we will turn to the Finns." He was unwilling to accept any treaty connected with the decisions of the United Nations, because the UN might end up being turned "against us," just like in 1939 when the League of Nations judged the Soviet Union to be the aggressor in the "argument" (*ssor*) with Finland.[49] In other words, the specter of the Winter War arose in Molotov's mind as soon as the security agenda touched on Finland.

In his letter Stalin suggested that Finland agree to an analogous treaty to those just struck with Romania and Hungary, "our involuntary allies," as Khrushchev labelled them. Stalin's signature at the bottom of the letter made it clear that the Soviets would not back out. It was nevertheless better to accept an initiative from Stalin than to show up "as a suppliant on his doormat."[50] This was how one experienced British diplomat described the Generalissimo's preferred terms of engagement: he would make people ask, then make them wait and, in the end, make them an offer they could not refuse. He applied these techniques even to Mao Zedong, whose victory in the Chinese Civil War made it necessary to receive him in Moscow.[51] Mao was from the same negotiating school as Paasikivi: open to agreement, but knowing his worth and keeping the trump cards close to his chest.

Finland, therefore, had a slightly stronger starting point than a suppliant would have had. Paasikivi was still playing for time: he delayed the publication of the letter and then invited the leaders of parliamentary groups and military and judicial experts to hear it. It was evident to the President that the matter had to be dealt with through a tête-à-tête with Moscow; no concrete Western support was available, nor had the Finns really hoped for it, since most likely it would only have hardened Russian attitudes.

The West's very existence was critically important to Finland, but any visible Western activity in the country entailed notable risks, all the more so if requested or tacitly approved by Finnish leaders or officials. The Soviet Union followed such actions with vigilance and mistrust, and it might deem it necessary to respond with severe countermeasures, either to exert its authority as a Great Power or as a deterrent. And in a full-blown emergency, the West could not or would not have time to help Finland, such was the country's geopolitical position and value after the Second World War.

The most significant Western Power for Finland was still Britain. At that time it was also one of the three best-informed foreign powers on Finnish affairs, alongside the Soviet Union and Sweden. The latter was, of course, a special case, since it was the only state in the world for which the fate of Finland was a crucial issue. Moreover, Sweden was not seen by the Finns as a completely foreign country in the same way that other countries were.

Britain's intelligence gathering was impressive, even on a par with the Soviet Union's. In January 1948, Rex Bosley, the head of SIS (MI6) station in Helsinki, boasted that "it's very rare that even matters of the slightest importance in this country escape our notice."[52] That said, the two best intelligence services both suffered from the same problem: mere information did not help if interpretation was colored by ideological (or other detrimental) presumptions. The Soviets certainly had their own biases, but the perspicacity of the British was hindered by their disproportionate belief that Communism would inevitably triumph in Finland. When informed about Yrjö Leino's behavior ("taking to *Wein* and *Weib* in a big way"), they concluded that he was celebrating in advance the transfer of power.[53] In reality, Leino had more reason to be scared of Communist power than to celebrate it.

The British advised Paasikivi on delaying tactics, which helped to reinforce the course of action already chosen by the President.[54] Already the previous fall, when they had heard from Paasikivi that Moscow was pushing for a military agreement, the British had been inclined "to do some wrecking," but in practice they lacked the means to interfere.[55] Granted, the British military leadership did want to incite Finland to remove all Communists from its army (although it did not really contain many, except for conscripts) and police force, but the Foreign Office opposed the idea. Better "to keep the 'cold war' away from Finland" and be wary of instigation, for the Finns "are pretty wild people; and we can't help them if the Russians turn sour."[56] The British remained reticent and did not bring up the possible impact of a military agreement on Finland's trade relations with Britain. They considered it dangerous to appeal to the United Nations on Finland's behalf and viewed a Baltic Sea naval visit premature and even harmful. "It might well provoke the Russians into going far further with Finland than they currently intend on going, and it would inevitably make it more difficult for the Finns to resist Russia's pressure."[57]

The main reason for British reticence was that from a military security standpoint Finland's case was interpreted as utterly hopeless. In London the Joint Intelligence Committee opposed the sale of airplanes to Finland, because then "Finland, and through it the Soviet Union, would get technical information," and most importantly, the Soviet Union's aircraft production industry would be freed from supplying a satellite state.[58] The British military leadership summarized this assessment in a single phrase, declaring that Finland had long since "been written off."[59]

Besides suggesting Paasikivi play for time, the British Minister to Finland, Oswald Scott, had other advice: the Finns should not negotiate in Moscow, where they would be isolated and unable to talk freely even among themselves. In the House of Lords, one member warned that Stalin's letter was an invitation "to visit Bluebeard's castle." The reference to the old French folk tale was topical— Chaplin's *Monsieur Verdoux* had been released only the previous year—but the allusion was ill-fitting, for as a murderer Bluebeard paled in comparison to Stalin. Moreover, having endured two wars against the Soviet Union, Finland was no longer a convincing choice for the role of innocent maiden.[60]

Paasikivi chose to ignore this advice and sent his men to Moscow, since in Helsinki a high-ranking Soviet boss would not have time for proper negotiations. This would be Finland's line of action for a long time to come: you must climb to Mount Calvary itself and aim for discussions at the highest possible level, preferably at the very top where the decisions were actually made, and where there was room to maneuver. The President himself stayed at home to avoid direct pressure and to insert another roadblock: the negotiators did not have full powers, but had to seek his permission and confirmation before agreeing to anything.

Stalin's letter launched the first wave of the Finnish Communist Party's offensive. At first this took the usual form of industrial action in the big workplaces, involving walk-outs and strikes. Concurrently, the Communists began to form special bodies to undertake so-called brisk action in the election campaign, as their purpose was explained to the members, who did not know that the target was 101 seats. These bodies were very similar to those used by the Czech party in Prague, and the idea clearly derived from Moscow, as can be concluded from Pessi's detailed report to Savonenkov's deputy.[61] The first instruction letter to the "groups" was sent immediately after this meeting, giving orders that opponents of the security pact with the Soviets should be exposed as enemies of democracy, and the groups should "prepare to strike [them] without mercy."[62] On 7 March a small maverick party demonstration against Stalin's proposal was dispersed by these groups, but it is obvious that this Communist organization was not firm or ready for any serious confrontation. The network never became fully formed and it was probably mainly concentrated in Helsinki.

Sergey Istomin, the Soviet intelligence official who oversaw Valpo, hinted to the secretary of Finland's Foreign Ministry that radical changes were to be expected in relations between the two countries due to a pro-Western plot having been exposed. Members of the government were involved, and from the background it was approved by Paasikivi. When Foreign Minister Carl Enckell complained about these comments to Savonenkov, the envoy replied: "There's no smoke without fire. Look at what you've got brewing."[63]

Valpo delivered the outline of the fabricated conspiracy ("The Finnish Resistance Movement's Organization") to Interior Minister Yrjö Leino. This was allegedly a right-wing conspiracy plan for a new pro-Western government, which would include former leaders of Finland, condemned to prison as war-guilty, and the right-wing Social Democratic leaders Unto Varjonen and Väinö Leskinen. At the same time Valpo's ability to carry out the arrest operation was improved by making Erkki Tuominen the organization's permanent head; he was the first (and last) card-carrying Communist to hold the post. His predecessors since 1945 had been fellow travelers. This was now the Hungarian case desired by Zhdanov and others in January. Leino included this paper in his memoirs, intended for publication in 1958, but avoided the topic of its origins, authors and plausibility.[64] Now it is clear. This plan was warmed up in Moscow in late 1949, when the Soviets prepared for a new hard-pressure campaign against Finland. Deputy Foreign Minister Andrei Gromyko, who coordinated the preparations, sent this plan to Stalin. It was prepared by the *Komitet informatsii*, which was a short-lived attempt to house under one roof all organizations involved in foreign intelligence. The alleged plot itself was similar in 1948 and 1949, but the warm-up included some new elements, like more efficient spreading of rumors and an anti-Soviet leaflet for the Finns, written and planned to be printed by the Soviets themselves. Another difference was that in 1949 the Communists no longer controlled any police organization in Finland, so the arrests as planned in 1948 were no longer possible.[65]

Leino took care of the appointment of a chief for Valpo, but on 9 March he made an unexpected move, hinting to General Aarne Sihvo that a possible plot was in the works. Sihvo was the Chief of the Finnish Defense Forces, and had already quelled one uprising, the Mäntsälä Rebellion in 1932, an attempt by the far-right Lapua Movement to topple the Finnish government. Unaware that he had just been labeled a Red fellow traveler by the British, the general initiated the army's emergency measures against the Communists.[66] The Social Democrats also began precautionary arrangements. Without going into details, Sihvo informed the Soviet military attaché, Major-General Sergey Tokarev, of his measures. Both sides thus dispensed servings of intelligence information in an attempt to influence one another. Sihvo's announcement to Tokarev was a reminder of Finland's capacity for resistance, and at the same time a cautionary measure in case the Soviets would somehow come to hear about the army's emergency measures. Istomin for his part warned what was in store for anyone who would say no to Stalin.

Let's stop for a moment to consider Yrjö Leino. Although he had been pushed out of the party, the roots of his world view did not disappear, as revealed by his notes in the 1950s.[67] As in the case of the party secretary general Arvo "Poika" Tuominen in Stockholm during the Winter War, Leino's secession was slow. In spring 1948 he was still, for the most part, a Communist and a client of the Soviet Union. Even after all that had happened, Hertta Kuusinen proclaimed: "Don't turn yourself into a 'gentleman,' but stay a man of the proletarian world view." Hertta saw that her soon-to-be former husband still wanted to support Communists as he understood them.[68] As often happens with those marginalized or forced to leave a political group, Leino saw himself as being true to ideology, unlike the party leaderships in Moscow or Helsinki, which were dominated by traitors, Jesuits, gangsters and crooks. He wrote that "the worst opponents of Communism (after the Second World War) are in Moscow," and asserted that the Muscovites were more culpable of the sin of nationalism than those they accused, representing, as they did, "the highest class of national Communism."

Of the core leaders from the SKP, Leino was the only one who never lived in the Soviet Union. Those who had resided there had learnt fear, silence and loyalty without asking questions. Having seen Soviet leaders, Leino's assessment was that Marx and Engels would not feel happy even a week in such a company. A week—too generous? He was surprised when Hertta told him, after her visit in fall 1945, that the imposing and broad-shouldered Stalin of the statues was, in reality, "only a small, hunched-up old man." In spring 1946, Yrjö saw with his own eyes that Stalin really was "a physically stunted tiddler with sloped shoulders."[69] His opinion was that small men were hardly cut out for leadership.

Leino realized that Stalin was responsible for his removal, but it was the incompetent and unmanly Malenkov who had done the dirty work. He arrived at Stalin's dinner in the Malachite Hall at the Kremlin in a collarless peasant shirt while Stalin and his comrades were in their finest uniforms and the Finns were in evening dress. Leino felt pity for this "trousered diva."[70] As for Beria, at the Bolshoi Theater he kept glancing around, playing the fool and flattering this Malenkov-nobody. The face showed what sort of man he was: a crook.

The main reason for Leino's dislike was not the foreign nature of the regime, but rather its tyranny. "It is not Communism," he asserted, "to murder and execute fellow human beings." Over the eastern border, the spirit of Ivan the Terrible lived on; Peter the Great, an obvious despot, was worshipped there.[71] Leino's hostility does not, however, seem to have extended to the Soviet people, whom he viewed as victims. "A person who has traveled along the S[oviet] U[nion]'s road of suffering is comparable to Jesus Christ."

His own acrid tale of the Soviet Union's injustice centered on the fate of Finnish Red refugees. Hertta's siblings knew the gulag. Her sister, Riikka, had a breakdown after successive husbands were sent to the camps, and her brother, Esa, was held in one until he was dispatched to be secretary of the Terijoki government. Hertta "warned [Leino] not to speak to her mother" about her brother's sentence. When Pessi plucked up the courage to ask Zhdanov about Hannes Mäkinen and other Finns who were swallowed up in the Great Terror, the Soviet answered: "Such old matters shouldn't be spoken of." At a meeting between Churchill and Stalin, the British Prime Minister expressed his regret for his perpetual anti-Communism, causing his Soviet counterpart to utter: "He who recalls the past should lose his eyesight."[72] Stalin could remember other people's sins if need be, but he also had a great deal to forget.

Zhdanov reminded Leino of F.A. Seyn, the last Russian Governor-General of Finland, in 1917. During this revolutionary year, a Russian seaman was pointing his Nagant revolver "at Seyn's face" on a platform at Helsinki railway station. Did Leino see it himself as a young man? Still clad in his uniform, the Governor-General spread out his arms in remonstration, just as Zhdanov was in the habit of doing. Of course, the posts held by these two men in Finland bore more than a passing resemblance to each other.

As for Molotov, Leino considered him sensible, "even comparatively flexible." Moscow's second-in-command was more familiar to Paasikivi, who would sometimes—in tête-à-têtes with Leino—launch into animated critiques of Stalin and Molotov, such as when he proclaimed of "these neighbours" that "more stupid men I've not met. *Saatana!*" An example of their idiocy was opposition to Scandinavian cooperation, as Paasikivi saw that this only pushed the Scandinavians to seek support from the West.

Leino knew more personally than anyone in the Finnish government that "the Russians are not satisfied with Platonic love only."[73] He would have recognized the later counter-espionage slang term *clean*: a diplomat who was not an intelligence officer. The contacts he had made around 1940 were anything but clean, and his connections with them continued even after Moscow had ordered his banishment from the SKP.[74] A tarnished record was easy to overlook if the source was still useful to Soviet intelligence. Leino was also careful to hold his tongue, and did not even include details of his intelligence relationships in his own notes.

Among Communists, or "friends," the Soviets did not adopt the tone of reserved politeness that they used with other foreign politicians. As Interior Minister, Leino saw this on many occasions: "Strict summons for any sort of report, even striking the table with their fists." The worst one took place right after he assumed his ministerial post in 1945, when the Soviets insisted that the emigrés—"dangerous war criminals"—be detained and then immediately handed over to them.

Political conflicts overlapped with Leino's personal tragedies. Booze played its familiar part. He fondly reminisced about Mannerheim's visit to a meeting room at the opening of the newly elected parliament in spring 1945. Pointing to a festive carafe, the Marshal-President asked, "What does that contain?" When informed that it was water, he commented: "Lousy substance." He was well versed in heavy consumption at a young age, and could certainly hold his liquor. In contrast, Leino, then forty-eight years old, was a novice, a former abstainer, quickly inducted into the governmental drinking culture by Kekkonen and others.[75] It is possible to write a history of Finland's Eastern relations from the perspective of alcohol tolerance: success demanded the ability to drink to excess, but many fell by the wayside: Leino, Mauno Pekkala, later others; Soviet casualties included Zhdanov, later Ambassador Belyakov and many KGB officers quietly recalled.

Leino's marriage was breaking up. Hertta's letters are full of emotion, pain and a tragic rationality, but Yrjö only describes his former *Tillottaja* (from the Swedish *tillåta*, to allow) with insipid negativity and vulgarity. He repeatedly brought to mind one particular dance his wife had done with a Swedish military attaché. Longing was concealed under indecent language, not to mention his jealousy that Hertta (or Gerta Ottovna) had had so "many men, adventures— some love, too." Leino claimed that her love life would make a fitting subject for a master's thesis by a young social scientist.

In his mind, the female genitalia, especially when neglected, was an animal, a beast, governed purely by "the instinct of the organ." Montaigne shared this viewpoint, although it is unlikely that Leino was familiar with his essay on the topic.[76] Leino's notes point rather to Elias Lönnrot, the nineteenth-century compiler of *Kalevala*, who, unlike those who came after him, did not shy away from collecting sexual ballads or including in his dictionary even the harshest four-letter word. Not that Leino needed any dictionary to use it: "The cunt has, to a large part, defined O.V. K[uusinen]'s politics, and H[ertta] K.'s fate is the same." Female beauty would continue to captivate Leino's father-in-law even as an old man.

Of Finland's leaders, Leino's preferred choice was Mannerheim, although he remembered the Marshal's procrastination when it came to his own ministerial appointment. Mannerheim's foremost merit was the active approach to withdraw Finland from the war. Also, the fight for independence had necessitated action; it would not have been reached under Paasikivi's old policy of "licking the Tsar's boot tip." Leino might well have grown equally disillusioned with Kekkonen, if his note from 1955 pointed to the soon-to-be President: "A political 'con-man' might even climb to become a presidential candidate, just by exhibiting humility and foolhardy bravery as the situation demands."

Leino's notes are dominated by bitterness and hindsight. He also had an exalted opinion of his own role, which he spelled out:

"Although I, too, was on the list of those kicked out in 1948, I saw it as my concern to save Finland as an independent nation and state."

The Military Treaty

Paasikivi did not say no to Stalin, but responded on 9 March 1948 that Finland agreed to enter into negotiations with Moscow. The decision went against the advice of the first President of the Republic, K.J. Ståhlberg, as well as against the will of parliament and the nation, although the matter was not put to a vote. Paasikivi reminded the Soviets that parliamentary approval would be needed before signing any agreement, and required that the treaty's contents be "freely considered and decided" in the negotiations. This part was deleted when the answer was published in *Pravda*.

The Finnish Communist offensive abated to wait for the outcome of the negotiations. An embarrassing disclosure was reported to the Soviets: the party district leaders believed that the target of 101 seats could be reached only with foreign (that is, Soviet) aid. Without that, the election defeat would be even more serious than in local elections in December.[77] The election target was reduced to eighty seats, and for the moment, the SKP "groups" received tamer instructions, focusing on economic and social issues. However, the slogan of the week reminded people of that of the Bolsheviks in 1917: *For peace, bread and land!* Now the decisive day would be the parliamentary reading of the pact with the Soviet Union. The Communists believed that the rightists, including the right-wing Social Democrats, would oppose the pact, which should then be pushed through by a powerful stand of the masses.[78]

The negotiations that led to the Treaty of Friendship, Cooperation and Mutual Assistance (the Finnish abbreviation YYA) have been the subject of detailed research, also using available Soviet material.[79] It should be noted that the Soviet Union negotiated in earnest with

Finland, and that Moscow's most important concession came at the very beginning. In a confidential meeting with Mauno Pekkala on 26 March, Molotov announced that the Soviet Union was prepared to accept Finland's draft as the basis for the treaty, if doing so would ensure its ratification in parliament.[80]

Finland's treaty ended up being a special case, *sui generis*. It was not a generic military treaty like the ones Moscow had signed with various Eastern European countries, for it was only pertinent in the event of an attack by Germany or its ally against the Soviet Union *through Finnish territory*.[81] Then Finland would have to defend itself, if necessary in cooperation with the Soviet Union. Unlike in Soviet treaties with Eastern Europe, Finland *was not obliged to consult with Moscow* when making foreign policy. This was reinforced by the treaty's statement of purpose, which outlined Finland's aim to keep clear of the contradictions between the Great Powers.

Soviet intelligence got precise information about Finland's position and the delegation's room for negotiation both in advance and during confidential meetings in Moscow. Stalin seems to have been most strongly influenced by information about the assessments of Finnish military experts. Generals Erik Heinrichs and Oscar Enckell considered that Finland would have no realistic prospect of staying neutral if a large-scale war broke out. Its location and, most significantly, the Soviets' military base at Porkkala, meant that the country would inevitably end up fighting on the side of its eastern neighbor. As ever, Stalin placed more store in secretly obtained back-channel information than in claims voiced over a negotiating table. Heinrichs was close to Mannerheim and a central strategist in the recent war, and Oscar Karlovich Enckell was the brother of the Finnish Foreign Minister and had served as chief of the special office of military intelligence in Imperial Russia on the eve of the First World War.[82] The opinion of such men carried weight.

Stalin decided to settle for what the Finns were ready to accept, although it was less than had been agreed with Hungary and

Romania, and less than he had been intending to get at the start of the year.

Intelligence information from Finland carried some weight, but Stalin was more efficiently influenced by the shift in the general international situation. Paasikivi's play for time paid off, for things looked very different in late March 1948 than they had at the start of the year. The Western Powers and their protégés reacted quickly to the coup in Prague: already on 17 March, Britain, France and the Benelux countries signed the Treaty of Brussels, creating the Western European Union (WEU). It was focused on national security cooperation, contained a mutual defense clause, and was supported by President Truman.[83]

The very next day, Soviet intelligence reported to Stalin about information from Washington suggesting that talks were beginning about the creation of an Atlantic bloc. This would include the United States, Britain, Canada, Denmark, Norway, Ireland and Iceland. On British Foreign Minister Ernest Bevin's recommendation, Sweden had been left out of the proposal. Further, the report claimed that the Western Powers had spread the rumor in Stockholm and Oslo that Moscow would seek a treaty with Norway once it was done with Finland.[84]

Secretly obtained British memos, classified minutes from Cabinet meetings, and details of British and American military negotiations[85] made Stalin see that too severe a line towards Finland would have serious consequences in the West and the Nordic countries, especially in Sweden. Even the Swedish Foreign Minister Östen Undén, champion of the policy of neutrality, rapidly hardened his attitude towards the Soviets due to events in Czechoslovakia and Finland.[86]

As the Soviets' negotiations with Finland heated up, A.N. Abramov, former Helsinki envoy and current departmental head at the Ministry of Foreign Affairs, was asked to provide a summary of the situation in the North. He depicted Scandinavian cooperation in an entirely negative light, claiming that these states' coordinated efforts since the start of the year were being openly used by the Anglo-Americans to help construct the Western Bloc. The reactionary and anti-Soviet nature of the cooperation could be seen, he argued, in Sweden's policy towards Finland, which aimed to "neutralize" the Soviet influence. In Finland, reactionaries rested on relations with the Nordic countries. The Finnish Social Democrats followed direct instructions from their ideological brothers in Sweden. Abramov's report saw the Scandinavian bloc as being "at present" to the disadvantage of the Soviet Union and to the advantage of American and British interests. In this situation, Finland and its democratic circles were seen as tools that the Soviets could employ to slow down these developments and to try to make Scandinavian cooperation more progressive in character. The report suggested that, over time, the Soviet Union should try to get its northern republics—Russia, Estonia, Latvia and Karelian Soviet Republic—included in this Nordic cooperation.[87]

According to the Soviet envoy to Stockholm, Sweden's foreign policy had clearly changed for the worse. The country was now actively advocating for a Scandinavian defense alliance, which would inevitably become affiliated with the Western Bloc. Moscow was careful with how it touched on the topic in public: Sweden was still keen to emphasize its neutrality, and the Soviets did not want it to follow Denmark and Norway in a more Westerly direction.[88] Although Paasikivi, in one of his fits of rage, might rant about the foolishness of the Soviet leaders, Stalin did realize that it was not in his interest to push Sweden further to the West.

As for the general developments in the international situation, acutely the most important were the passing of the Marshall Plan by the United States' Congress and the escalation of tensions in Germany. The latter resulted in the first Berlin crisis, in which the Soviets blockaded the West-controlled zones of the city. To gain support for its stance on the German question, the Soviet Union sought to establish a nine-state "peace front that opposes the West's military bloc and involves a majority of European countries," as the Deputy Minister for Foreign Affairs optimistically calculated. Finland was included among nine countries that had signed a treaty of friendship, cooperation and mutual assistance, even though at that time Paasikivi had only agreed to enter into negotiations.[89] The Soviets already planned to frame their agreement with Finland as an example of their peace-loving efforts. After the treaty was signed, Molotov told the American ambassador that it demonstrated "yet again [*lishnii raz*]" that the Soviet Union was not a remotely aggressive state. He was careful to add that, of course, the Soviet Union's treaties with its other neighbors were also proof of this.[90]

It is difficult to discern if Moscow's Finnish line was influenced by the fact that its relations with Yugoslavia were swiftly worsening. Maybe it was, in the sense that the Soviets had yet another awkward and urgent foreign policy dilemma on their hands.

More evident is that Italy's fraught parliamentary elections contributed to Soviet caution. The outcome—victory for the Christian Democratic party—determined the country's place on the Western side in the Cold War.[91] The election campaign overheated so that Palmiro Togliatti—leader of the most powerful Communist Party in Western Europe—had a secret meeting with the Soviet ambassador in a forest just outside of Rome. Assuming that the left would win the elections and the reactionaries would then try to nullify the result, Togliatti asked, should the left initiate an armed insurrection in order to seize power. This would probably bring about a big war in the area. Molotov's response came extremely quickly: the Central Committee of the Bolshevik Party (that is, Stalin) approved the use of weapons by the Italian Communists only in self-defense, if the party offices or leaders were attacked. "Under no circumstances" were they to start an armed rebellion.[92] Molotov's secret cable arrived in Rome on the same day that he informed Pekkala that the Soviets would accept Finland's draft treaty as the basis for the negotiations.

Stalin and Molotov must have understood how a vice-like grip on Finland would have exacerbated matters elsewhere in Europe. They had to draw a line somewhere, rather than agitate indiscriminately. This could be seen in Greece, too, where the Communist Party started to receive signals from Moscow in March that they should bring an end to the civil war. In April they did offer to negotiate with the Greek government, but the initial response from Athens was hostile.[93]

The long list of different factors brings to mind Boccalini's old observation that in the soul of tyrants resides and governs another true tyrant: interest.[94]

The Treaty of Friendship, Cooperation and Mutual Assistance was signed in Moscow on 6 April 1948. The next evening at dinner, Stalin—"in a brilliant mood"—returned to the topic of iron, which he had already raised with a Finnish government delegation in March 1946. Then, the Generalissimo had made vague promises about placing orders in Finnish shipyards, and had asked whether or not the armor on the big coastal defense ships *Väinämöinen* and *Ilmarinen* was Finland's own. Now he enquired again as to whether Finland had its own iron, and, when met with a negative reply, he commented: "That's bad, you ought to strive towards having your own iron, since you certainly can't produce your own guns, if there is no iron. Who would bother to defend such a country, if it did not have guns itself? Get your army in good shape."[95]

Before the Finnish team left for home they paid a visit to the former Stockholm envoy, Aleksandra Kollontay, considered a friend of Finland. She informed Stalin that Prime Minister Mauno Pekkala had, with great emotion, told her that henceforth all Finnish school-children would have to learn and remember his name, because it was he who had signed the new treaty.[96] This never happened.

The prevailing reaction in Sweden and further west was relief. Paasikivi explained in detail to the British Minister to Finland, Sir

21. The annual anniversary celebrations of the signing of the 1948 security treaty, organized by the Communists, 6 April 1949.

Oswald Scott, what sort of treaty had been achieved and what threats averted as a result. The President did not, however, write his analysis down, not even in his own diary. Perhaps it only dawned on the British at this point quite how valuable Paasikivi was to Finland, as well as how "physically and mentally tough" the old man was.[97] In contrast, Foreign Minister Carl Enckell—also known as Uncle Kalle or Karl Karlovich—was on his last legs—the Soviets had "worn him down" at last.[98]

In London, the Foreign Minister Ernest Bevin adjudged that Finland's uncompromising attitude had resulted in a treaty that "protects Finland from the Soviet Union interfering in its internal affairs and treats it rather as a buffer state than as a Soviet satellite." At the very least the Finns had got room to breathe. Although one senior civil servant at the Foreign Office did not think there would be much room at all: the Soviets would probably not allow free elections in Finland "if they can only avoid it."[99]

The British delivered memos to Paasikivi and a few other trusted persons detailing what happened in Czechoslovakia, which had caused considerable unease in Helsinki. The documents were conveyed secretly, and this perhaps inflated the message's importance. Scott, the British Minister to Finland, recommended open correspondence, especially as Finland's leading newspapers were even prepared to pay for the material, which was rejected as propaganda in the Western press and censored in Transcurtainia, that is, behind the Iron Curtain.[100]

When to Stop?

The second wave of the Communists' spring offensive was launched as negotiations in Moscow neared their conclusion. To lay the groundwork for the secretly planned arrests, revelations were published in the press about the Social Democratic leaders' wartime cooperation with the former state police. The SKP's "groups" received instructions that, when the treaty came before parliament, they should attack the reactionary objections against it "in all shapes and forms." In an even sterner letter of instruction in mid-April, the people's democratic government was demanded, as well as huge street demonstrations. "The solution," it declared, "whether forwards or backwards is near at hand. Comrades, it depends on you which path we take." The slogan of the day was: *Crush the intentions of the reactionaries!*[101]

Details of the Communists' plans, some of them exaggerated or erroneous, were obtained by their opponents' intelligence operations. This caused the Social Democrats, Paasikivi and the army to take urgent preparatory action to prevent any disturbances when the treaty would be brought for parliamentary approval. However, after mid-April the revolutionary fervor of the Communist groups' instructions had already abated; the crushing of reactionary forces was no longer demanded, nor was a people's democratic government.

The slogan had softened, and was now simply: *We want to construct.* The moment for acute action had passed: "Comrades! Our revolution has neither a date nor a clock's time stroke set in advance, it will begin at the moment when social development has created the occasion."[102]

The SKP leadership had obviously received new instructions from Moscow. An offensive was no longer necessary, not even to ensure the treaty's ratification, since the Soviet leaders now saw that this would happen in any case. The Finnish Communists' ascent to power would have required considerable and conspicuous military support from the Soviet Union, but Stalin did not want to go down this road when a tolerable military treaty with Paasikivi was in sight. As he had at the Bolshoi Theater during the Winter War, Stalin changed tack midway through the process.

This time there was no diarist to record the Soviet leader's volte-face. However, Stalin's comments and actions in other contexts help illuminate the reasoning behind his decision. As the Second World War was entering its final stages, during a meeting break he had chatted with British Foreign Minister Anthony Eden about their principal foe. "Hitler is a genius," Stalin said, "but he does not know when to stop." Eden responded: "Does anyone know when to stop?" Stalin: "Me."[103] This, in a nutshell, exemplifies his attitude when resolving Finnish issues in 1940 and 1948: when your own intentions lead to difficulties that threaten to snowball, it is worth taking stock and changing direction. The ability to perform abrupt U-turns was integral to Stalin's political skill.

Another example of his pragmatic attitude comes from February 1948, when the Bulgarian Communists visited Moscow. They asserted that they owed a debt of honor to the Greek partisans, whom they (and the Soviet Union) should continue to support. Stalin disagreed, justifying himself in terms of Kantian philosophy: "We don't have such categorical imperatives. The whole question comes down to [*zakluchaetsya*] the balance of power. If you are in the condition to do so, strike. If you're not, don't start a fight. We don't start fighting when the opponent wants, but only when it is in our own interest."[104] As this attitude is summarized by Jonathan Haslam: "When no obvious gains could be made and where relations became needlessly exacerbated, Stalin brutally cut his losses. The converse was, however, that now he had no hesitation to strike where the adversary was weak."[105] At this stage, Stalin's two-camp policy was governed by the defensive aspect, in which "caution, rather than aggression, was the word of the day." The main concern was to secure the Soviets' own zone; causing delays and obstructions in the West was secondary.[106]

Stalin ruled out direct participation in revolutionary projects within the West's sphere of interest, since that involved the risk of another great war. The Soviet Union had good reason to avoid this, for the country's resources had been heavily depleted by the previous war. It was in far more dire straits than outside observers could see, and at times even on the verge of a famine.[107] The Greek partisans would have to get by on their own. As for the French and Italian Communists, who had hardened their stance and organized strikes and demonstrations to cause problems for their governments, Moscow made it clear that they should not take things too far. Armed uprisings or antics that risked the Communist parties being declared illegal were out of the question. When the French party leader, Maurice Thorez, returned from his holiday at the Black Sea, he had a message for his comrades: "If we continue like this, Stalin will wash his hands [of us]."[108]

Finland did not belong to the Western camp, but nor to the Eastern one as had been supposed. It was, instead, an in-between zone, where the border between east and west was initially blurred and porous. Finland and Austria were states in this category, and caution proved to be the stronger instinct. In February, Zhdanov criticized Austrian Communist leaders for having too much faith in the Red Army and for being too reliant on the Soviet occupation zone. "A country's independence can't rest on foreign troops," he advised.[109] The Soviet Union did not want to commit additional military resources to Finland any more than it did to Austria, since the firepower might be required elsewhere, and neither of these small countries currently posed any threat.

The countermeasures arranged by Paasikivi, the Social Democrats and the military culminated on the night before 27 April, when the treaty was to be discussed and approved in parliament. The measures were based on intelligence observations and conclusions on that basis; what was lacking, however, was the information that the danger was over. The Communists were no longer preparing for anything exceptional. The solution was now seen in elections only, and the SKP tried to convince the rank and file that "the soil for our work has now softened, it is more favorable for us now, if we are able to till." There were "conditions of victory hidden in the present situation." The enemy was not supported by the American Navy, police terror and millions of dollars, as in Italy. "In Finland, the reactionary forces have their own strength only."[110]

And that was enough. In addition to strength, the "reaction" as led by President Paasikivi also possessed tactical skill and flexibility. In February most of the right wing and the Social Democrats had been against a security treaty with the Soviet Union, and that would have been the opinion of the majority of the people, if asked. In April they were ready to agree to the treaty in the form achieved in the negotiations. The treaty was accepted by the parliament with a large majority.

Surprised by the extent of countermeasures, the SKP secretary general Ville Pessi took himself off to Moscow on 13 May to explain the situation and to ask for help. Since the SKP did not have sufficient forces to produce a turn-around on its own, he requested the Soviet Union to apply pressure, most of all on the Finnish Army. As was habitual for the Finns, Pessi was woolly and vague, Zhdanov reported to Stalin. He did not consider that the Finnish Communists' actions could be taken seriously while Leino continued to be involved. The Interior Minister had been banished by Moscow and in no uncertain terms. Surely the Finnish comrades were not harboring sympathies for their former leader?[111]

Stalin did not consider that exerting intense pressure on a state with whom the Soviets had recently signed a fresh treaty of friendship to be a brilliant idea. Instead, Moscow offered the SKP the consolation of accepting the Communist ministers' petition (with Yrjö Leino the first signatory) to significantly reduce the amount of remaining reparations. This was believed to be something that would support the party at the ballot box. Although the SKP got the carrot rather than the stick on this occasion, it was still hard to stomach. In Russian the two alternatives are more extreme: *knut ili pryanik*, the knout (whip) or the gingerbread.

Leino's notes contain a surprising entry, according to which in the aftermath of the treaty, "I was urged to take charge of the SKP. I was not really willing." He did not specify—or did not know—the precise powers behind the suggestion, but did mention that the initiative came "from a high authority in Moscow."[112] This would not be totally out of the question, even though high-ranking comrades had only just repeated their January call for him to be ousted. Beria would later develop a similar scheme, so it is not unreasonable to suspect that he was already behind this proposal as well. Even if Moscow wanted a less vague and more capable leader for the SKP, the idea should not necessarily be taken at face value. Maybe the idea was to provoke Leino into raising his head to make it easier to remove him.

Five years later, straight after the death of Stalin, Beria launched a series of quick reforms. These included the strengthening of national elements in the Baltic republics and people's democracies. Imre Nagy took the reins in Hungary: although a former NKVD informant, he was still more a product of his nation than the Moscow-educated (mostly Jewish) party leadership in Budapest.[113] Beria ordered intelligence officers in Helsinki to sound out Yrjö Leino about the prospect of his return to the highest echelons of the Communist Party. As with Nagy, on the one hand Leino was a tried former agent, on the other he represented a more national mindset than the Soviet-educated party leaders. In his notes, Leino wrote: "Still years later [than in 1948] they tried the same, in a roundabout way—not to me directly. But I didn't want to anymore."[114]

There was one more surprise turn before the elections. Leino's potential for influence was fundamentally damaged on 20 May 1948, when the parliament voted in favor of a motion of no-confidence in him during the discussion about the government's annual report of the year 1945. The motion concerned Leino's decision in April 1945 to arrest and hand over to the Soviets twenty anti-Bolshevik activists. Not even Prime Minister Mauno Pekkala defended his Interior Minister, being angry about the petition to the Soviets to reduce Finland's reparations, which was signed by only three Communist ministers and not also by their allies. Neither the government nor even the ministers of the Finnish People's Democratic League had been informed in advance.[115] Whether this was the fault of Stalin, Zhdanov or Pessi, it thus proved to be a tactical blunder. When Leino lost the vote of confidence, Paasikivi was furious at the National Coalition Party and the Social Democrats for rocking the parliamentary boat at a delicate moment, yet he had no choice but to remove the Interior Minister from his role in Cabinet. In Finland only the innermost circle of the SKP knew that parliament and the President were unknowingly carrying out the demand that Moscow had made back in January.

The supporters did not know about this backstory, so the SKP had to kickstart widespread strike action in support of their secretly fallen lion. Pent-up social pressures made for a surprisingly tempestuous strike, which caused the President to make preparations for a state of emergency. He instructed the military and the police forces that, for the time being, they should only obey his orders.[116] However, the crisis was over before it began, for the SKP leadership agreed to a compromise almost on the spot: Hertta Kuusinen would enter the government as a minister without portfolio. "We got advice, and followed it with aching hearts," Hertta explained to her father.[117] In other words, the Soviets had told their Finnish comrades not to rock the boat.

In early July regular and free parliamentary elections were held. The Communists and their allies lost thirteen seats and got only thirty-eight instead of the hoped-for 101 or at least eighty. The Communist-led bloc SKDL was immediately removed from the government. Usually, the negotiations for coalition governments had been lengthy, but this time they had barely begun when the President appointed a Social Democrat minority government. The most volatile period was over. Nonetheless, the situation would remain unpredictable for at least a further couple of years.

The outcome in Finland bruised the Soviet officials involved. The Soviet way to wage war had eaten up men, as a Finnish general said in the government when military cooperation with the Soviets was first pondered, but even in peacetime it wasted human resources. But there was no Helsinki curse here, rather a Kremlin curse, if any. However, it did not strike everyone: the careers of intelligence officers Aleksandr Sakharovsky and Mikhail Kotov received a boost, and they both rose to the rank of general. Kotov's advancement was entirely the product of his work in Finland: he was made a deputy chief on foreign intelligence straight after Kekkonen's election as President in 1956. As for Sakharovsky, the shadowy councillor in Helsinki in early 1948, his two decisive promotions were linked to Finnish operations. In 1948 he was appointed as deputy intelligence chief, and in 1956 he became head of the KGB First Chief Directorate, the foreign intelligence.

Many others met with tribulations after trying to solve the Finnish question. From their fates can be glimpsed with what kind of political system Finland, as a neighbor, had to contend.

Zhdanov was already in a tight spot when he had scolded Pessi in May 1948. Zhdanov's son, Yuri, a scientist, had taken a critical position against the superstar biologist Trofim Lysenko in the battle over science in the Soviet Union. The latter's ideas had helped reform Soviet agricultural policy in the 1920s; they had also led to disastrous famines, but, in spite of this, he remained in favor with Stalin (and later with Khrushchev, too). In June 1948, Stalin—typical of his habits—forced Zhdanov to draft a statement denouncing his son's opinions.[118] Not long after, Stalin received a recommendation from doctors that Andrei Aleksandrovich Zhdanov would soon enter into medical care. The Soviet leader prevaricated at first ("To where? What care?"), but then gave his mark of approval and allowed Zhdanov to go to the sanatorium. There, after two heart attacks, the Soviet politician died on 31 August, aged fifty-two. He was buried at the Kremlin Wall, and the city of his birth, Mariupol, was renamed Zhdanov (changed back in 1989). The 70th infantry division, which had charged on Vyborg at the end of the Winter War and on Tallinn in 1944, was renamed in his honor. The Zhdanov division has since served in Cuba during the missile crisis and in Afghanistan after the Soviet invasion in 1979. More recently, it has undertaken operations in Abkhazia and in both Chechen wars.[119]

In the early 1950s, Stalin made use of this death during his last purge, in which mostly Jewish doctors at the Kremlin were accused of murdering Zhdanov and other high-ranking officials. This fabricated conspiracy came to be known as the Doctors' Plot, and it was not the only occasion on which Zhdanov's demise was connected to a purge. Half a year after his passing, his former faction was dismantled in the so-called Leningrad Affair. The matter did not seem like much in the beginning, but soon members of the Politburo and high-ranking officials in Leningrad were caught up in it. The primary targets were arrested on 13 August 1949 in Malenkov's office, where they had been invited for negotiations. As former rivals of Zhdanov, Malenkov and Beria were instrumental in this political operation, but Stalin was still pulling the strings. In addition to the main defendants, the affair resulted in at least 214 death sentences, and numerous prominent Leningrad residents were forced into exile.[120]

Perhaps connected with this affair, Major-General Sergey Tokarev, the military attaché in Helsinki, was arrested on a visit to his homeland at the end of 1949. Even after he was imprisoned, his name appeared as the official military attaché for a long time. In April 1952 he was stripped of his military rank; there is no information about any other sentences, although he remained behind bars until Stalin's death, after which he was released. His reputation and rank were reinstated, but the forty-nine-year-old Siberian general was no longer fit for service. He passed away in 1969.[121]

After leaving Finland, the envoy Grigori Savonenkov was appointed chief of administration and logistics at the Ministry of Defense and promoted to colonel-general. For "Iron Tooth" Fyodorov, on the other hand, Helsinki was his final posting. His iron teeth were not a sufficiently distinctive mark in the city's Soviet circles, where he was known as "Big Belly" Fyodorov. Alongside his official role as councilor, he acted as the embassy's party organizer, or rather the supervisor of others, and in so doing he was to cut short the career of Lieutenant-Colonel Juho Pakkanen. The Ingrian Finn had served as Stalin's interpreter in the 1948 negotiations, and on other occasions. However, after one official meeting Pakkanen stayed on at a sauna with Kekkonen, and from there the two went on to chase women. When Big Belly got word of this night of absence, he dispatched Pakkanen to Moscow, where he was expelled from the party. Pakkanen then got a position as translator from Finnish in Petrozavodsk, the capital of Soviet Karelia.[122] As for Fyodorov, he returned to his homeland in December 1950 and took early retirement, at the age of forty-five, in Leningrad. In 1959 he was expelled from the party.[123]

Sergey Kozhevnikov, Fyodorov's boss and the head of the Smersh group in Finland that abducted Leino's prisoners, continued flying high until 1951, when the arrest of Viktor Abakumov sent his career into a tailspin. Kozhevnikov was dispatched back to Ukraine as MGB chief to Zaporizhzhya: a steep, sudden fall from grace. After Stalin's death he first waited for a new job and was then made to resign. Abakumov and his close subordinates were executed, found guilty of illegal interrogation methods and baseless executions, but Kozhevnikov was allowed to live out his retirement in Zaporizhzhya and died at the age of fifty-seven.[124]

Malenkov and Beria were no specialists on Finland, but they had a background role in the Communist offensive in 1948. Malenkov was part of the leadership troika that seized power in Stalin's wake. As Prime Minister, he seemed to be in the most dominant position, but in less than two years he was forced to resign, unable to keep up with Khrushchev's pace. He was sidelined after a failed coup attempt in 1957 and expelled from the party in 1961. His fate was to manage a hydroelectric plant in Kazakhstan. In his notes, Leino expressed satisfaction at this downfall.[125]

Beria did not lack the ability to lead, as demonstrated by the Soviet atom bomb project. He was, however, so feared that he was ousted from the troika by Stalin's followers less than four months after the leader's death. He was arrested in a Politburo meeting, accused of being a British spy and shot. This was the last time that the loser of a power struggle in Moscow was to face fabricated charges and death sentence. In addition, Lavrentiy Pavlovich had an extensive list of unsavory acts to his name, like suspected treason during the civil war in the Caucasus, as well as torture, executions and rapes.

In addition to Yrjö Leino's comeback, Beria had another plan for Finland. According to the head of his secretariat, Colonel Boris Lyudvigov, his former boss had proposed "defeatist ideas [*kapituly-antskie idei*]." On 23 June 1953, Beria said that the Karelian Isthmus should be returned to Finland, and then, warming to his theme, suggested giving the Kuril Islands back to Japan and even Königsberg (Kaliningrad) to the Germans. He reasoned that such handovers of territory would help improve Soviet relations with these states. Two other officials had heard their fallen leader say such things. The prosecutor was taken aback. Really, to give Soviet land to capitalist states? Beria denied these allegations.[126]

Beria's downfall came only three days after his comments about Karelia, so it remained unproved whether or not he would really have attempted to carry out the idea. It would not have been easy, but Finland was the easiest place to start. Saying it out loud, the best-informed Soviet leader showed he was aware that Finland's scars had not yet healed. Moreover, it serves to remind one that Soviet policy was not so strictly planned and immovable as it appeared. The surface calm belied the commotion below, where there was space for whims and improvisation.

What Was It?

Did Stalin see forcing Finland down the road to a people's democracy as a realistic option? The available sources do not provide a conclusive answer. Obviously, it was not a "categorical imperative" for him, but neither something to rule out completely. In short, it was dependent on how the situation developed. *If you're in the condition to do so, strike.*

The preparations for the Communist power grab in spring 1948 were serious enough. Had Paasikivi and Finland rejected the security treaty demanded by the Soviet Union, the plan could have been put into action. However, Stalin ultimately settled for a less substantial treaty than he had originally intended. In other circumstances he might have allowed the Finns even more room for maneuver, although there was little leeway left with the first two articles of the agreement. In Paasikivi's mind, two articles about military issues were the only ones that really mattered; the rest of the text could be as "thick" as necessary. Stalin surely felt the same way.

To get the Finnish Communists into power, the Soviet Union would have had to invest substantial resources over a long period of time. In any case, Stalin had to ponder carefully the possible acute consequences of his action in the broader international context. As for the geopolitical position, viewed from the West, Finland was practically an island, and seen from the East it only had Sweden lying the other side of it. Sweden's mere existence helped protect Finland. George Kennan saw that the captivating fate of Finland came down to two factors: Finland's capacity for resistance, and Sweden.[127]

Had Finland not agreed to the security treaty, from a purely military standpoint it is not a given that Moscow would have found it necessary to undertake immediate coercive measures. As long as the Soviet Union had the base at Porkkala, Finland and its heartland were inescapably in the grip of their eastern neighbor, regardless of what agreements were or were not struck. That said, a moderate Soviet response to an act of Finnish defiance would have required a particularly benign international situation.

Why was Finland such a hard nut for Stalin to crack? The answer lies in both the 1944 peace process and the Winter War.

In summer and early fall 1944, Finland escaped Soviet occupation as a result of its geopolitical position, its military endurance, and the swift developments in the world war on other fronts. On the Finnish side, the single most decisive actor in that moment was Mannerheim. Avoiding occupation meant that Finland enjoyed exceptional continuity: institutions, the state and its administration, the political system and the media all survived relatively unscathed. Of course, there were some changes, but these were not extensive enough to throw the country into disarray. For example, the rise of the brothers-in-arms Social Democratic trend and its dominance in the SDP would have been impossible under Soviet occupation.[128] The basic political situation would then have been utterly transformed. On the acute political scene of 1948, combat-effective Social Democracy and President J.K. Paasikivi were the most decisive forces.

In Finland a large majority of the population saw the state and the society as their own (or at least as preferable to the alternatives), and were motivated to defend them. In this way Finland was more reminiscent of Sweden than of those countries that were occupied or on the losing side in the war, and/or in the killing fields between Germany and the Soviet Union. As Mikko Majander succinctly put it, Finland did not become a people's democracy because it was a Nordic country.[129]

Equally important was the Finnish and Soviet experience of the Winter War. The Finns' resilience and defensive capabilities stayed with the Soviet leaders for the rest of their lives. As will be recalled, when an elderly Molotov was being pressed as to why the Soviet leadership did not "do it" to Finland after the war (that is, impose a people's democracy or simply annex the country), he asserted that it was correct not to do it. Coercion to bring such a stubborn nation under control would only have produced a perpetual wound in the Soviet body. It does not matter much whether Finland was any longer in the same shape as during the Winter War; it was enough that the Soviet leaders believed it might be.

Finland's leaders knew the weight of the Winter War, but did not mention it to the Soviets, at least not when sober. It was as taboo as Alsace-Lorraine should have been in France after 1871: never said, but constantly in mind. When a British representative in the control commission was about to return home, Paasikivi told him that the Soviet Union would never force a Communist government on Finland, as it would require thirty divisions to keep the country in check.[130]

The policy of appeasement adopted by Paasikivi and other politicians was necessary because of the outcome of the wars.[131] It was possible because the nation had come through the conflicts with relatively modest losses, which had left it with sufficient self-assurance to stand up to Soviet pressure. The Finnish leadership had the courage to appease. The impact of the wars was also felt in

Moscow, of course, and the Soviet leaders treated Finland with more respect than those countries that had been overwhelmed by the Red Army. Due to their worse locations or unrepresentative and authoritarian governments, these nations had been unable to defend themselves in the Second World War with the same success.

In mid-eighteenth-century Sweden two parties had opposed each other over the correct policy towards Russia. The bellicose "Hat" party of the nobility nursed revenge and a reconquest of areas lost to Peter the Great, whereas the "Cap" party (mainly of peasants and priests) supported appeasement. The official Finnish policy since 1944 was indisputably that of the Cap tradition, but in the situation of 1948 a successful approach required the Finnish leaders to wear both soft Caps and hard Hats, the latter ones a bit hidden. Their appeasement helped create a situation where Stalin was able to accept Finland's draft treaty, which met the Soviet Union's absolute minimum security needs. However, this approach needed to be counterbalanced by the capacity to resist, best carried out by the Social Democrats and potentially the army. For Moscow it was wise to content itself with what could be squeezed out of the Finns currently in power, for if no agreement was reached then less amenable forces could rise to take their place.

The eastern policy of first Sweden and then Finland has traditionally been characterized by the conflict between the Caps and the Hats, which has often led to domestic strife and dysfunction. When one side has been too dominant, it even contributed to catastrophes, such as Sweden's disastrous defeat to Russia in the War of the Hats, 1741–43. It was to Finland's advantage that the two competing approaches were fairly well balanced in 1948. In some cases, individuals or authorities could even play both roles, being one by day and the other by night.

The Winter War confirmed Stalin's distrust of the Finnish Communists. He certainly had not forgotten what had transpired with the Terijoki government. It is less certain that he saw particularly clearly that he himself had played a large part in the debacle, by ordering the murder of the main group of Finnish Red refugees. In his mind the blame lay, as ever, elsewhere. Although genuine support for Communism in Finland was much stronger than in Poland or Hungary, Stalin remained unconvinced: he did not want to put all his chips on red, as it were. His caution was not unfounded: the Great Hate,[132] as it was called, was fresh in the memory of the Finnish Communist leadership. Its members were alive and now leading the party, because they were safe in prison in Finland in 1937–38. Everybody had lost somebody in Stalin's Terror. It was the source of silent doubts in Communist minds and diluted their lust for power. They were afraid of their own victory.

In spring 1948 the SKP was a tool deployed by Stalin as and when required, and then cast aside. Should he have deemed it necessary, he could have ordered the Communists to go further, perhaps even as far as seizing control of the government. Had this been attempted, one can only imagine the scale of the destruction that would have ensued.

Stalin changed tack in his policy towards Finland in March 1948. The country was repositioned, not on the map like Poland had been, but geopolitically and symbolically: from the group where it was possible to strike to that where it was not, at least for the moment. This turned out to be a long-term decision, but there is good reason to suspect that Stalin originally intended it to be temporary. The policy shift was brought about by a rapidly changing international situation and the urgent political evaluation that it necessitated. A further change in international relations with reassessment of the Soviet Union's priorities could have suddenly made the establishment of a people's democracy in Finland pertinent again. Stalin was not afraid to make dramatic U-turns. He even flashed the chance to O.V. Kuusinen in 1951, when he prepared for a great war and was at the same time afraid of it.

In later decades, in particular during the 1970s, it was typical to stress the stability and permanence of the 1948 treaty. It is, however, doubtful that Stalin saw the treaty in this light, rather it was a temporary deal, the true value of which could be weighed up in a crisis situation. For him, the treaty underlined that Finland was in the Soviet Union's sphere of interest, nothing more. During Stalin's remaining time in power, the Soviets did not really suggest, let alone demand, joint military preparations under the pretext of the stipulations in the treaty. They did not even propose mutual visits of the military top brass, nor any coordination of the plans or drills of military staffs. Moscow first began to apply such pressure in 1954, when Deputy Premier Mikoyan visited Finland. For the next thirty years Finland had to put the brake on these suggestions. Under Stalin, the Soviet priority had been to use their intelligence networks to ensure that Finland was not, after all, undertaking military cooperation with any other country.

Time and again, researchers on the early period of the Cold War have ended up rejecting the idea that Stalin had a well-thought-out (and secret) plan for Europe, for the world, or even for certain countries that he methodically and precisely carried out. The Soviet Union constantly aimed to present its policy in this way, but no such grand plan existed. It operated within a broad ideological framework, of course, and its consistent objective was to secure and strengthen its own power, but in practice that meant, for the most part, taking tactical steps and reacting to foreign irritants by exerting force or influence. It functioned according to the situation at hand.

It was a close thing for Finland in spring 1948. It could have gone differently, and that was acutely felt at the time. On one occasion, in a small park in Töölö, just north of the center of Helsinki, two girls started swinging skillfully, talking to each other in Russian, in defiantly loud voices. They caught the attention of a young schoolgirl from an emigré family, used to speaking in whispered Russian in the city. When some boys arrived and started calling the swinging girls *ryssä*, they responded by singing a Russian song. The emigré girl recognized it and joined in. Then the bigger of the two girls addressed her: "If Stalin gets to know how they mock Russians, then he will send tanks to put things in order! All will be avenged! The *Chukhnas* [derogatory Russian term for Finns] will cry yet!" The emigré girl felt scared: for her, Stalin was bad, a foe.[133] This may not reveal precisely the official diplomatic or intelligence tasks of the swinging girls' fathers, but it does reflect the climate of the time, and even the tone at home when the adults were consuming vodka and *zakuski* late in the evening at the kitchen table.

IV
Pendulum Motions
1950–51

With the January 1950 presidential elections approaching in Finland, word circulated in Moscow's foreign-policy circles: it was time to get rid of J.K. Paasikivi. He had been the central actor in the determination of Finland's political orientation in spring 1948, as well as the decisive influence when the Communists ended up out of office and the Social Democratic minority government came to power, classed as their enemy by the Soviets, but the President had been unwavering in his support for it.

To Get Rid of Paasikivi

To justify the removal, a memo was composed about Paasikivi's reactionary activities. There was no shortage of examples to pick from, since he had committed sins as a reactionary politician for the past half-century. No mercy was given even to his policy of appeasement towards the Russian Empire; this was condemned as adulation of tsarism. Paasikivi's 1935 tax report showed his income as Chief Executive Officer of a big bank and the large amount of shares that he held there. A capitalist, that is. Then, his pro-German attitudes. In 1918, Paasikivi was Prime Minister of the White Government that came to power after defeating the Reds in the Finnish Civil War; as such, the memo argued, he was just as responsible as Svinhufvud and Mannerheim for punishing the workers. The Whites had won the civil war with the support of Germany, and Paasikivi had been eager to make Finland a German colony by installing a German king in Helsinki. Thus, he was known "as the rabid opponent of Soviet Russia and a bare-faced falsifier of the history of Finland's independence."

As for the years 1934–41, the memo listed Paasikivi's official positions without comment. This way it avoided saying anything positive, since in that period he had been instrumental in steering the Coalition Party away from far-right politics. With regards to the Winter War, the memo included only an excerpt from a speech Paasikivi gave in 1942, in which he criticized the Soviet Union for its Great Power machinations and harsh peace terms. It declared that Paasikivi had maintained his hostile anti-Soviet line during the Continuation War, with opinions not materially different from those of pro-war politicians. In March 1942, Paasikivi even gave a speech on an occasion "where Tanner also spoke."

The last period of the war was framed in a more favorable light. Paasikivi's attitude at that time was seen as more positive, but only because he wanted to withdraw Finland from the conflict. It again became negative immediately after his appointment as Prime Minister in November 1944. As a politician "untarnished" by government responsibility during the war, he came into power "to defend the interests of big capital and Finnish reactionaries." He "tried by all means to prevent" the war responsibility trial from progressing and openly opposed the mass movement in late spring 1946. Astonishingly, the memo even claimed that Paasikivi was the real inspiration behind the Karelians' hopes for border checks.

In his speeches Paasikivi assured his friendship with the Soviet Union, but in reality—as seen in the memo—he had directed Finland's foreign policy to the general framework of an Anglo-American, anti-Soviet line. This was seen in the preparations for the 1948 treaty, when Paasikivi raised hopes of Western aid and steered Finland back onto its old anti-Soviet course. On 26 February 1948 he slanderously characterized Stalin's letter as pressure. The next day, he provocatively claimed, to the parliamentary groups, that the Paris Peace Treaty (1947) already covered everything necessary. A new treaty would solely benefit the Soviet Union, because Finland had no enemies and it wanted to stay out of international conflicts. The President proceeded with the matter only when the government's Foreign Affairs Committee, led by Prime Minister Mauno Pekkala, supported the treaty on 1 March. However, by instructions to the delegation he aimed to make the agreement as convenient (*udobnyi*) to the Finnish bourgeoisie as possible. Even on 1 April, in the final stages of talks, he announced to the government that if there was no parliamentary majority in sight, then it would be wisest to break off the negotiations. Or, he suggested, they could go down an alternative route, and sign the treaty solely in the name of the President and the government. Once the agreement had been struck, Paasikivi was one source of the rumors that were swirling about the threat of a Communist coup. A fresh black spot was his support for the Social Democratic government, including pardons and even job appointments for those involved in the weapons cache case and "fascists." By pardons to wartime leaders convicted in the war responsibility trial, he had brought the Soviet Union's enemy-in-chief (*materyi vrag*)—Väinö Tanner—back into politics.

The memo referenced the occasion on 20 August 1948, straight after the government had been formed. Three MPs of the Finnish People's Democratic League (SKDL), Hertta Kuusinen at their head, went to complain about their treatment in the negotiations. Paasikivi responded that the new government was better qualified than its predecessor. As the argument grew more heated, he laid bare his anti-Soviet feelings—as it was seen in the memo—by letting an insult spew from his mouth: "We must always remember that in

1939 there was an aggressor, who has thus far not been punished."
Last but not least, a warning against going down the Czechoslovakian
route: "Well, if the Soviet Union wants to do it to us, it will first have
to kill half a million Finns, and myself."[1]

In Paasikivi's diary this discussion is civilized and prudent, no sign
of any fit of rage.[2] However, in this case the Russian document is
more believable. "And myself!" The President's message was intended
for Moscow, and it was duly delivered. Most of the Russian document, for instance the description of Paasikivi's role in the creation of
the 1948 treaty, picks, chooses and interprets details to serve its
purpose, and reflects how those events had to be portrayed at the
turn of 1949–50.

The indictments were harsh, but there was harsher stuff still. A shorter
report to Stalin about anti-Soviet policy of the SDP was similar in
tone; it was assessed that Communist and progressive propaganda is
"clearly insufficient and defeated by enemy propaganda." Additional
resources were badly needed.[3] This was followed by a ten-point
proposal about possible measures against Finland, sent on 21 November
1949 by Deputy Foreign Minister Andrei Gromyko to Stalin.
Diplomatic measures concentrated on articles in the 1947 peace treaty:
handing over Soviet citizens; building a new railroad in Lapland from
Kemijärvi to the border; transferring remaining German property to
the USSR. Secondly, there was pressure on the Finnish government
not to give any positions to "war guilty" politicians (now released from
prison) or leaders of former pro-German organizations abolished in
1944. This would be helped by spreading rumors that the Soviets
would demand handing over such persons for a trial in the USSR. On
the economic side, trade negotiations would be protracted and rumors
spread that a new agreement would not be signed as long as the present
Social Democratic government was in power in Helsinki. Propaganda
against Finland would be intensified and the Communist Party be
given 30 million FIM for presidential elections.[4]

The core operation was prepared by Komitet informatsii (KI), which was a rather short-lived attempt to combine main foreign intelligence channels (MGB, GRU, MID and others) under one roof. The arrest plan of spring 1948 was recycled. First, a reliable KI agent would mail fifty to sixty anti-Soviet leaflets to bourgeois politicians and three to five copies to known democratic influencers, who would certainly bring the mail to the Soviet Legation. Envoy Savonenkov would then go to President Paasikivi to complain about leaflets and to tell him that the Soviet government possessed information about an illegal "Resistance Organization," which performed espionage and hostile actions against the Soviet Union and prepared a coup d'état to form a pro-fascist government with the participation of Social Democratic politicians Väinö Tanner, Unto Varjonen and Väinö Leskinen, as well as General Lars Melander, the wartime chief of Finnish military intelligence. Government ministers Aleksi Aaltonen and Unto Varjonen had participated in preparations. As the leaflet proved, the resistance organization was moving to an active stage. Savonenkov should demand determined measures against this conspiracy. If this would not happen, the Soviet Union will act "according to its own discretion."

Even the planned anti-Soviet leaflet was already written, but not yet translated into Finnish. The text flows as follow:

Finns!

Russian Bolsheviks for decades have mocked our heroic nation and humiliated us. Here they are helped by the local Communists, those agents of Moscow.

We call all brave men and women to prepare for the decisive battle against the Bolsheviks, to get back our beloved Vyborg, Petsamo, Porkkala and the flowery Karelia.

The day is not far away when all patriots take up arms and put an end to the command of the *ryssä*.

In that battle we are not alone, we are supported and aided![5]

It defies belief that a plan of this sensitivity could have been written by lower-level chiefs on their own. There was at least a hunch of what the boss wanted, and probably even instructions. However, for the time being Stalin did not give his green light. In the plan, it was not specified what would be the next Soviet step in case Paasikivi would not act against the fabricated conspiracy of the extreme right wing and the SDP. The sole efficient next step would have been to use Soviet military force, and Stalin was not yet ready to take that risk. If the immediate goal was to intimidate Paasikivi to step down and force Finland to return to a government with Communist participation, as seems likely, this weapon was probably too strong for that purpose and even counterproductive. In addition, Stalin was absent from Moscow for almost three and half months until 10 December and then occupied by his bombastic 70th birthday celebrations. He was able to make decisions, but the occasions for consultations were limited.

In the proposal to Stalin it was planned to gather all Soviet complaints connected with the Paris Peace Treaty in one extensive

22. Children celebrating Stalin's seventieth birthday, December 1949.

198

note, which would then be delivered to President Paasikivi. This did not happen; the measures were realized as separate acts. The most important of these was the demand—presented by Gromyko on New Year's Eve—to hand over nearly three hundred Soviet citizens, "war criminals" allegedly hiding in Finland. Most of them had served in the Finnish military and intelligence during the war and were no longer available in Finland.

No advance in trade negotiations was visible in Moscow, where the Finnish minister of trade had already spent six weeks. The Soviets also protested against any official or public positions given to the "war guilty" politicians now pardoned and former members of abolished organizations, in particular the Brothers-in-Arms Association, where Social Democrats had held prominent positions. This potentially far-reaching ban was a new Soviet interpretation, not required in the peace treaty. Propaganda campaign against Finland in general and President Paasikivi in particular reached record heights.[6]

The main Soviet target was the presidential election. Stalin had already twice interfered in that process. First, when the SKP proposed to put up Hertta Kuusinen as their candidate because of her huge appeal among voters, in particular among women, Stalin responded that it was inappropriate to nominate a party member and wanted instead a non-Communist ally. Thus, he ruled out the first-ever female candidate for the President of the Republic in Finland and forced the Communists to turn to former Prime Minister Mauno Pekkala, whom the SKP leaders had already considered impossible because of his growing disloyalty.[7] Second, advice was asked by the SKP when Prime Minister K.-A. Fagerholm proposed to cancel the elections altogether and re-elect Paasikivi simply by passing a law to that effect in the parliament, as had been done four times during and after the war. The tyrant in Moscow took a stand for elections "according to the constitution."[8] In case occasion allows, it has not been rare even for sworn tyrants to give an appearance of honoring legal formalities and not breaking the protocol. However, Stalin's decision was not dictated by any democratic mindset, but by the fact that it was possible to get rid of Paasikivi only through elections, and that was now the goal.

The idea to remove Paasikivi was not new. Already in March 1947, after Zhdanov's farewell visit to Helsinki as the chairman of the Allied Control Commission, the Soviet envoy A.N. Abramov had pondered the chances of replacing the President. Zhdanov had probably at least signaled that this was now a proper topic. Since Paasikivi had been chosen in 1946 by the parliament rather than by electors, Abramov saw that one way to campaign against him could be to demand regular presidential elections. This should of course be done through Finnish organizations. Although the President may not perhaps be unseated, this "could scare [*napugat'*] him."[9] This project was shelved at that time, perhaps as too risky for the continuation of the big three government. When the idea was raised again in 1949–50, there was no longer a need to protect a government, but it was still useful to scare the President and others. .

Paasikivi of course understood that the Soviets wanted him to give up, and he came quite close to it, even writing a text to use in case the Soviets would officially declare that his selection would be an unfriendly act. However, each time he contemplated the issue, the conclusion was the same: "It is difficult for me to give up, because that would mean a dangerous precedent, we would give the Russians the power to determine who will become the President of Finland."[10] Had he seen the whole dark and disparaging portrait of himself now depicted in Moscow, for example how the pleasant envoy Abramov was calling him an enemy already in early 1947, he might have lost all hope and thrown in the towel. Or not, not even then.

In the Finnish presidential elections of that time, the voters first elected a 300-member electoral college. It was not compulsory even to announce in advance the party candidate for the high office; in 1949–50 the SDP did not appoint any candidate, because they supported Paasikivi but did not want to present such a capitalist to their worker voters. The 300 electors would then assemble to elect the president. In the first and second round you were free to vote for anybody you chose, and if somebody received the majority, 151 votes or more, he was elected. If not, then the decisive third vote was between number one and number two of the second round.

Six days before the electoral college meeting in Helsinki, the Soviet Foreign Minister Andrey Vyshinsky delivered a proposal to Stalin about different ways of putting pressure on Finland's governing circles. Freezing trade negotiations was again repeated, as also was the complaint about public positions held by those responsible for the war, war criminals, and former members of the disbanded right-wing organizations. In the event that Paasikivi did not win outright in the first round, Vyshinsky suggested that the Finnish Communist leadership consider instructing their electors to change tack in the second round. Instead of voting for Mauno Pekkala, the SKDL candidate, they should transfer their support to the Agrarian League's Urho Kekkonen.[11]

Kekkonen had emerged as the favorite non-Communist politician of the Soviets during the Social Democratic government, when the Agrarian League was in the opposition. In 1945–46 the Soviets were still rather critical of his way of conducting (as Minister of Justice) the war-guilty trial, and in 1946 Kekkonen's rise to the premiership was prevented by the lack of Soviet and Communist support. However, he had confidential contacts with Soviet political intelligence since 1944 and was even mentioned as a Komitet informatsii agent in Gromyko's November memo to Stalin. The later category "agent of influence" was not yet used. Since 1948, Kekkonen had been free to criticize the Social Democratic government and drop hints about the return of the big three.

The transfer of votes as suggested by Vyshinsky would have brought Kekkonen to the final third round. Three bourgeois parties supporting Paasikivi had 107 electors, but the second place was taken by the Communist-controlled alliance SKDL (67 electors), followed by Social Democrats (64) and the Agrarians (62). Strengthened by pro-Communist votes, Kekkonen would still have only 129 elector votes, not enough to win, but this was still a strong and unambiguous demonstration against Paasikivi, who might have considered it necessary to give up. However, this was repelled by the Social Democrats, who had voted for the President already in the first round. Paasikivi got 171 votes and was elected. The idea of transferring and dividing SKDL elector votes was then used in 1956, when Kekkonen was elected by the narrowest majority possible, 151 votes.

The Moscow campaign was not enough to force Paasikivi to step down, but it made him attempt to soothe the inflamed relations by changing the government, even including the Communists. The task of forming the government was given to Urho Kekkonen. Unlike him, Paasikivi did not have direct contact with the MGB officers in the Soviet Legation (he said he did not want to touch an ugly fish), but he was aware of the significance of this channel and used middlemen, primarily former second Foreign Minister, Reinhold Svento, who now traveled to Moscow to sound out the vistas.

When Svento told Foreign Minister Andrei Vyshinsky about the intentions of the President, the latter said that a new government was Finland's internal affair and belonged to the domestic affairs of Finland. This was less than a month after he had written a plan about how to influence the final election in Helsinki. An old Russia hand, Svento interrupted him and said that he knew very well the standpoint of the Soviet government of not meddling in the internal affairs of other states. So, he was not expecting any advice but only wanted to offer his own opinion. Vyshinsky then said that the Soviets hoped that Finland would stay on the road of peace, democratic forces would not be discriminated, and the government would oppose the warmongers. "Everything else is the Finns' own business."[12] Svento had a more substantial discussion with his case officer Elisei Sinitsyn, former *rezident* in Helsinki, and of course "in Beria's service," as the President needed to be reminded. When Svento had spoken out about Soviet campaign against the Finnish President, Sinitsyn blamed the local Communists and leftists for it. Truth was indeed a rare commodity in mutual relations. Perhaps it was more important to sense the atmosphere, since Paasikivi and Svento now agreed that without a general war "the Soviet Union will not engage in violent deeds" in Finland.[13]

Korea and Kekkonen

Urho Kekkonen set about his task even before the Social Democratic minority government had officially resigned at the start of the President's new term of office. His aim was a government of the big three: the Social Democrats, the Agrarian League and the SKDL. He wanted to ensure that the Communists would not be as powerful as they were between 1945 and 1948, but that they still had sufficient influence, so that relations with the Soviet Union would be improved.

The SKP's Ville Pessi and Hertta Kuusinen informed the Russian envoy Savonenkov about this project of the "young wing" of the Agrarian Party (Kekkonen was forty-nine). The People's Democrats were being offered three or four ministerial portfolios, one of which would be high-ranking (defense, trade and industry, or agriculture). The Communists presented the proposal cautiously, but they were inclined to accept it. In the event of Moscow's reluctance, the SKP announced that they would use their participation in government to strengthen support for mass movements.[14]

After Hertta Kuusinen met with Kekkonen on 5 March 1950, she again rushed to the Soviet Legation with an update. The forthcoming Prime Minister had informed her that Paasikivi was prepared to allow the SKDL to return to the government. This did not mean that the President was particularly supportive of the idea, for he had shown some resistance. Having made this clear, Kekkonen went on to enquire what the Communists were hoping for. In addition to matters of policy, Kuusinen mentioned that they wanted pardons for strikers convicted of insurrection after their bloody clash with the police in the northern town of Kemi in August 1949. Kekkonen agreed: the Social Democrat Ministers of Justice and the Interior should not have authorized such an aggressive response; their mistake should be corrected and "these working men ought to be pardoned." Then discussion turned to the portfolios: Kekkonen stated that the President had barred the SKDL from the positions of Prime Minister and Interior Minister, but all others were open to them, even that of second Foreign Minister. Kekkonen was ready to offer this, along with the Ministries of Social Affairs and Education. While the SKDL would get three ministers, the Social Democrats and the Agrarian League would get five apiece, the Swedish People's Party of Finland would get two, and Sakari Tuomioja, of the National Progressive Party, would be the Minister of Trade and Industry.

The Finnish Communists asked Moscow if it was appropriate for them to enter this government. For their part, these "friends" (the usual Soviet term for foreign Communists) were amenable to doing so if they could get four ministerial portfolios, membership of the government's Foreign Affairs Committee and certain policies in the government's program.[15]

Upon receipt of the message, Stalin underlined the number of seats and ministerial positions offered to the SKDL and made a snap decision: agreed (*soglasen*). This was transmitted to Helsinki on 8 March 1950 via a secret cable from "Filippov."[16] As Filippov, Stalin took care of all sorts of international matters, whether big or small: in one moment he was cautiously preparing for the Korean War with Mao Zedong; in the next he was permitting the Communist-led labor unions in Finland to participate in a Nordic meeting.[17] Filippov was also required to take the role of judge when the Finnish Communist leadership was arguing over whether to split from the Central Organization of Finnish Trade Unions (SAK), which was under the heavy-handed direction of the Social Democrats.[18]

In spite of the blessing from the Kremlin, a Finnish government made up of the big three did not come into being. The Social Democrats were reluctant to be in the same cabinet as the Communists, especially with Kekkonen at the helm. So, on 17 March, the President appointed Urho Kekkonen to lead an Agrarian minority government, which also contained a couple of independent politicians.

The first reaction of the Soviet press and the Finnish Communists to the new government was as negative as it had been towards its Social Democrat-led predecessor in 1948. Trade negotiations remained on ice, the SKP began to organize large-scale strike action and even took measures to prepare for war. The efforts by Kekkonen's government to mollify Moscow failed to have the desired effect.

Then, all of a sudden, everything changed. Envoy Cay Sundström was invited to meet Vyshinsky on 8 April 1950. In a meeting lasting just seven minutes, the Minister of Foreign Affairs declared that the Soviets were now prepared to receive Finland's trade delegation. Only five days earlier, Deputy Minister Gromyko had curtly dismissed the Finns' request. And when the new Foreign Minister, Åke Gartz, had made his first visit to the Soviet Legation and hoped for better relations, Savonenkov responded coolly that "it depends completely on him as Foreign Minister and on the Finnish government as a whole."[19]

The change of government in Finland was a necessary condition for this abrupt change of Soviet mind. But it was not sufficient. What more was needed was an international and strategic factor, this time the Korean War. During the same early April days Stalin finally relented to the repeated pleas of the North Korean leader, Kim Il Sung, and permitted him to attack the south.[20] As a new war was hovering into view at the far eastern extremity of the Soviet Union, it made sense for Moscow to repair relations at its opposite border, the north-west, where the situation had been tense for almost two years already. A precaution was reasonable, for a war—and a rather big war at that—always carries unintended consequences.[21]

Moscow was making preparations for a far sharper change of direction in its Finnish policy than the Finns realized. In happy ignorance the Finns began to negotiate the trade deal, not knowing that the fundamental position of their country in the Soviet Union's security politics was to be transformed. Moscow's aim was to extend trade relations with Finland, also in terms of temporal scope. Instead of a five-year arrangement the Soviet foreign trade officials were tasked with planning for up to ten years of orders from its neighbor, until 1960. Once Finland was finished with the reparations, Moscow wanted it to continue as a large trading partner. Ships remained the most important Finnish export, but there were also machines and apparatuses, prefabricated buildings, even cellulose. In addition, Moscow's intention was to recruit Finns to build three power stations along the Finno-Soviet border. To plan the trade, the Soviets prepared comparative statistics of the payment of war reparations from Finland, Romania, Italy and Hungary. Finland was the most punctual with its payments, while Italy had barely coughed up anything. Statistics on Finland's foreign trade led to the conclusion that the Soviet Union and the people's democracies ought to increase their share.[22]

Most ships were intended for military use, but they would be ordered without cannons, torpedoes, radio stations and other classified equipment. These would only be put in place in the Soviet Union once the Finns had delivered the orders.[23] In connection with the trade plans, the Soviet leaders ordered a review of the defense capability of Finland. This was signed by the head of the GRU military intelligence service, General Matvei Zakharov, with whom Finland was familiar due to his post as Chief of Staff of the Leningrad Military District before the war.

The memo began in much the same way as a war does: with mobilization. Finland's new plans in this regard had been under development for some time; progress had been in fits and starts, and they were still not ready. In an emergency the Finns would proceed from the same starting point as in the recent war, when they had 550,000 men at arms, of whom 90 percent were in the army. The Soviets clearly considered this to be a sizeable force. They estimated that Finland could muster fourteen infantry divisions, one armored division and seven infantry brigades. In terms of equipment, the army would need 250,000 rifles, 36,000 automatic weapons, 100 tanks and 550 airplanes.

The Finns' stockpile of weapons was significantly greater than that permitted by the Paris Peace Treaty. Their supply of rifles was 605,550, thirteen times the amount allowed (46,100), and they had 68,437 automatic weapons (only 11,000 allowed). Molotov underlined these illegitimately large figures. Furthermore, the Finns had a large supply of airplanes, including sixty-five bombers that had been banned outright by the peace treaty. Finland was allowed a total of sixty planes, and this amount happened to be in service, so formally the peace terms were not broken. However, the Soviet report noted an additional sixty-four flightworthy planes in storage, and another 250 that could be brought into flying condition. The review continued in a similar vein, going through every aspect of Finland's defense in detail: tanks, artillery with each type listed separately.

In conclusion, the capacity of Finland's arms industry was estimated. The eighty-seven companies active in wartime had mostly switched to civilian production, but it would only take three or four months for them to reassume their role as military industries. The biggest companies were listed by name, and their production capacity estimated: the Tampere airplane plant, for example, was able to make sixty-seven planes per year.[24]

In fall 1946, Sweden's Chief of Staff, General C.A. Ehrensvärd, had a pessimistic view of the impact of the peace treaty on Finland's military. The army would become a drill organization without its own supply of weapons or ammunition, unable to carry out its own mobilization. The Soviets would train the troops and arm them during wartime, if the Finns proved themselves dependable.[25] These fears had not come to pass: the Finns had kept their store of excess weapons; they had not given them up of their own initiative, nor had the Soviets put pressure on them to do so. When the new Finnish Foreign Minister asked about them in May 1950, the Soviet envoy still avoided the topic, apparently under instructions.[26]

The GRU chief and his superiors in the General Staff did not make any recommendations, but they certainly had an idea of what was expected from them. Their tone was to the point and blame-free: Finland was not presented as an aide to imperialists making preparations for war, nor as a weapon hoarder flagrantly in breach of the peace treaty. The material presented could easily have been deployed for such propaganda purposes, if the decision makers had seen fit to go down that route. It actually made reference to earlier official letters by Soviet military authorities that had been produced with that sort of motive in mind; in the end, however, these were left unsent.

The restraint is replicated in the draft negotiating mandate that Molotov and Mikoyan sent to Stalin for his approval. In addition to trade, it touched on political and military issues. Concerning the excess weapons, it was suggested that Finland be allowed to keep them, but not to hand them over to any other nations. New weapons would have to be procured from the Soviet Union, or at least in accordance with the spirit of the 1948 Treaty, which presumably meant the Finns would have to make purchases from a Moscow-approved source, such as Czechoslovakia.[27]

The conclusion is obvious: Stalin was preparing for a time when the Korean War would develop into a wider conflict, even in Europe. In such a scenario, the Soviets now believed that they could get Finland on their side. The country's military capacity was not, therefore, inspected as if it were an enemy, but rather viewed as a resource. The Soviets would not have got Finland to join in an attack, nor would they have required that; they simply wanted the country to defend its own territory against the West.

Considering the harsh assessments of Paasikivi only five months earlier, it seems incredible that the Soviets were now envisaging his country as an ally. Even if they did so with some reluctance, this was quite a volte face—but not uncommon in Stalin's foreign policy. On the eve of the Korean War, Moscow saw Finland's national security orientation in an auspicious light: for a short time, Finland was a potential ally and a country of economic opportunities. The trade agreement was signed on 13 June 1950 for five years, not for ten, and it was not as broad as the Soviets outlined when serious negotiations began.

Before the signature, Stalin received Kekkonen, and the next evening he hosted a dinner for the whole Finnish trade delegation. The military materials prepared for him and quoted above help to understand what was behind his words. "How can you defend your country, if you don't have a steel industry, if war breaks out and the borders close?" he asked, then announcing that in this respect he was a nationalist. Stalin clarified to Kekkonen—but not to the other Finns—that he was talking about Finland's dependence on Swedish iron production, which provided the steel plates needed for Finnish-built ships. What if the borders were shut and the supply of iron and steel should run dry? "Foreign steel is blunt steel," Stalin declared, and suggested a joint steel company: the Soviets would provide orders and expertise, but would not impose themselves as stake-holders, "as you Finns are scared of us Russians." The new company could target China's limitless markets, alongside others. It was no coincidence that China was mentioned: over the course of the dinner, its development was a frequent topic of discussion.[28]

Stalin did not broach the matter of Finland's excess weaponry nor another peace treaty paragraph still to be implemented: the repair of the Salla track. This was the railway line cutting across from Finland's west coast to its border with the Soviet Union; the Treaty of Moscow had required its construction after the Winter War, but sections of it had been destroyed by the Germans withdrawing from Lapland in 1944. The Soviet Foreign Ministry had included both themes in a briefing for the meeting. Most likely, the plan was to let the Finns keep their weapons but not to broadcast this out loud. That way, the issue could be used for pressure in the future; if need be, the Finns could even be accused of breaking the peace treaty.

Once again, Stalin remembered the military man who was seminal at the beginning of this road in 1944, raising a toast to the envoy in Helsinki, G.M. Savonenkov: "To You, friend of Mannerheim!"[29] At the heavy-drinking dinner were the eight-man inner circle of the Politburo, among them Khrushchev, recently returned to Moscow and now forming his first impressions of the Finnish leadership. No Finn, however, seems to have paid him much attention. In addition to high-ranking officials from ministries of foreign affairs and foreign trade, most conspicuous was the presence of the military: Deputy Prime Minister, Marshal Bulganin, responsible for the arms industry; the Defense Minister, Marshal A.M. Vasilevsky; and the Naval Minister, Admiral I.S. Yumashev.[30] This time, the presence of the military was not seen as a threat by the Finns, about whom Stalin said, "It is no business of the Soviet Union, what kind of political system there is in Finland."[31]

With the presence of the military leadership, and through the conversation topics and other hints, Stalin was showing the Finns the strategic significance of the trade deal. Nevertheless, military matters were not discussed directly and there was no attempt to strike an agreement about them. While the danger posed by the present global circumstances was often mentioned, barely a word was uttered about Korea. However, both Kekkonen and the SKP's Ville Pessi seem to have been informed by the Soviets about overarching risks of the situation, without mentioning any location. The Finns returned home only ten days before the Korean War would break out.

The notion of making Finland an ally was left untested, because the Korean War did not spread to Europe. In other respects, too, the

23. The Finnish delegation, in the Soviet Union to hold trade talks, leaves Moscow, June 1950. In the front row, from left to right, are Minister Sakari Tuomioja, Prime Minister Urho Kekkonen, interpreter Rudolf Sykiäinen, Minister of Foreign Trade Anastas Mikoyan and Deputy Foreign Minister Andrei Gromyko.

conflict went differently from how the aggressors had calculated, certainly not for the first nor the last time in military history. The big trade agreement with Finland was but one offshoot of the strategic deliberations and war preparations for the Soviet Union, whereas it was the most significant outcome for its Nordic neighbor. Slowly but surely, over time, trade came to play an increasingly influential role in neighborly relations.

Third World War?

In contrast to what Stalin had hoped and expected, the United States responded assertively to the challenge in Korea. Preparations for an intervention began immediately, and it was carried out under the flag of the United Nations. This was possible because the Soviet Union was boycotting the Security Council meetings to protest the fact that China was still represented in the UN by the government-in-exile in Taiwan rather than by the newly formed people's republic.

The leader of Czechoslovakia, Klement Gottwald, ventured to speculate that the boycott was perhaps a tactical misstep. "Filippov" responded with a cable from Sochi, and gave a vigorous defense of Soviet actions. As might be expected, Stalin denied that any mistakes had been made; quite the contrary, the events had revealed to every honest person that the United States was the aggressor. The main thing, Stalin asserted, was that American attention had been redirected from Europe to the Far East. "Is this a plus for us in respect of the global balance of power? Without a doubt it is." It can be assumed, he continued, that the United States will end up embroiled in a war with China. (For Stalin this was closer to a certainty than an assumption.) "America, just as any other state, will not cope [*spravit'sya*] with China," since the latter's armed forces were in fighting shape and extremely large. Tied up in the East, "America will not, in the near future, have the capacity for a third world war." With such a conflict postponed, the Soviets had time "to strengthen socialism in Europe," and, moreover, improve the prospects of revolution in the Far East. "Is this a plus for us in respect of the global balance of power?" Stalin repeated. "Without a doubt it is."[32] In early October 1950, when it was necessary to nudge China into the Korean War, Stalin sent a cable to Mao Zedong, enquiring, rhetorically, whether a third world war ought to be feared. "In my opinion," he stated, "it needn't be, because we are, together, more powerful than the USA and England. [...] If war is inevitable, then let it come now, not in a few years' time," when the West would have grown stronger and Japan would be back on its feet.[33]

In January 1951 the party leaders and defense ministers of Eastern Europe's people's democracies were invited to Moscow for a four-day conference held entirely in secret. Archive materials and memoirs about the discussions have been published in the Czech Republic, Hungary, Poland and Romania, and even Albania, whose delegates visited Moscow separately. The Soviet Union was represented by Stalin, Molotov, Malenkov and Beria, as well as by the Defense Minister, Marshal A.M. Vasilevsky, and Chief of Staff Sergei Shtemenko.[34]

Addressing the Korean War, Stalin declared that the United States was not ready to start a third world war, nor was it even capable of fighting a small one. America would be kept busy in Asia for two or three years, which, as Stalin saw it, created exceptionally auspicious circumstances for Europe. Seeking to exploit this opportunity, Stalin considered it was abnormal that the people's democracies had armies both too small and in bad condition, so he and Shtemenko outlined a dramatic two-year armament program. When the allies from the people's democracies started to squirm uncomfortably and to ask for more time, predominantly for economic reasons, Stalin demanded a cast-iron guarantee from Polish and Bulgarian representatives that war would not break out within the next two years. They admitted that they were unable to give this, and, with that, the matter was settled.

So, Stalin saw a large-scale military clash in Europe as a distinct possibility in the near future. The conference launched a flurry of rearmaments. After the war, the number of Soviet troops had dropped to below 3 million, but, by the time of Stalin's death in March 1953, it had already doubled in size, to 5.6 million. Furthermore, the Soviets developed the capability of mobilizing 10 million people in just thirty days. To bolster their camp's offensive strength, Stalin required each ally to provide one full bomber division, and delivered nippy Tupolev Tu-2 planes for the purpose. Even just before Stalin's death, the Soviet government decided that the number of such divisions would increase from thirty-two to 106 within two years. To meet this target they would have to build 10,300 new bombers.

Finland's position in this pattern was in stark contrast to how Moscow had viewed it on the eve of the Korean War. A number of memos sent from the Soviet Mission in Helsinki confirmed that Finland's reactionary circles were calculating that war was on the horizon in spring 1951. They also located the country, more or less explicitly, in the enemy camp. It is hardly likely that the diplomats serving in Helsinki had a precise understanding of Stalin's scheme for Eastern European leaders, but they could see which way the wind was blowing, and knew the sort of reports that were expected.

In the Finnish security atmosphere of the time there was some basis for Soviet suspicions. After lively discussion about regional defense, in September 1951 the Finnish General Staff was ordered to prepare a new operative plan, which was then approved by the Commander on 19 June 1952 and given the title "Operative Order no. 8: Fuel procurement." The idea of this extensive plan (over 100 pages) was regional defense against a surprise attack, based on four areas able to act independently even after the highest command had been disabled. This was a defense plan against possible Soviet attack, an extremely sensitive issue, since officially the Soviet Union should have been exclusively an ally. It is unlikely that Soviet intelligence got its hands on the plan itself, but they surely detected the scents in the atmosphere, as it was necessary to inform civilians about some measures connected with the plan, for example the idea of transferring weapons to regional arms depots instead of central depots. The existence of a "fuel procurement" plan was made public only in 2018.[35]

There was also a political reason for Moscow's changed attitude to Finland. In January 1951, Kekkonen formed a new government together with the Social Democrats. Although he did it because of domestic political issues, "the Tannerites' return to power" (as a Soviet memo put it) set alarm bells ringing in Moscow. This supposedly fulfilled the primary aim of the Anglo-Americans: unseating the Agrarian League government. According to the Soviets, "even" Kekkonen had classified the Social Democrats as "the American party," but this did not prevent him from entering a coalition with them. The Americans' next goal, the memo claimed, was to ensure that their pro-Western "agent parties" win the parliamentary and central labor union elections for which they were investing substantial financial resources. They had enough money also for the Agrarian League. In the United States, W. Averell Harriman—the former American ambassador to the Soviet Union—had promised Finland's Social Democratic trade-union leaders all (*vsemirnuyu*) the help they needed.[36]

Stalin took on the Americans' challenge. From February 1951 he summoned western Communist leaders to Moscow, starting with Italy's Palmiro Togliatti, whom Stalin wanted to leave Italy to lead Comintern's successor, Cominform.[37] Then came the turn of Ville Pessi, who appeared before Stalin for the first time as the party leader. Such a meeting had been requested by the Finns for years. On the night of 25 April 1951, in the presence of the inner circle of the Politburo and the new envoy to Helsinki, V.Z. Lebedev, the main theme was the general elections in Finland.

The Soviet leader's primary demand was to take a shrewder fight to the Social Democrats. In the draft instructions for the SKP that formed the basis of the conversation, it was unambiguously stated that the main enemies were the Social Democrats, who "want war and strive to unleash it [*razvyazat'*]." Stalin approved the slogan, "*Every vote for right-wing Social Democrats is a vote for war*," but was dissatisfied when he saw that Tanner was the only person labelled a Nazi ally and an American agent in Pessi's papers. He insisted on more names (*kto imenno?*).

Secondly, Stalin required, as before, that the Communists make a clearer distinction between their approach to the Social Democrats and the Agrarian League. This was tricky, since the Social Democrats' policies and economic demands were closer to those of the Communists, but the interests of Soviet foreign policy made it necessary to support the Agrarian Kekkonen. The instructions considered the policy of peace as decisive, for this was something that Kekkonen had continued to follow "loyally." It was "an obvious mistake" to refuse to support him simply because of the government's reactionary economic line.

Thirdly, Stalin demanded that the Communists make the peace policy the most important issue in the elections. He hardly informed Pessi about the January conference, but he undoubtedly stressed that world peace was in great and immediate danger.[38]

Stalin's amendments to the SKP's election manifesto would not, at least, be held back by a lack of money. The SKP received a grand total of $874,000 from the relief fund administered by the Communist Party of the Soviet Union, that is, approximately 40 percent of all financial aid distributed to Communist parties and organizations all over the world that year. This was a $500,000 increase on the previous year, since the Finnish comrades were given two years' support, paid in full in advance.[39]

Next evening Pessi was again escorted to Stalin's office, where he found Molotov and O.V. Kuusinen waiting. This was the latter's first time there in eleven years, having been dispatched to Petrozavodsk in ignominy after the Winter War. Now Stalin had just decided that Kuusinen would not be allowed to travel to his former home-land in fall 1951, even though the SKP had invited him over to celebrate his seventieth birthday. Kuusinen might have been the party's founder, but Stalin had not forgotten the failure of the Terijoki government. The Soviet leader casually inquired, as if he did not know, "What are you, Otto Vilgelmovich, up to nowadays?" Having heard Kuusinen's answer—still the leader of the Karelo-Finnish Soviet Socialist Republic—Stalin announced that the Karelians would surely get by without him, and suggested that Kuusinen ought to aim to become Finland's President. This information comes from the recollection of interpreter Rudolf Sykiäinen.[40]

Kuusinen was not required for Finland's forthcoming elections. Stalin had already given Pessi a clear brief, and the SKP leader could be trusted to accurately convey Moscow's message to his party. Taking into account Stalin's pronouncements about bolstering socialism in

Europe (in his cable to Gottwald and in the conference with the Eastern Europeans), it is possible to discern his plans for Kuusinen, even without Sykiäinen's wry anecdote. Kuusinen was probably brought back into the fold in case imposing socialism upon Finland again became a viable option. Stalin did not necessarily put it so bluntly to Kuusinen, and especially not to Pessi, but, at the very least, he wanted to ascertain with his own eyes if these were the men for the job. V.Z. Lebedev's appointment as Soviet envoy to Helsinki was connected to this potential scenario, for he replaced the incompetent and bumbling Savonenkov. Lebedev had served for six years in an identical posting in Poland, and socialism, of the sort condoned by Moscow, had been foisted upon the country during his tenure.[41] Furthermore, he had begun his international career as a military intelligence officer, so he had a good understanding of the secretive side of diplomacy.[42]

In light of Stalin's scheming, a misunderstanding by Molotov at the very start of 1951 is worthy of note. While reading the SKP manifesto submitted by Pessi and Hertta Kuusinen, his eye caught the phrase "people's democratic politics." Molotov did not recall that in Finland this was often a reference to the SKDL, the name coined for this alliance party in 1944 before there was any talk of people's democracies. Interpreting the phrase instead as alluding to Finland being or becoming a people's democracy, he circled "people's," wrote in the margin his comment "too early! [*rano!*]," and ordered "people's democratic" to be struck out.[43] If implementing people's democracy in Finland had really been the order of the day, it would not have been mentioned only in passing in a manifesto.

Less than a year had passed since the extensive trade agreement between the countries, yet Moscow's position on Finland had swung from one extreme to the other. It now eyed its Nordic neighbour as a potential enemy rather than as a potential ally, and as a target for coercive measures rather than as a cooperative partner. Back then, Urho Kaleva Kekkonen had been invited into Stalin's office, now it was Otto Ville Kuusinen. These new arrangements had their roots in the top-secret January conference, and the possible military conflict in Europe. The Soviet camp would have to go on the offensive, although any attack launched would naturally be presented as pre-emptive and in self-defense. In practice, it would have been impossible to get the government of Finland to participate in such military action, hence Stalin was weighing up alternative options.

This scenario was never realized. Was it the balance of terror that prevented it, or something else? It is enough to note here that Europe did not descend into war once again, and so the Soviets' preliminary arrangements for Finland were never tested.

Finland's Third Way

During Stalin's final years, Moscow thus viewed Finland as a potential ally at times, and as a potential enemy and a target of subjugation at others. Even a third scenario emerged in connection to Stalin's last great foreign-policy initiative: the so-called March Note.

On 10 March 1952 the Soviet Union suggested to the three Western occupying powers that Germany be unified. Along with this, it proposed a peace agreement, in which the country would be declared neutral. One of the most analyzed and contested topics of historical research on post-war Germany has been whether Stalin's initiative was sincere, or rather a deceptive piece of propaganda. The debate has centered on the motives behind the proposal, and what precisely it aimed to achieve. A merciless battle of chasing references has been waged between scholars on the subject.[44]

The project gradually took shape over 1951. It included a new Soviet attitude towards Nordic identity and neutrality, which it had until then looked upon with disdain. In fall 1951, Soviet officials in the Scandinavian capitals began to sound out the possibility of detaching Norway and Denmark from NATO under the banner of neutrality. In Helsinki the intelligence officer V.V. Zhenikhov mentioned in passing the idea of a Swedish–Finnish "defence and neutrality alliance," one that Norway and Denmark could join at a later date. Prime Minister Kekkonen started to prepare a big foreign-policy speech in support of Nordic neutrality.[45]

In early January 1952, Kekkonen told the envoy Lebedev of his intention to give a speech on uniting the Nordic countries "around the idea of neutrality, as it is understood in Finland." Moscow approved his initiative, even the notion of neutrality, and ordered Lebedev to inform Kekkonen of this as the envoy's own personal opinion.[46] This gave rise to the "Pajama-pocket speech," so-called because Kekkonen was in hospital and unable to deliver it as planned. It was published on 23 January.

On the Soviet Union's part, the purpose was to procure additional support for the March Note. In this connection, the Soviets were even ready to invite Paasikivi to Moscow, provided that the initiative came from the Finnish side.[47] That moment soon passed, as did the Soviet interest in Nordic neutrality. In Stalin's final year, Moscow readopted a policy of heightened mistrust towards Finland. Deputy Minister of Foreign Affairs Zorin even warned Lebedev not to be too gullible in his dealings with Kekkonen.[48]

The neutrality ideas connected with the Stalin note were significant, both in principle and with regards to future developments. Earlier scenarios—Finland as an ally or as an enemy—came from the standpoint of Soviet national security, but on this occasion the Soviets took Finland more clearly on the country's own terms and tried to make use of them. The Soviets attempted to get Finland to start initiatives that could benefit their own foreign policy and be exploited in their propaganda. For Kekkonen's part, he tried to adapt his schemes to the Soviet Union's explicit or presumed wishes in order to strengthen Finland's position in the process.

After Stalin's death, this became a central theme in Finnish–Soviet relations. One feature of it was its strong connection to Kekkonen himself. Although Paasikivi's fundamental policy towards the Soviet Union stemmed from broadly the same premise as that of

Kekkonen, this was a clear difference. The old President was not at all inclined to take initiatives beyond that which was strictly necessary for survival. Kekkonen, on the other hand, was, and for a long time he was the only one who had the space and the ability to play in this kind of system.

The Soviet Union's fundamental aims in Finland remained essentially constant for the entirety of the end period of Stalin's rule (1939–53). The first was to ensure that its neighbor was secured and remained under Moscow's political sphere of influence, with the help of a so-called friendly government that would do its bidding. And the second was to limit Western (and until 1944 also German) influence in the country and make certain that foreign powers hostile to the Soviet Union could not make it a part of their military or geopolitical projects. Unlike three earlier stages, the last period, shortly described in this part, was by nature potential rather than feasible, "cold" rather than "hot."

Why, then, did Moscow's line towards Finland oscillate so wildly?

There are at least two reasons. From the Winter War onwards, Finland was a special case, one that did not fit neatly into a generic foreign-policy framework. In that sense, it was more reminiscent of that much larger and much more troublesome neighbor, Mao's China, which no state could handle, to borrow Stalin's utterance. China was a case of its own if ever there was one, and so was Finland, albeit on a much smaller scale. Moscow tried different approaches to Finland in different situations, but it was many years before the Soviet leadership came to anything like a comprehensive understanding of what worked and what did not. Even then, there remained gaps in their knowledge.

The second factor was the Soviet state's underlying ideological character. The expectation was that the type of socialism propagated by the Soviet Union would, in the end, come to win out across the whole world. The very fact that Finland continued to exist was a regrettable marginal note that tarnished this theory, especially when it was a country right next door, where the Soviet Union's influence and example ought, without doubt, to have had an effect if it were anything like as compelling as Moscow claimed. Moreover, the voluntary support of Communism was much stronger in Finland than anywhere in Eastern Europe, post-war Czechoslovakia and Yugoslavia excepted. In spite of everything, the prospect of Finland embracing socialism remained shrouded in doubt. In Moscow, this periodically gave rise to the feeling that something ought to be done. Even Stalin was occasionally susceptible to this impulse, although he had long been accustomed to assuming the role of cynical realist in matters of power politics.

It might be futile to try and find a rational explanation for every-thing. An in-depth analysis of a historical event may well indicate that "contingency, irony and straight Machiavellian fortune often have a major role to play."[49] The last fifteen years of Stalin's reign were a time of extremes in the relationship between Finland and the Soviet Union. The experiences from this period are not, in and of themselves, applicable to other eras and conditions. Nonetheless, they left deep imprints, ones that are still visible, even today.

To an extent, the preservation of states is undoubtedly something unattainable by reason, but in Finland's case the weightiest factors seem to have been the nature of Finnish society, the war experience both in Finland and in the Soviet Union, and the fast-changing international situation, where the most important stable element, in relative terms, was Sweden.

President J.K. Paasikivi believed that the survival of a small state required much stronger political skill than leading a great power. Frightened by the outbreak of the Korean War, he pondered if this was the beginning of a new era, the era of Communism. He raged against the Western leaders: "What kind of people they have had by way of world politics. [...] Baldwin, Chamberlain, Roosevelt, Attlee, Bevin—ignorant, naïve, easily cheated. Do they know history? No. Do they know geography? No. Do they know foreign languages? No.

Пролетарии всех стран, соединяйтесь!

ПРОПУСК № 492

Тов. *Кекконен*

для ПРОХОДА на КРАСНУЮ ПЛОЩАДЬ
НА ПОХОРОНЫ
Председателя Совета Министров СССР и
Секретаря Центрального Комитета КПСС
Генералиссимуса
**Иосифа Виссарионовича
СТАЛИНА**
ПРОХОД ВСЮДУ

*24. Prime Minister Kekkonen's pass allowing him to participate in
Stalin's funeral.*

They have had one capable man, Winston Churchill, but they got rid
of him immediately after the worst danger was over. Then they gave
everyone to understand that South Korea had great weight for them,
but forgot to give weapons to those unhappy numskulls [*pässinpäät*].
If our fates of small nations would be directed by such amateurs, we
would have perished long ago."[50]

This much-needed political *savoir faire* boils down to boldness
and the ability to deal with multifaceted unclear situations, to play on
through uncertainty. No harm was done by timing and a dose of
fool's luck. In 1940 and 1944, and again in 1948, Finland ended up
being the country of unfulfilled catastrophes, as it was later described
by a perceptive Swedish diplomat.[51]

Notes

Introduction

1. S. Kotkin, *Stalin*, vol. 1: *Paradoxes of Power, 1878–1928* (2014), 138.
2. At that time, the Finnish labor movement was not yet divided, so everybody on the Red side was more or less social democrat. The division into social democrats and communists came only after the Civil War.
3. Memo by Kekkonen about the talks in Moscow, no title, not dated (late June 1950), Urho Kekkonen archives 21/30 (quotes); Memo by A. Gromyko and R. Sykiäinen (interpreter) on Stalin's talk with Kekkonen on 13 June 1950, RGASPI, f. 558, op. 11, d. 389, ll. 120–25.
4. Ville Pessi (FCP secretary general) to dear comrade Stalin, 26 Apr 1951, RGASPI, f. 558, op. 11, d. 389, ll. 141–43. Margin notes in the Russian translation. Stalin was not famous for any successes in competitive elections, but the huge amount of US dollars sent by him certainly helped campaigning.
5. A. Rieber, *Stalin and the Struggle for Supremacy in Eurasia* (2015), 32.
6. Politburo decisions in 1928–34 on western neighbors in O. Ken and A. Rupasov, *Zapadnoe prigranits'e* (2014).
7. Vladimir Genis, *Nevernye slugi rezhima: Pervye sovetskie nevozvrashchentsy (1920–1933)*, kn. 2 (2012), 320–82; K. Rentola, *Neuvostodiplomaatin loikkaus Helsingissä 1930* (2007).
8. The original Great Hate (*isoviha* in Finnish) was experienced during the Great Northern War in the beginning of the eighteenth century, when Russian troops under Tsar Peter I occupied Finland, then belonging to Sweden.
9. Report by M. Frinovski (border troops commander) on the work of a commission on the northwestern border, Feb 1935, V.N. Khaustov and L. Samuelson, *Stalin, NKVD i repressii 1936–1938 gg.* (2009), 50–51. The area was sparsely populated, so there were probably not many more families to take.

10. A collection published in Finnish as *Varjo Suomen yllä: Stalinin salaiset kansiot*, ed. by Timo Vihavainen, Ohto Manninen, Kimmo Rentola and Sergei Zhuravlyov (2017). A Russian edition does not seem to have appeared.

I The Winter War (1939–40)

An earlier version of this part is in Kimmo Rentola, "Intelligence and Stalin's Two Crucial Decisions in the Winter War, 1939–40," *International History Review* 35:5 (2013), 1089–1112. Other versions are in Finnish, Norwegian and French.

1. C. Van Dyke, *The Soviet Invasion of Finland 1939–40* (1997), 66.
2. Copy of General Staff Order (Voroshilov, Shaposhnikov) to Leningrad Military District, no. 256, 2 Dec 1939, in Washington DC Library of Congress (LOC), D.A. Volkogonov Papers, Box 1.
3. For good overviews on this war in English, see: D. Kirby, *A Concise History of Finland* (2006), 197–216; and O. Vehviläinen, *Finland in the Second World War: Between Germany and Russia* (2002), 30–73. Deeper scholarly analysis now in Stephen Kotkin, *Stalin: Waiting for Hitler 1929–1941* (2017), 702–61.
4. Reports of the NKVD's military secret police (OO), quoted in several reports from Beria to Stalin and others, 12–15 Dec 1939, Central Archives of the Russian Federal Security Service (TsA FSB), f. 3, op. 6, d. 35, published in A.N. Sakharov, V.S. Khristoforov and T. Vihavainen (eds.), *Zimnyaya voina 1939–1940 gg.: Issledovaniya, dokumenty, kommentarii* (hereafter *ZV*) (2009), doc. nos. 85, 82, 94, 97, 88, 91 and 100. The Finnish version is: T. Vihavainen and A.N. Sakharov (eds.), *Tuntematon talvisota: Neuvostoliiton salaisen poliisin kansiot* (hereafter *Tuntematon*) (2009), doc. nos. 129 and 162.
5. Beria to Stalin, no. 5547/B, 16 Dec 1939, attached with NKVD Order no. 1478, 15 Dec 1939, 'O sformirovanii semi polkov voisk NKVD SSSR', *ZV*, doc. no. 98.
6. Finnish General Staff Office of Statistics, Memo on the combat ability of the Red Army, 28 Oct 1939, National Archives of Finland, War Archives, General Headquarters 1587/23. On Finnish military intelligence in 1939–44 there is now a comprehensive dissertation by Toni Mononen, *Saadun tiedon muokkaajat* (2023).
7. A.I. Kolpakidi (ed.), *Entsiklopediya sekretnyh sluzhb Rossii* (2004), 711–12; and E. Sinitsyn, *Rezident svidelstvuyet* (1996). Sinitsyn's posthumously published memoirs are, unfortunately, rather confused.
8. Copy of Leningrad Military District (LVO) cipher telegram report to the General Staff, no. 39419/39418/sh, 29 Nov 1939, LOC, Volkogonov, Box 1.
9. Copy of order by Voroshilov, Stalin (member of the War Soviet) and Shaposhnikov to the commanders of the 7th, 8th, 9th, 23rd and 14th Armies, 29 Dec 1939, LOC, Volkogonov, Box 1. According to the Gori Parish Registers, Stalin was born on 6 (18) December 1878, meaning that he was over a year older than his official birthdate. It is not known why this incorrect birthday was taken into official use.
10. Osmo Jussila, *Terijoen hallitus* (1985).
11. Kimmo Rentola, "The Finnish Communists and the Winter War," *Journal of Contemporary History* xxxiii (1998), 591–607 (and dissertation in Finnish in 1994).

12. V.A. Nevezhin, *Sindrom nastupatel'noi voiny* (1997), 133, quoting Mekhlis's report to Zhdanov on the work of the Red Army's Political Directorate, 23 May 1940.

13. On the Leningrad NKVD: S.K. Bernev and A.I. Rupasov (eds.), *Zimnyaya voina 1939–1940 gg. v dokumentakh NKVD* (2010). Despite the titular similarity, this is a different collection to *ZV* (2009). On the GRU military intelligence: V.A. Gavrilov (ed.), *Voennaja razvedka informiruyet: Dokumenty Razvedupravleniya Krasnoi Armii. Janvar'1939– ijun' 1941* (2008), 173–248 (the section on the Winter War).

14. See, for example: Z. Steiner, *The Triumph of the Dark: European International History 1933–1939* (2011), 867–922; and G. Roberts, *Stalin's Wars: From World War to Cold War, 1939–1953* (2006), 30–60.

15. See e.g. Richard Overy, *Blood and Ruins: The Great Imperial War, 1931–1945* (2021), 81–86.

16. Leningrad-area state security (UGB LO) memo, 'Germanskaya rabota v Finlyandii', 13 July 1939, in Bernev and Rupasov (eds.) *Zimnyaya voina 1939–1940 gg.*, 85–112; Beria to Stalin, Molotov and Voroshilov, no. 2995/B, mid-July 1939 (based on Japanese military-intelligence cables from Helsinki), in *ZV*, doc. no. 4.

17. Draft resolution by the Politburo outlining which experts should travel to Germany, 17 Oct 1939; memcons of A.M. Mikoian's talks with Ritter and Schnurre, 20–31 Oct 1939, in *Moskva-Berlin: Politika i diplomatiya Kremlya 1920–1941*, 3: 1933–1941 (2011), doc. nos. 231, 234–5, 239–40 and 243.

18. Beria to Stalin, Molotov and Voroshilov, no. 4600/B, 13 Oct 1939, in *ZV*, doc. no. 15. On Chief of Military Intelligence Colonel Melander's trip to Berlin, see Report, including attachments from Helsinki, by Swedish Military Attaché to Riga Karl Lindqvist, no. 351, 11 Oct 1939, Krigsarkivet, Stockholm (hereafter KrA), Försvarsstaben, Underrättelseavdelningen (hereafter FST/Und), Serie E II A: 1.

19. Beria to Stalin, Molotov and Voroshilov, no. 4647/B, 17 Oct 1939, in *Tuntematon*, doc. no. 22. Cf. the German memo (3 Oct 1939) quoted in R. Peltovuori, *Saksa ja Suomen talvisota* (1975), 116. Soviet intelligence did not come to hear that the Finnish probing trip to Germany was made on Mannerheim's initiative.

20. Beria to Stalin, Molotov and Voroshilov, no. 4705/B, 21 Oct 1939, in *Tuntematon*, doc. no. 24. For analysis of Germany's policy, see M. Jonas, *Kolmannen valtakunnan lähettiläs* (2010), 107–51.

21. Beria to Stalin, Molotov and Voroshilov, no. 4600/B, 13 Oct 1939, in *ZV*, doc. no. 15.

22. Beria to Voroshilov, no. 4243/B, 14 Sept 1939, and no. 4343/B, 23 Sept 1939, copies in LOC, Volkogonov, Box 16; Tim Bouverie, *Appeasing Hitler: Chamberlain, Churchill and the Road to War* (2019); M.J. Carley, *1939: The Alliance That Never Was and the Coming of World War II* (1999).

23. Report by Swedish Military Attaché to Moscow Major Vrang, no. 44, 4 Oct 1939, KrA, FST/Und, E I: 15.

24. Beria to Stalin, Molotov and Voroshilov, no. 4490/B, 5 Oct 1939 (referring to Foreign Office telegrams dated 28 and 29 Sept 1939), in *ZV*, doc. no. 10; Voroshilov's copy with handwritten date 05 Oct 1939 (LOC, Volkogonov, Box 16), quoted in D. Volkogonov, *Stalin: Triumf i tragediya* (1989), 488–89.

25. Jonathan Haslam, *The Spectre of War* (2021), 341.
26. Agents were considered the most valuable sources, cf. the NKVD report of foreign intelligence 1939–41, April 1941, in V.P. Yampol'skii et al. (eds.), *Organy gosudarstvennyi bezopasnosti SSSR v Velikoi Otechestvennyi voine: Shornik dokumentov* I:2 (1995), 130–32.
27. Major Vrang's successor, Major Engelbrekt Flodström, was rather more discerning, and not convinced by the Soviet agent, voicing his suspicions of this "old, inherited, secure" source: Reports by Major Engelbrekt Flodström, no. 43, 24 Feb 1940, and no. 69, 7 Apr 1940, KrA, FST/Und, E II: 15; U.A. Käkönen, *Sotilasasiamiehenä Moskovassa 1939* (1966), 137–38. In Beria's report no. 4589/B (quoted below), a handwritten note in the margin reveals that the source's codename was "Keit" and that his handlers were Department 3 of the GUGB, i.e. the counter-intelligence section of the Main Directorate of State Security.
28. Käkönen, *Sotilasasiamiehenä*, 62; Erik Norberg, "Det militära hotet. Försvarsattachéernas syn på krigsutbrottet 1939" in B. Hugemark (ed.), *Stormvarning. Sverige inför andra världskriget* (1989).
29. Beria to Stalin, Molotov and Voroshilov, no. 4589/B, 12 Oct 1939, *ZV*, doc. no. 12; Voroshilov's copy (with its handwritten note), LOC, Volkogonov, Box 1. Vrang's report series in the Military Archives of Sweden is missing nos. 45–47, between 4 and 12 Oct 1939.
30. Beria to Stalin, Molotov and Voroshilov, no. 4591/B, 12 Oct 1939, *ZV*, doc. no. 14.
31. At the time of these negotiations Molotov's wife, Polina Zhemchuzhina, was facing charges of spying and sabotage. The accusations were found to be slanderous by the Politburo on 24 Oct 1939, but her disposition was adjudged to be sufficiently at fault that she lost her post in the People's Commissariat of the Fishing Industry. See O. Khlevniuk, *Master of the House* (2009), 220.
32. The Soviet source would claim to Vrang's successor that only 21 divisions would attack Finland: Flodström's report no. 54, 1 Nov 1939, in KrA, FST/Und, E II: 15.
33. Beria to Stalin, Molotov and Voroshilov, no. 4605/B, 14 Oct 1939, *ZV*, doc. no. 16.
34. M.I. Semirjaga, "Neuvostoliittolais-suomalainen sota v. 1939–40" in T. Vihavainen (ed.), *Talvisota, Suomi ja Venäjä* (1991), 187; O. Manninen, "Neuvostoliiton operatiiviset suunnitelmat 1939–1941 Suomen suunnalla," *Sotahistoriallinen Aikakausikirja* (1992), 92–93 and 98.
35. Born to a Jewish family in Odessa, Lev Mekhlis (1889–1953) was originally a Zionist-Socialist and a Menshevik. He made Stalin's acquaintance during the Russian Civil War, and was his assistant between 1922 and 1927. Stalin even inscribed his book on Leninism with "to my young friend." He worked to build Stalin's cult of personality as editor-in-chief at *Pravda*, 1930–37. As head of the Red Army's Political Directorate (PURKKA), 1938–40, he played an active part in the military purges. He was an insatiable workaholic and taskmaster, a fanatic, and, in Stalin's view, someone ready to carry out any order without question. However, he was lacking in military prowess. S. Kotkin, *Stalin: vol. I* (2014), 456–57; O.V. Khlevniuk, *Stalin: New Biography of a Dictator* (2015), 220–21 and 360.

36. Volkogonov, *Stalin: Triumf i tragediya*, 359; D.E. Murphy, *What Stalin Knew: The Enigma of Barbarossa* (2005), 30.
37. Mekhlis's report to Stalin and Voroshilov, 28 Sept 1939, his billet to Zhdanov, 3 Oct 1939, and the decision of the Politburo of the Communist Party of the Soviet Union, 3 Oct 1939, in *Rodina: Rossiiski istoricheski zhurnal* (2014), no. 9, 34–37. These politburo documents were published by Zoya Vishnyakova of the Russian State Archive of Socio-Political History.
38. Copy of order by Voroshilov, Stalin (as member of the War Soviet) and Shaposhnikov to the commanders of the 7th, 8th, 9th, 23rd and 14th armies, 29 Dec 1939, LOC, Volkogonov, Box 1.
39. The *rezident* (the head of the intelligence outpost) Boris Yartsev (Rybkin) was no longer permanently based in Helsinki; after April 1938 he only visited to carry out probing missions on Stalin's orders. His predecessor Genrikh Iosifovich Brzhozovsky (who went by Henrik I. Bayevich in Finland) was invited to Moscow to be an aide to one of the departmental heads in intelligence, but was arrested on 24 Nov 1936 and shot on 21 Aug 1937, accused of being a spy, possibly for Poland, since he was Polish himself; this charge was baseless. See K. Degtyarev and A. Kolpakidi, *Vneshnyaya razvedka SSSR* (2009), 377; Bayevich's ID card, The Archives of Foreign Ministry of Finland (UMA), 6 O.
40. Stalin to Head of Military Intelligence I.I. Proskurov, 25 Aug 1939, in *Lubyanka: Stalin i NKVD–NKGB–GUKR "Smersh," 1939–mart 1946* (2006), 123. It is not known who the Finnish Voroshilov was.
41. Special notification of the GUGB's Foreign Department no. 250304, 2 June 1936, in L.F. Sotskov (ed.), *Pribaltika i geopolitika* (2010), 48. The documents that Soviet intelligence acquired from Finland's Ministry of Foreign Affairs include: Foreign Ministry report of a ministerial visit to Lithuania and Prague, no. 205, 22 May 1936 (distributed to Stalin, Molotov and Litvinov 15 Aug 1936); Envoy Palin's report on Latvian internal politics, Foreign Ministry summary of report, no. 342, 24 Sept 1936 (to Stalin, etc., 3 Nov 1936); report of the Finnish Envoy to Kaunas on Lithuanian–Soviet relations, 29 Mar 1937 (to Stalin, etc., 23 Apr 1937); Envoy Palin's report from Riga, 19 July 1937 (to Yezhov, etc., Aug 1937). News about Major General Sotskov publishing documents from 1938: 'Russian Foreign Intelligence Service declassifies Munich Agreement Papers' (RIA Novosti, Valery Yarmolenko), 2 Oct 2008, *Russia Beyond*, https://www.rbth.com/articles/2008/10/02/021008_munich.html (accessed 12 May 2022).
42. Finnish state police reports on popular moods published in the *ZV* collection (e.g. 30 Oct 1939, doc. no. 23, lacking archival codes) are not from Russian archives but delivered for publication by the National Archives of Finland.
43. Zoya Voskresenskaya (Rybkina), *Pod psevdonimom Irina* (1997), 90–91 and 104–05. The book is Rybkina's memoir.
44. Beria to Stalin, Molotov and Voroshilov, no. 4590/B, 12 Oct 1939, *ZV*, doc. no. 13. Two lines were redacted, but they remain in Voroshilov's copy, identifying the source as Sundström: LOC, Volkogonov, Box 1. For more on Erkko's role, see O. Manninen and R. Salokangas, *Eljas Erkko* (2009).
45. Beria to Stalin, Molotov and Voroshilov, no. 4647/B, 17 Oct 1939, *ZV*, doc. no. 22. The source for this was Helsinki cipher cable no. 959 from Irina (i.e. Zoya

Rybkina). On Irina's relationship with Wuolijoki, see Voskresenskaya, *Irina*, 112–18. Wuolijoki's codename is ANNA in Sinitsyn's memoirs, but POET in Helsinki telegrams from 1941 published in V.K. Vinogradov et al. (eds.), *Sekrety Gitlera na stole u Stalina* (1995), notes 94 and 112, and index 240.

46. Beria to Stalin, Molotov and Voroshilov, no. 4687/B, 19 Oct 1939, *ZV*, doc. no. 20.

47. M. Majander, *Pohjoismaa vai kansandemokratia?* (2004), chapter entitled "Sota-Tannerin synty."

48. S. Beria, *Moi otets Beria* (2002), 75.

49. Beria to Stalin, Molotov and Voroshilov, no. 4815/B, 27 Oct 1939 (Tanner in a SDP meeting, 26 Oct), *ZV*, doc. no. 22.

50. Major Vasilyev's reports, 5 and 21 Oct 1939, *Voennaya razvedka*, 197–198, 201–202; Beria to Stalin, Molotov and Voroshilov, no. 4875/B, 1 Nov 1939, *ZV*, doc. no. 24.

51. Sinitsyn's report to V.G. Dekanozov, 12 Nov 1939, quoted in Viktor Vladimirov, *Kohti talvisotaa* (1995), 163–64. Sinitsyn made a personal visit to Stalin's office on 27 Nov 1939: A.A. Chernobaev et al. (eds.), *Na prieme u Stalina* (2008), 282. V.M. Vladimirov served as KGB *rezident* in Helsinki in 1970–71 and again 1977–84.

52. C. Gerrard, *The Foreign Office and Finland* (2005), 88–93, quoting Lascelles's and Lawrence Collier's observations in a report from Helsinki, 8 Oct 1939.

53. Cipher telegram from Maisky to the People's Commissariat of Foreign Affairs (NKID), 7 Oct 1939, in *Dokumenty vneshnei politiki* (hereafter *DVP*), xxii: 2, 1939 (1992), 167–69. More details in I.M. Maisky, *Dnevnik diplomata: London 1934–1943*, 2: 1, A.O. Chubarian et al. (eds.) (2009); in English *The Maisky Diaries*, ed. G. Gorodetsky (2015).

54. Maisky's diary, 26 Oct and 10 Nov 1939, *Dnevnik diplomata*. Not included in the English translation.

55. Cipher telegram to the NKID, 13 Nov 1939, *DVP* xxii: 2; cf. D. Carlton, *Churchill and the Soviet Union* (2000), 70–74. Churchill also commented to the British government that a stronger Soviet Union in the Baltic Sea region would be advantageous to Britain, as it would limit Germany's influence. L. Rees, *World War II Behind Closed Doors: Stalin, the Nazis and the West* (2008), 42.

56. Maisky's diary, 30 Oct 1939, *DVP* xxii: 2.

57. Maisky's diary, 29 Nov 1939, *DVP* xxii: 2, and *Dnevnik diplomata*, where also his discussions with Halifax and Butler, 27 and 28 Nov 1939.

58. See Jonathan Haslam, *The Spectre of War: International Communism and the Origins of World War II* (2021).

59. Georgi Dimitrov's diary, 7 Nov 1939; G. Dimitrov, *Dnevnik* (1997).

60. Nevezhin, *Sindrom*, 84, 119, the source being Mekhlis's speech in a closed meeting with the Union of Soviet Writers, 10 Nov 1939.

61. Quoted by Haslam, *The Spectre of War* (2021), 333.

62. Rentola, "The Finnish Communists" (1998); the source for Dimitrov's comments is his discussion with the Comintern Commission on Germany, 29 Nov 1939.

63. R. Garthoff, *Soviet Leaders and Intelligence* (2015), 12–13. The chapter on Stalin extends to a mere 16 pages, but manages to cover all the most essential points.

64. For example, Wuolijoki's information about the views of the French military attaché to Helsinki, Commander Paul Ollivier, in the aforementioned reports sent to Stalin by Beria, nos. 4647 and 4687.

65. Beria's order no. 001445, 1 Dec 1939, in N.S. Lebedeva et al. (eds.), *Katyn: Plenniki neob'yavlennoi voiny* (1997), doc. no. 122. The need for additional space in the camps was one of the background factors leading to the massacre of the Poles in Katyn and elsewhere.

66. Flodström's report no. 69, 7 Apr 1940, KrA, FST/Und E II: 15.

67. Paasikivi's notes from the Finnish government's Foreign Affairs Committee, 2–3 Dec 1939, in O. Manninen and K. Rumpunen (eds.), *Murhenäytelmän vuorosanat: Talvisodan hallituksen keskustelut* (2003).

68. Beria to Stalin, Molotov and Voroshilov, no. 4984/B, 9 Nov 1939, *ZV*, doc. no. 33; Communist attitudes outlined in Rentola, "The Finnish Communists."

69. Quoted in D. Volkogonov, *Sem vozhdei: Galereya liderov SSSR* 1 (1995), 296.

70. Report of the NKVD GUGB OO on the opinions of the intelligentsia, 7 Dec 1939, in *ZV*, doc. no. 70.

71. Report by Major P.V. Fedotov of the Moscow region UNKVD to the 2nd section of the GUGB NKVD, 2 Dec 1939, in *ZV*, doc. no. 55; and the original in the Central Archives of the Russian Federal Security Services (TsA FSB RF), f. 3, op. 6, d. 85, II. 385–89. On the fate of the four Starostin brothers in the Gulag 1942–54, see A. Vlizkov, "Lagernaya planida Aleksandra Starostina," *Molodezh Severa* 45 (6 Nov 2003), available at www.mskomi.ru/arhiv/new078. htm (accessed 12 May 2022), based on documents from the Komi KGB archives; R. Edelman, *Spartak Moscow* (2009), 125–35.

72. Vernadsky's diary, 2 and 19 Dec 1939, V.I. Vernadsky, *Dnevniki 1935–1941 v dvukh knigakh*, vol. 2, V.P. Volkov (ed.) (2006).

73. Report by Captain M. Baskakov (Commissar for Internal Affairs in Soviet Karelia) to the 2nd section of the GUGB NKVD, no. 21113, 10 Dec 1939, *ZV*, doc. no. 76. "Siihen perkeleen puna-armeijaan," Honkanen probably said. The Finnish word "perkele" is much stronger than "devil."

74. Copy of Eric von Rosen's memo on conversations with Hermann Göring on 5–6 Dec 1939 (dated 8 Dec 1939), Swedish Labor Archives, Stockholm (Arbetarrörelsens arkiv—ARAB), Per Albin Hansson Papers, vol. 8.

75. Head of Military Intelligence (GRU) Proskurov's letter to BINE (N.M. Zaitsev), 27 Dec 1939, *Voennaya razvedka*, 214. NKVD intelligence networks in Berlin ran into problems when A.Z. Kobulov was appointed *rezident* in 1939: E.M. Primakov et al. (eds.), *Ocherki istorii Rossiiskoi vneshnei razvedki*, vol. 3, 1933–1941 (1997), 419.

76. Beria to Stalin, Molotov and Voroshilov, no. 208/B, 13 Jan 1940, including attachment of Ambassador Blücher's report from Helsinki to Berlin, 11 Dec 1939, *ZV*, doc. no. 158.

77. Beria to Voroshilov, 1 Jan 1940, quoted in Bushuyeva, *Krasnaya armiya* (2011), 359–60.

78. Beria to Stalin, Molotov and Voroshilov, no. 5823/B, 29 Dec 1939, *ZV*, doc. no. 133; cf. Ambassador Steinhardt to the State Department, 1 Dec 1939, *Foreign Relations of the United States (FRUS)*, 1939: I (1956), 1014–15.

79. Memo by F.H.R. Maclean entitled "Propaganda with regard to the Soviet Union," 15 Dec 1939, and comments on it; updated version of Maclean's

memo (printed and circulated), entitled "Line for Propaganda with regard to the Soviet Union," 3 Jan 1940, again with added comments on it, The National Archives of the United Kingdom (TNA), Foreign Office (FO) 371/24845.

80. Quotation from Maclean's aforementioned memo, 3 Jan 1940; Minutes of the Joint Intelligence Committee Sub-Committee meeting at the Foreign Office, 5 Jan 1940; Foreign Minister Lord Halifax to Chamberlain, 12 Jan 1940, and the written response from No. 10, signed by the Prime Minister's assistant, TNA, FO 371/24845; Y. M. Streatfield's paper, "The Major Developments in Political Warfare throughout the War, 1938–1945" (1949), TNA, Records of the Cabinet Office (CAB) 101/131; P. Osborn, *Operation Pike: Britain versus the Soviet Union, 1939–1941* (2000), 17, 30, quoting Knatchbull-Hugessen's report from Angora, 18 Nov 1939, and Collier (FO) to Angora, 1 Dec 1939.

81. Stalin "interview," *Pravda*, 30 Nov 1939.

82. J. Nevakivi, *The Appeal That Was Never Made* (1976), the original book was published in Finnish in 1972 and an updated version in 2000; T. Munch-Petersen, *The Strategy of Phoney War* (1981).

83. Quotes from Brigadier Ling, "Notes on Interview with Field Marshal Baron Mannerheim at Finnish G.H.Q. on 8-1-40"; Ling's notes in his notebook; his report on the overall situation; letter dictated by Mannerheim to Ironside, 9 Jan 1940, TNA, War Office (WO), 208/3966.

84. K. Jeffery, *MI6: The History of the Secret Intelligence Service, 1909–1949* (2010), 371–72; Beria to Stalin, Molotov and Voroshilov, no. 210/B, 13 Jan 1940, *ZV*, doc. no. 155; J. Haslam, *Near and Distant Neighbours* (2015), 98–99.

85. General Ironside's memo, "Operations in Scandinavia," 12 Jan 1940, TNA, WO 208/3966.

86. H. Tala, *Suomea pelastamassa* (2012); J.-B. Duroselle, *Politique étrangère de la France. L'Abîme, 1939–1944* (1986). Duroselle's book cites *Documents diplomatiques français, 1939* (2002) and *1940*: tome I (2004).

87. Beria to Stalin, Molotov and Voroshilov, no. 54/B and 55/B, early Jan 1940 (both based on reports from the acting *rezident* in London), *Tuntematon*, docs. no. 141 and 142.

88. N. West and O. Tsarev, *Crown Jewels* (1999), 144, 163. On Gorski's career, K. Degtyarev and A. Kolpakidi, *Vneshnyaya razvedka SSSR* (2009), 403. Two of the Cambridge Five, Donald Maclean and Kim Philby, spent most of their time in France, the former in the Paris Embassy and the latter as a journalist with the British Expeditionary Force. It seems improbable that the decision to close the London *rezidentura* would have been due to two defection cases in which the defectors A. Orlov and V. Krivitsky knew the Cambridge Five. These defections occurred in July and October 1938, so it was not very sensible to wait until February 1940 with any Soviet countermeasures. J. Haslam, "'Humint' by Default and the Problem of Trust: Soviet Intelligence 1917–1941," in *Secret Intelligence in the European States System, 1918–1989* (2014), 30–31.

89. The expression used by Maisky in his diary, 30 Oct 1939, *DVP* xxii: 2.

90. Cipher telegram from 9th Army OO to OO GUGB (Moscow), no. 42164vh, 12 Dec 1939, *ZV*, doc. no. 84.

91. Copy of Stalin's cipher telegram to Mekhlis, no. 1184/sh, 9 Jan 1940, LOC, Volkogonov, Box 17.

92. Beria to Stalin, Molotov and Voroshilov, no. 203/B, 12 Jan 1940, *ZV*, doc. no. 152.

93. R. Self, *Neville Chamberlain: A Biography* (2006), 404–08; A. Gat, "Containment and Cold War before the Nuclear Age: The Phoney War as Allied Strategy According to Liddell Hart," in M. Clemmesen and M. Faulkner (eds.), *Northern European Overture to War, 1939–1941* (2013), 15.

94. Beria to Stalin, Molotov and Voroshilov, no. 225/B, 13 Jan 1940, *ZV*, doc. no. 159.

95. Telegram no. 71 from London to British military attaché in Finland, forwarded to Brigadier Ling, 18 Feb 1940, TNA, WO 208/3966.

96. Beria to Stalin, Molotov and Voroshilov, no. 227/B, 13 Jan 1940, *ZV*, doc. no. 160. For Beria's son's account of Stalin's reaction to this information, see Beria, *Moi otets*, 76.

97. Meeting of the Soviet Command Personnel at the Central Committee, Verbatim Record, Sixth Session, 17 Ape 1940, in A.O. Chubaryan and H. Shukman (eds.) and T. Sokokina (trans.), *Stalin and the Soviet-Finnish War 1939–1940* (2002), 201.

98. Osborn, *Operation Pike*, 82–83, quoting from the Joint Intelligence Committee's memo "Measures to Deceive the Enemy," 6 Feb 1940. This mentions that false evidence had already been delivered to the enemy.

99. M.I. Meltyukhov, *Upushchennyi shans Stalina* ("Stalin's Missed Chance") (2000), 262–65.

100. G. Gorodetsky, *Grand Delusion* (1999), 17. At the turn of 1940 Molotov had already accused the British government of destabilizing Turkish–Soviet relations: Telegram of William Seeds from Moscow to the Foreign Office, no. 1, 1 Jan 1940, TNA, FO 371/24845.

101. R.A. Leeper (FO Political Intelligence Department) to Sir H. Knatchbull-Hugessen (Angora), 1 Feb 1940, TNA, FO 371/24845; M. Thomas, "Imperial Defence or Diversionary Attack? Anglo-French Strategic Planning in the Near East, 1936-1940," in M.S. Alexander and W.J. Philpott (eds.), *Anglo-French Defence Relations between the Wars* (2002), esp. 176–77.

102. Knatchbull-Hugessen to Leeper, 10 Feb 1940; Knatchbull-Hugessen to Lawrence Collier (FO), 7 Feb 1940 (discussion with Kerim Oder, the former Musavat leader), TNA, FO 371/24845; additional British diplomatic correspondence quoted in N. Tamkin, Britain, Turkey and the Soviet Union, 1940–45 (2009), 16.

103. Memo by F.H.R. Maclean (FO) on Sir Campbell Stuart's proposals concerning Ukrainian separatism, 12 Feb 1940, TNA, FO 371/24845. For more about the subsequent British/German interference in the Organization of Ukrainian Nationalists (OUN), see J. Armstrong, *Ukrainian Nationalism 1939–1945* (1955), 54–58.

104. Report by the Party Secretary of Chechnya-Ingushia, N. Mihailenko, c. 22 Nov 1939, and other reports from the Caucasus and Central Asia sent to G.M. Malenkov in Moscow, in L.S. Gatagova et al. (eds.), *TsK VKP (b) i natsional'nyi vopros*, vol. 2, 1933–1945 (2009).

105. Georgi Dimitrov's diary, 21 Jan 1940, *The Diary of Georgi Dimitrov 1933–1949*, ed. Ivo Banac (2003), translation amended.

106. Stalin's speech in the party central committee session, 19 Jan 1925, quoted by Kotkin *Stalin: vol. I*, 556–58. A redacted version published in Stalin's works, vol. 7.

107. Notes by Zoltán Schönherz in the Comintern, 30 Dec 1939, published by Krisztián Ungváry, *Jahrubuch für historische Kommunismusforschung* (2010), 269–74. The notes were seized by Hungarian military counter-intelligence in May 1940 and preserved in their archives. Issue of Hungary in Dimitrov's diary, 28 Dec 1940.

108. V. Krévé-Mitskevičius, "Conversation with Molotov" [29 Jun 1940], *Lituanus* 11 (1965), no. 2, p. 18. http://www.lituanus.org/1965/65_2_02_KreveMitskevicius.html. Published 11 years after the death of the author.

109. Statement by former foreign minister, Rickard Sandler, *Social-Demokraten* (19 Jan 1940).

110. O. Manninen, "NKVD:n henkilökohtaiset kontaktit Moskovan rauhan taustalla," *Sotilasaikakauslehti* 2014: 2, 50–52. The article was based on notes by Russian scholars from Beria's memo to Stalin; these were shown to Professor Manninen in the early 1990s, but have since then been unavailable for scholars.

111. S. Sebag Montefiore, *Stalin: The Court of the Red Tsar* (2003), 293. Stalin received nobody in his office between 13 and 28 Jan and again between 30 Jan and 3 Feb. *Na prieme u Stalina*, 290.

112. VKP(b) Central Committee Politburo resolution no. 208, 17 Jan 1940, original in Arkhiv Prezidenta Rossiiskoi Federatsii (AP RF), f. 3, op. 24, s. 177, ll. 116–36, here used electronical copies published by this archive and Memorial, Stalin.memo.ru/images/introt.html

113. Maisky diary, 11, 25 and 26 Jan 1940, *Dnevnik diplomata*; Maisky's letter to Molotov, 26 Jan 1940, *DVP* xxiii: 1, 53–56; on Maisky's views, S. Pons, *Stalin and the Inevitable War 1936–1941* (2002), 195; on opinions at the Foreign Office Northern Department, M. Folly, *Churchill, Whitehall and the Soviet Union, 1940–45* (2000), 7–8.

114. Nevezhin, *Sindrom*, 115. The source is the diary of the director of Mezhdunarodnaya kniga publishers, A.G. Solovyov, 22 Jan 1940.

115. Hella Wuolijoki's report to Andrei G. Graur (NKVD), Stockholm, 21 Jan 1940, a copy attached in V. Merkulov's (NKGB) letter to S.A. Lozovski, no. 4945/M, 2 Aug 1945, The Archives of Foreign Policy of the Russian Federation (AVP RF), fond 0135 (Referentura po Finlyandii), opis 29, papka 158, delo 9, ll. 9–15.

116. Beria to Stalin, Molotov and Voroshilov, no 685/B, 26 Feb 1940, ZV, doc. no. XXX. Kollontai was talking with her councillor, Plakhin.

117. Yuri Rubtsov, *Mekhlis: Ten' vozhdya* (2007), 213–14, based on directives for PU RKKA, early Feb. 1940.

118. Gorodetsky, *Grand Delusion*, 12.

119. Maisky's diary, 30 Jan 1940, *Dnevnik diplomata*; Maisky's memorandum on conversation with Butler, 30 Jan 1940, *DVP* xxiii: 1, 61–63.

120. Chiefs of Staff Committee, draft report, "Military Implications of Hostilities with Russia," Feb 1940, printed copy no. 17, TNA, FO 371/24845; one version partially published in H.-J. Lorbeer, *Westmächte gegen Sowjetunion 1939–1941* (1975), 102–11.

121. First quote from the Chiefs of Staff Committee report mentioned above; the second one from Sargent to Knatchbull-Hugessen, 23 Feb 1940, TNA, FO 371/24845.

122. Meltyukhov *Upushchennyi shans Stalina*, 262–64, on the basis of General Staff orders to air force; Nevezhin, *Sindrom*, p. 120, on the basis of an order to the Central Asian military district. "Afghan" corrected into "Pashto" in the text.

123. At the farewell visit of Ambassador Sir William Seeds, Molotov even accused Britain of instigating a people of 3.5 million against one of 180 million.

124. E.g. "England treibt zu einem neuen Weltkrieg," *Die Kommunistische Internationale* xxi:1 (Jan 1940), 9, 15–17.

125. Molotov to Maisky, 21 Feb 1940, with attachment on 22 Feb; Maisky's memoranda of conversation with Butler, 22 and 24 Feb 1940, *DVP* xxiii: 1, 101–05, 107–08.

126. Jonas, *Blücher*, 118, 130.

127. Natalia S. Lebedeva, "The Process of Revealing the Truth and Commemorating" (2015), 251.

128. V.F. Tributs, *Baltiitsy vstupayut v boi* (1972). Winter War is not included in a later volume putting together this and the next part of the memoirs, V.F. Tributs, *Baltiitsy srazhayatsya* (1985). This order, dated 26 Feb 1940, is mentioned in the chronology prepared for the memoirs of the people's commissar for naval affairs N.G. Kuznetsov, *Krutye povoroty* (1995), but not at all in P.V. Petrov, *Krasnoznamennyi Baltiiski Flot* (2016).

129. Manninen's article, mentioned above.

130. B.V. Sokolov, "The Soviet Policy Towards the Baltic States in 1939–41," *Northern European Overture to War* (2013).

131. Report by Maj Flodström, no. 23, 5 Feb 1940, and no. 26; 9 Feb 1940, KrA, FST/Und E II:15. The source was very eager to certify that his information would be duly reported.

132. Lasse Laaksonen, *Todellisuus ja harhat* (1998).

133. Memo (by Maj J. Magill) on the conversation between Mannerheim and Lt. Gen. King-Salter, 4 Mar 1940, TNA, WO 208/1966.

134. Beria to Stalin, Molotov, Voroshilov and Mikoyan, no 901/B, 8 Mar 1940. This document is not included in the Russian version of the Winter War documentary collection (*ZV*), but published in the Finnish one (*Tuntematon*, doc. no 219). Sender's copy of the original in TsA FSB, f. 3, op. 6, d. 13, ll. 81–82.

135. Maisky's diary, 21 Feb 1940, *Dnevnik diplomata*.

136. Molotov's entry in his office diary, 5 Mar 1940, quoted by J. Kilin, *Suurvallan rajamaa* (2004), 174, original in AVP RF, f. 06, op. 1, papka 25, d. 318, l. 36.

137. Steinhardt's report from Moscow, 9 Mar 1940, *FRUS* 1940: I, 592.

138. Beria to Stalin, Molotov and Voroshilov, no. 550/B, 10 Feb 1940; no. 688/B, 26 Feb 1940; no. 851/B, 5 Mar 1940, *ZV*, nos. 185, 193, 197.

139. Beria to Stalin, no. 794/B, 10 Feb 1940; no. 688/B, early Mar 1940; Minute of the VKP(b) Central Committee politburo, 5 Mar 1940, in *Katyn*, ed. Lebedeva (1997), docs. no. 216, 217; N.S. Lebedeva. "Katynskoe prestuplenie," in A.V. Torkunov and A.D. Rotfeld (eds), *Belye plyatna—chernye plyatna: Slozhnye voprosy v rossiisko-polskikh otnosheniyah* (2010), 204–05;

Lebedeva, "The Process of Revealing" (2015), 250–54. The number 25,700 is from Beria's proposal and not the actual number shot.

140. Beria to Stalin, Molotov and Voroshilov, no. 969/B, 14 Mar 1940, *ZV*, doc. no. 213.

141. Dimitrov's diary, 25 Nov 1940.

142. Elena Zubkova, *Pribaltika I Kreml 1940–1953* (2008), 93–94.

143. Dimitrov's diary, 21 Jan 1940.

144. Quoted by K. Wahlbäck, *Jättens andedräkt* (2011), 165.

145. Introduction by O.I. Nazhestkin in Primakov et al. (eds.), *Ocherki* (1997), part iii, 17–18, quoting a report by the NKVD's Chief of Foreign Intelligence P.M. Fitin. He had 18 intelligence officers in the United States, 17 in Finland and 13 in Germany.

146. Memo by Knatchbull-Hugessen, 1 Apr 1940, quoted by Tamkin, *Britain, Turkey and the Soviet Union*, 19; Osborn, *Operation Pike*, 129, 133–34, 143–53 and 165.

147. Miner, *Between Churchill and Stalin* (1988), 45. "By late May 1940, the Allies no longer had the military power to deal the Soviet Union a serious blow while simultaneously fighting the Germans."

148. Wahlbäck, *Jättens andedräkt* (2011), 254.

149. West and Tsarev, *Crown Jewels*, 223; Y. Modin et al., *My Five Cambridge Friends* (1994), 17, 104.

150. J. Förster, "The German Military's Image of Russia," in *Russia: War, Peace and Diplomacy*, ed. L. and M. Erickson (2004), 123–24.

151. Iz akta o prieme narkomata, May 1940, published in *Voennaya razvedka*, p. 717. In the next Politburo criticism against Voroshilov on April 1942, the failure of the Finnish war was again mentioned. O. Khlevniuk, *Khozyain: Stalin i utverzhdenie stalinskoi diktatury* (2009), 456.

152. Ivan Josifovich Chernyi (1894–1943) lost his post in London in May 1940, was arrested on 7 June 1941 and died in prison. M.A. Alekseyev. A.I. Kolpakidi et al., *Entsiklopediya voennoi razvedki 1918–1945 gg.* (2012), 823–24.

153. D. Murphy, *What Stalin Knew: The Enigma of Barbarossa* (2005), 238–39.

154. Khlevniuk, *Stalin* (2015), 40. Kira Kulik-Simonich was arrested on 3 May 1940 and shot after lengthy interrogations. Kulik himself was arrested in 1947 and shot in 1950. On unnatural sexual appeal to former persons there was a Politburo decision 3 May 1935 on Abel Yenukidze, the chief of the Kremlin administration. D. Shearer and V. Khaustov, *Stalin and the Lubyanka; A Documentary History of the Political Police and Security Organs in the Soviet Union, 1922–1953* (2015), 184.

155. Dimitrov's diary, 21 Jan 1941. According to Stalin, Mekhlis was "a good man, hard worker, but unfit for military leadership." Dimitrov's diary, 28 May 1940. Despite this, he was allowed to lead the defense of Crimea in 1942 to a catastrophe. Even after that he continued in the government, died three weeks before the Boss, and was buried in front of the Kremlin wall, in the same row where Brezhnev later got his grave.

156. Bushuyeva, *Krasnaya armiya*, 288–93, 397–98; Roberts, *Stalin's Wars*, 53–55.

157. Khrushchev's memoirs, the part published later, *Voprosy istorii* 1990, no. 7, 104.

158. O. Khlevniuk, *Master of the House: Stalin and His Inner Circle* (2009), 234–35.

159. Stalin's remarks in the intelligence commission of the party presidium, Nov 1952, quoted by Y. Gorlizki and O. Khlevniuk, *Cold Peace: Stalin and the Soviet Ruling Circle, 1945–1953* (2004), 171; Khlevniuk, *Stalin*, 308.

160. Meeting of the Command Personnel, 17 Apr 1940, *Stalin and the Soviet-Finnish War, 1939–1940* (2002), 196.

161. Nikita Petrov, *Palachi: Oni vypolnyali zakazy Stalina* (2011), 158. Later, Shvartsman served as deputy head of the department of the most important cases in the NKGB/MGB and advisor in Berlin, Sofia and Bucharest, e.g. in the Kostov case. Next day after the arrest of the MGB head, V.S. Abakumov in July 1951, Shvartsman was arrested, and then not released after the death of Stalin. He was condemned to death for illegal interrogation methods and fabrications (e.g. the Leningrad case) and other crimes and shot on 13 May 1955.

162. *Vneshnyaya politika Sovetskogo Sojuza* (1940), Report by V.M. Molotov, 1 Aug 1940.

163. G.A. Gripenberg's diary, 26 June 1944, G.A. Gripenberg, *Dagbok 1944* (2019), 140. This was told to Gripenberg (the envoy of Finland) by UD Cabinet Secretary Erik Boheman, who said he "knew" the occasion. His probable source was the Soviet ambassador, Aleksandra Kollontay, possibly the first lengthy discussion on 20 November 1943 on the terms of the next peace. Erik Boheman, *På vakt* (1964), 248–51. Molotov's words, if uttered, should be in 1940.

164. Nevezhin, *Sindrom*, 139 (outlining Marshal Zhukov's outlook).

165. F. Chuyev, *Molotov: Poluderzhavnyi vlastelin* (1999), 21. This is an expanded edition of the book *Sto sorok besed*, first published in 1990.

166. Memo from Stalin's meeting with a delegation from the Finland-Soviet Union Friendship Society, 8 Oct 1945 (abridged), written by A. Karaganov, RGASPI, f. 558, op. 1, d. 5379, II. 1–9. Originating from Ukrainian, *khutor* means a single, sectioned-off farm located outside of a compact village. In pre-Soviet Russia it was specifically considered the agricultural model agreeable to Ingrians and Estonians.

II The Way to Peace (1944)

1. NKGB (V. Merkulov) to Stalin, Molotov and Beria, no. 2864/M, 12 Nov 1943, doc. no. 40 in V.S. Khristoforov, *SSSR—Finlyandiya: protivostoyanie 1941–1944 gg.* (2018), pp. 322–23. The original sender's copy in TsA FSB, f. 4 os.

2. NKGB (Kobulov) report to Stalin, Molotov and Beria, no. 130/M, 15 Jan 1944, doc. no. 45 in Khristoforov 2018, p. 363.

3. Jaakko Keto was a member of the SDP board and the leading figure in one leftist tendency; Ensio Hiitonen, former Finnish envoy to Prague, was from the Progress Party (as was President Risto Ryti); and Laurin Zilliacus was a school principal, a key activist in the SDP opposition and a native speaker of Swedish. Zilliacus' brother, Konni Zilliacus, had served in the League of Nations secretariat and became a Labour MP after the war, received even by Stalin, but in the Yugoslav issue he favored Tito. Young Laurin had lived with his family in the US and Britain, and after the war got a job in the US Embassy in Stockholm (press relations). Later he served as a Columbia University professor and a UN advisor in education issues.

4. Osmo Apunen and Corinna Wolff, *Pettureita ja patriootteja* (2009), 266–73; W. Agrell, *Venona* (2003), passim. During the Finns' visit, the Stockholm NKGB asked and got headquarters' permission to recruit a Finn, but the trio had already left the city when the answer was received.

5. E. Boheman, *På vakt* (1964), 248–51.

6. G.A. Gripenberg's diary, 5 Dec 1946. Gripenberg was a relative of the Marshal and they talked also about private issues. The discussion took place on the eve of Finland's independence day.

7. Memo from the People's Commissariat of Foreign Affairs concerning peace terms for Germany and its allies, c. 17 Oct 1943; Voroshilov to Molotov, 6 Oct 1943, in *SSSR i germanski vopros* I, doc. nos. 60 and 68.

8. Dimitrov to Stalin and Molotov, 3 Mar 1943, attached with Kuusinen's memo, in K. Anderson and A. Chubarian (eds.), *Komintern i Vtoraya mirovaya voin* II (1998), doc. no. 124.

9. Litvinov to Molotov, 3 Aug 1943, and to Stalin and Molotov, 9 Sept 1943, with an attachment on international and country-specific issues, in *SSSR i germanski vopros 1941–1949* I, doc. nos. 52 and 55; Dimitrov's diary, 30 Aug 1943.

10. O.V. Kuusinen's lecture, 'Finlyandiya kak vassal gitlerovskoi Germanii', 30 Nov 1943, Bulgarian Central State Archives (TsDA, Sofia), fond 146-B (Dimitrov's Papers), opis 5, a.e. 1930, II. 1–23.

11. T. Polvinen, *Barbarossasta Teheraniin* (1979), 285–86, quoting memos by Boheman about his meetings with Kollontay on 13 and 20 Nov 1943.

12. E. Carlsson, *Gustaf V och andra världskriget* (2006), 285.

13. The Tehran Conference has been very well researched—recent works on the topic include: F. Costigliola, *Roosevelt's Lost Alliances* (2012), 194–204; Susan Butler, *Roosevelt and Stalin* (2015); O.A. Rzheshevski, *Stalin i Churchill* (2004), 384–411; and G. Roberts, *Stalin's Wars* (2006). On Finland in particular, see: O. Apunen and C. Wolff, *Pettureita ja patriootteja* (2009); T. Polvinen, *Barbarossasta Teheraniin* (1979) and *J.K. Paasikivi: Valtiomiehen elämäntyö*, vol. 3, 1939–1944 (1995); and O. Vehviläinen, *Finland in the Second World War: Between Germany and Russia* (2002).

14. Unless otherwise stated, the sources on the Tehran Conference are American memos by Roosevelt's interpreter, Charles Bohlen, 1 Dec 1943. *Foreign Relations of the United States: The Conferences of Cairo and Tehran 1943*, docs. no. 376 and 378; Soviet memos on 1 Dec 1943 in *Tegeranskaya konferentsiya rukovoditelei trekh soyuznykh derzhav—SSSR, SShA j Velkobritanii* (1978), docs. nos. 62 and 63. On small but important redactions to the Russian texts, Roberts, *Stalin's Wars*, 408, fn. 68.

15. C. Bohlen, *Witness to History* (1973), 219.

16. Bohlen, *Witness to History*, 150–51.

17. Costigliola, *Roosevelt's Lost Alliances*, 292, quoting Ambassador Clark Kerr's advance obituary of Stalin for the BBC (1949). According to Stalin's visitor logbook, in 1943 Kerr last visited the Soviet leader's office on 21 October.

18. Memo of conversation between Zhdanov and Finnish Communist Party leaders Y. Leino, H. Kuusinen and V. Pessi, 28 Mar 1945, RGASPI, f. 77, op. 3, d. 53.

19. S. Cohen, *Bukharin and the Bolshevik Revolution* (1973), 346. Bukharin's observation: "genial'nyi dozirovshchik."

20. The envoy Ivan Zotov to Molotov, 12 Jan 1941, attached to an unsigned report from Hanko maritime base, late December 1940, AP RF, f. 3, op. 66, d. 582, ll. 1–7. Molotov forwarded this to Stalin. The matter was not taken up with the Finns.

21. Lars Rowe, *Pechenganikel* (2013), 54–57, quoting seven reports made by Soviet mine engineers and geologists in early 1940, held at the Russian Economic Archives (RGAE). The Soviet specialists were impressed by the mine's technical level and its high mineral content.

22. The preparatory material of fall 1943 mentioned, e.g., the punishment of the "war guilty," as well as the disbandment of the Civil Guards and their affiliate organizations, and the internment of their members. Memo on 3 Oct 1943; Voroshilov to Molotov, 6 Oct 1943, in *SSSR i germanski vopros*, I, doc. nos. 59 and 60.

23. M. Gilbert, *Winston S. Churchill, Vol. VII: Road to Victory, 1941–1945* (1986), 591.

24. Churchill's minute to Cadogan, 25 Oct 1943, quoted in H.P. Evans, *Diplomatic Deceptions* (2011), 24.

25. Geoffrey Wheatcroft, *New York Review of Books*, 9 June 2016. The full quote is: "his greatness matched by his meanness, his nobility by his brutality, his courage by his rapacity."

26. Apunen and Wolff, *Pettureita ja patriootteja*, 313.

27. V.S. Khristoforov, "Za kulisami sovetsko-finlyandskih peregovorov o peremirii. 1943–1944 gody," *Novaya i noveishaya istoriya* (2015), 25, quoting Soviet counter-intelligence materials in FSB archives. At the time, the Soviets claimed that Captain Nygren was planning to deliver Soviet military secrets to the Germans; V. Assarsson, *I skuggan av Stalin* (1963), 227–33.

28. See, for example, Ohto Rintala, *Yhdysvallat ja Saksan koalition pienet maat* (2014).

29. Ambassador William C. Bullitt's memo of his discussion with Otto von Habsburg, 16 Jan 1944, quoted in Costigliola, *Roosevelt's Lost Alliances*, 202–03. Habsburg had just come from a meeting with Roosevelt, who had, apparently, admitted to giving the Soviets a list of those "countries they could take over and control completely as their sphere—so completely that the United States could from this moment have no further policies with regard to them."

30. Roosevelt's letter to Cardinal Spellman, Sept 1943, quoted in Butler, *Roosevelt and Stalin*, 123.

31. Maisky's memo to Molotov, 11 Jan 1944, in *SSSR i germanski vopros* I, doc. no. 71, on Finland pp. 336, 352.

32. Memcon between Stalin and Eden, 16 Dec 1941, in *DVP* XXIV, doc. no. 71.

33. Notes by hand on the Headquarters Intelligence Dept discussion on 6 Jan 1944, top secret, Kansallisarkisto (KA) War Archives T-19932/20 The Headquarters (PM), Foreign Office (Ulk 1), Correspondence 1941–1944. For the development in general, Henrik Meinander's total history, *Finland 1944* (2009), 33–42.

34. Intelligence report received by SOE, no. 22, 1 Mar 1944, The National Archives (TNA, Kew), HS 2/125. The information was acquired on 7 Feb 1944 from a non-Finnish source working for the Germans in Helsinki.

35. Report no. 230, 14 Feb 1944 (opinions of clerk Peter Wolontis, 3 Feb 1944); report no. 374, 6 Mar 1944 (Britta Karlsson's comments, 29 Jan 1944); report no. 397, 10 Mar 1944 (on left-wing opinions), KA, EK-Valpo I, folder 970.

36. A.M. Aleksandrov-Agentov, *Ot Kollontai do Gorbacheva* (1994), 36–37.

37. V. Tanner, *Suomen tie rauhaan 1943–44* (1952), 163–64; Tanner's diary, 6 Feb 1944; E. Tuomioja, *Häivähdys punaista* (2006), 300. On the spy aided by Wuolijoki, O. Manninen, *Kerttu Nuorteva* (2006).

38. W. Agrell, *Venona* (2003), 305, quoting the NKGB cypher telegram (19 Dec 1943), in which the Americans made an obvious typo or error in Kollontay's code name, as it should be Khozyaika.

39. Report no. 386, 7 Mar 1944, KA, Valpo, personal file no. A4091 (Atos Wirtanen).

40. Kollontay's telegram to Molotov, no. 2565, 11 Feb 1944. Many Stockholm cables are copied in the Foreign Policy Archive of the Russian Federation (AVP RF), f. 012 (Dekanozov's secretariat), op. 5, p. 67, d. 67, ll. 1–5, the original is in AVP RF, f. 059, op. 12, p. 28, d. 172, ll. 23–25; W.M. Carlgren, *Svensk utrikespolitik 1939–1945* (1973), 491–92.

41. V. Erofeyev, *Diplomat: kniga vospominanii* (2005), 71–72.

42. In her 1922 pamphlet *Soon (In 48 Years' Time)*, Kollontay sketched out the future. In 1970 there would no longer be smoking, or swearing, nor constant talk about sex, since sexuality would have been neutralized. See G. Carleton, *Sexual Revolution in Bolshevik Russia* 2005, 57. On Kollontay and her relationship to the North, see Y. Sørbye (ed.), *Revolusjon, kjærlighet, diplomati: Aleksandra Kollontaj og Norden* (2008).

43. H. Rautkallio, *Pohjoinen liitto: Wallenbergit ja Suomi* (2021), 340–41.

44. Kollontay's aforementioned telegram to Molotov, no. 2565, 11 Feb 1944 (her characterization of Wallenberg as the King of Sweden came earlier); T. Polvinen, *Teheranista Jaltaan* (1980), 15–16; Ryti' diary, 7 Feb 1944.

45. J. Suomi, *Mannerheim—Viimeinen kortti?* (2013), 39–40; Ryti's diary, 8 Feb 1944.

46. Tanner's diary, 11 Feb 1944.

47. Kollontay's cable to Molotov, 13 Feb 1944.

48. Molotov's cable to Kollontai, no. 146, 15 Feb 1944.

49. Kollontay's cable to Molotov, 15 Feb 1944.

50. Kollontay's cable to Molotov, 17 Feb 1944; Polvinen, *J.K. Paasikivi*, 353–55. Of course, Kollontay did not compare Paasikivi to a lover in her cable to Molotov, but in later conversation with the Swede Boheman.

51. Molotov's cable to Kollontay, 19 Feb 1944; Kollontay's cable to Molotov, 20 Feb 1944; Molotov's cable to Kollontay, no. 1842, 20 Feb 1944; Polvinen, *J.K. Paasikivi*, 356–357.

52. Kollontay's cable to Molotov, no. 3253, 22 Feb 1944; Paasikivi's report, 22 Feb 1944, Archives of the Ministry for Foreign Affairs (UM), 110 B 2.

53. Gusev's cable no. 435 (entry number), 11 Mar 1944, copies of London cables, AVP RF, f. 0135 (Finland's referentura), op. 28, papka 155, d. 8.

54. Report no. 397, 10 Mar 1944, Freedy Kekäläinen (based on informant S. Leskinen's account), KA EK-Valpo I, folder 970 (Reports 1944). The informant was former Communist Sakari Bernhard Liimatainen.

55. NKID's 1st European Department's overview of Anglo-American media reaction (M. Sergeyev and G. Shumilov), 26 Feb 1944, AVP RF, f. 012, op. 5, papka 66, d. 202, II. 1–9.

56. SOE memo "Suggested Mission in Finland," undated and signed with a mark; and cover letter, to D/S from A/CD, 24 Feb 1944; L/IS to D/S (detailing opinion of the War Office), 23 Feb 1944; from Magill to ADP 1 A/CD, Mar 1944, TNA, HS 2/125.

57. MI3 memo, "Factors affecting operations of the Red Army in Finland," Most Secret, 6 Mar 1944, TNA, WO 208/583.

58. SS's comment, after 7 Mar 1944, TNA, HS 2/125.

59. "Russia/Finland," to ADP 1 A/CD, 6 Mar 1944, TNA, HS 2/125.

60. F.J. Harbutt, *Yalta 1945* (2010), 189–190.

61. "Question of Finnish–Russian Armistice, Attitude of Marshal Mannerheim and G.H.Q.," Northern Department, no. 18, 28 Feb 1944, TNA, HS 2/125.

62. O. Manninen, *Miten Suomi valloitetaan* (2008), 196–97.

63. The researcher who has seen the document gave the archive reference number, but not the source's title, author or date. Judging from the archival signum (TsA FSB f. 4os, op. 2, d. 2, ll. 1040–41), this is in the series of reports to Stalin, Molotov and Beria and from late March or early April 1944. The information placed emphasis on Paasikivi's opinions. V.S. Khristoforov, "Finlyandiya dolzhna dobit'sya mira, no sokhranit' nezavisimost'," in V.S. Khristoforov (ed.), *Velikaya Otechestvennaya voina: 1944 god* (2014), 150, 183.

64. Memcon of Stalin and Ambassador Kerr's discussion, 28 Feb 1944, extract, copy, AVP RF, f. 06 (Molotov's secretariat), op. 6, papka 32, d. 374, II. 1–2. Cf. Polvinen, *Teheranista Jaltaan*, 20–21, and Evans, *Diplomatic Deceptions* (2011), 34–35.

65. Gusev's cable to Molotov, no. 434 vh, 11 Mar 1944, the copies of London cables.

66. NKGB radiogram no. 66, Valerian to Viktor (V.F. Razin in Stockholm to P.M. Fitin in Moscow), 22 Feb 1944, Venona cables. From 1995, the United States National Security Agency (NSA) has published Soviet intelligence cables decrypted by the Venona Project (1943–1980); W. Agrell, *Venona* (2003); J.E. Haynes, *Venona: Decoding Soviet Espionage in America* (1999).

67. Partly decrypted NKGB cipher telegram no. 578, 25 Feb 1944, Valerian (Razin) to the 8th dept, Venona.

68. Wuori was identified in the author's 2001 article, Rentola, "Stalin, Mannerheim ja Suomen rauhanehdot 1944." The matter has been researched further in Agrell, *Venona*, and thoroughly in Apunen and Wolff, *Pettureita ja patriootteja*.

69. Partly decrypted NKGB cipher telegram from Stockholm to Moscow, no. 568, 24 Feb 1944, Venona.

70. Agrell, *Venona*, 302–28. When the Soviet spy couple, the Petrovs, defected in Australia in 1954, they identified Stridsberg as KLARA. She admitted as much to the Swedish State Police, but played down her role. In 1954 the Venona cables were not yet available.

71. Mrs Petrov's statement concerning her past intelligence history, 15 May 1954, TNA, KV 2/3456 (the Petrovs' personal file).
72. Partly decrypted NKGB cipher telegram from Stockholm to Moscow, Valerian (Razin) to the 8th department, no. 658, 4 Mar 1944, Venona.
73. D.Z. Manuilsky (former Comintern Secretary) to Dekanozov, 30 Mar 1944, no. 144ss, with two intelligence cables on Finland attached, AVP RF, f. 012, op. 5, papka 66, d. 202, II. 18–20. The radio connection was established after a lengthy break, so complicated follow-up checks were needed. Manuilsky to Molotov, 20 Apr 1944, and his markings in it, attached with Inkeri Lehtinen's draft reply for O.V. Kuusinen, RGASPI, f. 82 (Molotov), op. 2, d. 1339, II. 61–62.
74. The main culprit in the case was the Swedish intellectual, Per Meurling; Agrell, *Venona*, 182–84.
75. Confronted with the fierce opposition of the Director of the FBI J. Edgar Hoover, Roosevelt eventually abandoned the idea. A. Weinstein and A. Vassiliev, *The Haunted Wood* (1999), 242–44.
76. Agrell, *Venona*, 307–12. In the 1990s, I talked with this Finnish newswoman.
77. Cable no. 4174 from the Soviet Embassy in Stockholm, 7 Mar 1944; Tanner's diary, 6 Mar 1944; EK-Valpo card on Lindström, Harald Carl Albert Richard, s. 1/9-94, citizen of Sweden, Member of Parliament.
78. Partly decrypted NKGB cipher telegram from Stockholm to Moscow, no. 658, 7 Mar 1944, Venona.
79. The envoy Gripenberg's cipher telegram to Foreign Minister Ramsay, 19 Mar 1944, UM 110 B 2.
80. Report from NKGB (Merkulov) to Stalin, Molotov and Beria, No. 962/M, 17 Mar 1944, doc. no. 50 in Khristoforov, SSSR—Finlyandiya (2018), 373–75; Wirtanen was a maverick politician, originally from the Åland Islands, a keen anti-fascist and anti-nationalist. He is considered to have been the model for the adventurer and wanderer Snufkin in the Moomin stories by Tove Jansson, whose lover Wirtanen was for a period. Early Moomin books deal with small figures campaigning against huge catastrophes; the first one, *The Moomins and the Great Flood*, was drafted during the Winter War, finalized in 1944 and published in 1945; H. Meinander, *Finland 1944* (2009), the chapter on May.
81. In May 1945, when the Chairman of the Allied Control Commission Andrei Zhdanov asked the Minister of the Interior Yrjö Leino, what did the communists think about the future of Finland, the latter began his response by saying that "the general aim is the incorporation of Finland in the Soviet Union," but for the moment the position of the eastern European states was sufficient. Memcon between Zhdanov and Leino, Hertta Kuusinen and Ville Pessi, 10 May 1945, RGASPI, f. 77, op. 3, d. 63, quoted p. 33.
82. On the negotiations in Moscow, see Apunen and Wolff, *Pettureita ja patrioot-teja*, 338–42; Polvinen, *J.K. Paasikivi*, 368–85.
83. Commentary by H. Rautkallio on Tanner's diaries from 1943–1944, in V. Tanner, *Unohdetut päiväkirjat 1943–1944* (H. Rautkallio ed.) (2011), 119, 123.
84. Cable no. 5609 from the Soviet Embassy in Stockholm, 27 Mar 1944, Stockholm's cable summaries.

85. Memcon of Molotov's discussion with the Finnish delegation, 27 Mar 1944, AVP RF, f. 06, op. 6, p. 52, d. 709, ll. 1–18. Molotov was better prepared for the next negotiations, and was able to point to German troops also much further south, in the regions of Kandalaksha and Kalevala.

86. Captain Georg Enckell's memo "Thoughts, which on this occasion concern the Moscow trip," 18 Apr 944, Sota-arkisto, Pk 1172/46.

87. Khristoforov, 'Finlyandiya dolzhna . . .' 158. The Soviets were listening, when G. Enckell answered the question of Antti Hackzell, leader of the Finnish negotiators in September.

88. Khristoforov, 'Finlyandiya dolzhna . . .' 152–53. The sources are from the FSB archive. The reports combine at least two different quarrels.

89. Memo from Molotov's second discussion with the Finnish delegation, 29 Mar 1944, 4pm, RGASPI, f. 558 (Stalin), op. 11, d. 389, ll. 9–21.

90. Memo by P. Orlov (NKID's 5th European Department) entitled "Spravka o zadolzhennosti Finlyandii SSHA," 27 Mar 1944, AVP RF, f. 012, op. 5, papka 66, d. 203, ll. 1–2.

91. Gusev's cable no. 604vh, 2 Apr 1944, Stockholm cable summaries.

92. Kerr to Vyshinsky, 11 Apr 1944, translation, AVP RF, f. 0135, op. 28, papka 155, d. 3, ll. 4–9; Polvinen, *Teheranista Jaltaan*, 30–31.

93. Cadogan's diary, 10 Mar 1944.

94. Aforementioned memcon of Molotov's discussion with the Finnish delegation, 27 Mar 1944.

95. Stalin's comment quoted in V. Mastny, *Russia's Road to the Cold War* (1979), 18.

96. "Sravnitel'naya tablitsa uslovii peremiriya s Finlyandiei," undated, early April 1944, AVP RF, f. 012, op. 5, papka 67, d. 67, ll. 36–39. The source refers to the northern shore of Saimaa, but it is clear from the places mentioned that the area under discussion was, in fact, the lake's southern side.

97. "Sravnitel'naya tablitsa mirnyh usloviyah s Finlyandiei," undated, April 1944, AVP RF, f. 012, op. 5, papka 67, d. 67, ll. 40–43. Discussion and analysis of the draft treaty in the main text is based on this source.

98. J. Leskinen and P. Silvast, *Suljettu aika* (2001), 39–49.

99. A. Rieber, *Stalin and the Struggle for Supremacy in Eurasia* (2015), 298–99.

100. G. Shumilov, "Spravka o lapuastsakh i agrariyakh," 3 Mar 1944, AVP RF, f. 012, op. 5, papka 66, d. 201, ll. 1–4.

101. "Sravnitel'naya tablitsa mirnyh usloviyah s Finlyandiei," undated, April 1944, AVP RF, f. 012, op. 5, papka 67, d. 67, ll. 44–48.

102. "Report on a fortnight in Finland," T.1637, 21 April 1944 (quote), NA OSS Document no. 76824; abridged report by the chargé d'affaires in Finland (Gullion), 9 Apr 1944, doc. no. 529, *FRUS* 1944: III.

103. Kotkin, *Magnetic Mountain*, passim.

104. Extract of V.P. Roshchin's memoirs, in Zoya Voskresenskaya, *Pod psevdonimom Irina* (1997), 317. Soviet intelligence background is suggested also by Scott's wish to talk with the Ingrians, and by his various explanations for Stalin's policies. E.g. he said that Stalin had to be so hard on Poland and Finland because he envisaged a new war between the USSR and the Western allies soon after the current one. Report from Governor Kaarlo Hillilä to Mannerheim, no. 219, 22 Mar 1944, KA PM Ulk1, T-19932/20. Hillilä had

received the Swedish journalist Åke Sandler (son of the former Foreign Minister) who had just met Scott in Stockholm.

105. Security police report no. 1413, 30 June 1944, KA, EK-Valpo I, folder 974. Security police chief Paavo Kastari noted that Jarke had "herself explained that she was madam Kollontay's good friend."

106. Security police report no. 999, 18 May 1944, KA, EK-Valpo I, folder 972. The incident took place on 14/15 May 1944; the guard was A. Veinil, but the report does not mention where he was keeping watch. The lieutenant left for Malmi (a northern district of Helsinki). In this folder there are a large number of reports about Estonians.

107. O. Manninen, *Miten Suomi valloitetaan*, 224–28.

108. Manninen, *Miten Suomi valloitetaan*, 197 (Stavka quote), 219–21; Polvinen, *Teheranista Jaltaan*, 65–66, based on Shtemenko's and Meretskov's memoirs.

109. Tanner's diary, 19–21 May 1944; Molotov's cabled reply, 20 May 1944, and other details in Khristoforov, "Finlyandiya dolzhna . . ." 154; Sven Grafström's diary, 26 May 1944; J. Seppinen, *Hitler, Stalin ja Suomi* (2009), 285–86.

110. S. Sebag Montefiore, *Stalin* (2003), 404–05; Mikoyan, *Tak bylo* (2000), 563.

111. Molotov to the American chargé d'affaires Hamilton, 10 Apr 1944, AVP RF, f. 0135, op. 28, papka 155, d. 2, l. 1.

112. Kerr to Vyshinsky, 20 Apr 1944, AVP RF, f. 0135, op. 28, papka 155, d. 3, ll. 1–2. Vyshinsky underlined and added a question mark to the term "instrument of surrender." The Soviets ran up against a similar conceptual problem in Japan, for that language did not have the characters for the phrase "unconditional surrender." Colonel-General Terenty F. Shtykov was the Soviet Union's representative charged with solving the issue. As the story goes, he exclaimed to the Japanese: "Draw a samurai committing harakiri!" See K. Ranta, *Arpi korvassa ja sydämessä* (2000), 184.

113. Kerr to Vyshinsky, 18 June 1944, AVP RF, f. 0135, op. 28, papka 155, d. 3, ll. 15–17.

114. D. Mayers, *The Ambassadors* (1995), 158.

115. Memcon of Vyshinsky's discussion with Harriman, 7 Jun 1944, AVP RF, f. 0135, op. 28, papka 155, d. 2, l. 1.

116. "Obrashchenie s Finlyandie," translation, NKID arrival no. 108, 12 June 1944 (shared with: Molotov, Vyshinsky, Dekanozov), AVP RF, f. 012, op. 5, papka 67, d. 67, ll. 52–69. The date of the original was 8 May 1944, so the document had been obtained hot off the press. For the final version, see "The Treatment of Finland," 10 May 1944, no. CAC-141b/PWC-161, Library of the Parliament of Finland, Microfilm no. 181, Post World War II Foreign Policy Planning: State Department Records of Harry A. Notter, 1939–1945 (Notter File), no. 1090-CAC-141, no. 1411-PWC-160 and no. 1411-PWC-161. Originals available at the US National Archives, RG 59 (State Department).

117. Inter-Divisional Committee on Finland, Minutes 28 and 30 Mar 1944, 6 and 8 May 1944, Notter File, no. 1173–78. Among the committee members was L. Randolph Higgs, who had held diplomatic positions in Helsinki and Stockholm. Committee papers were available, e.g. for Alger Hiss and Philip E. Mosley.

118. "Treatment of Finland," 31 Mar 1944, Notter File, no. 1090-CAC-141.

119. A Russian-born lady in Helsinki had perhaps heard Stalin's radio speech, since she espoused similar views: if the Finns weren't sheep, they "would start an insurrection against the current government, they would overthrow it, because it did not accept the Russians' lenient peace conditions." Security police report no. 1220, 12 June 1944, KA, EK-Valpo I, folder 973. Her comments were overheard on 30 May 1944.

120. "Treatment of Finland," aforementioned memo, 10 May 1944.

121. Memcon of Vyshinsky's discussion with Harriman, 19 June 1944, no. 509-V, dated 20 June 1944, AVP RF f. 0135, op. 28, p. 155, d. 5, ll. 5–6; Harriman to the State Department, 20 June 944, no. 2197, *Foreign Relations of the United States (FRUS)*, 1944: I, 609–10.

122. Vyshinsky's note in the translation of the memo from the British Embassy, dated 7 Mar 1944, entry number 1040/2e0, dated 2 June 1944, AVP RF, f. 0135, op. 28, p. 155, d. 3, ll. 12–14.

123. Memo on Finnish trade in the first post-war year, 2 June 1944, quoted in T. Androsova, "Kauppapolitiikka," *Haik* 2002: 2, 153–54. The memo is held in the Russian State Archive of Economics (RGAE).

124. Apunen and Wolff, *Pettureita ja patriootteja*, 351–52.

125. Kollontay's cable to Molotov, no. 1984, 19 June 1944.

126. Gripenberg's diary, 18 and 19 June 1944. To the Finnish envoy, Boheman said during the occupation that Russian behavior would be very correct with full discipline observed. Gripenberg's diary, 20 June 1944.

127. Kollontay's cable to Molotov, no. 2004, 21 June 1944. Lindh spoke to military attaché Nikolai Nikitushev.

128. Kollontay's cable to Molotov, no. 2010, 22 June 1944. "chto s nashey storony vozmozhno takzhe trebovanie kapitulyatsii. No bol'shego byt' ne mozhet"; Gripenberg's diary, 22 June 1944. According to a Swedish source it was Kollontay who spoke about the insignificance of the new government's form. Ehrensvärd's diary, 21 June 1944.

129. Kollontay's cable to Molotov, no. 2011, 22 June 1944.

130. Apunen and Wolff, *Pettureita ja patriootteja*, 354, 358–59.

131. Grafström's diary, 20 June 1944. This high UD official commented: "The Finns seem to have hopelessly resolved to make every conceivable mistake before this wretched war has come to an end."

132. Kollontay's cable to Molotov, no. 2018, 22 June 1944. "oni v sushchnosti otdayutsya v Vashi ruki."

133. Stalin's visitor logbook, 22 June 1944. Around midnight Stalin and Molotov were alone together for a moment in the Soviet leader's office, then other members of the Politburo arrived before, finally, the generals were invited inside.

134. Ehrensvärd's diary, 20 June 1944.

135. Molotov's cable no. 7556 to Stockholm, 23 June 1944, Stockholm cable summaries, AVP RF, f. 012, op. 5, papka 67, d. 67, ll. 14–15; the same text was in Kollontay's statement to Boheman, 23 June 1944, AVP RF, f. 06, op. 6, papka 52, d. 710, l. 10; Polvinen, *J.K. Paasikivi*, 396.

136. S.T. Bazarov, secretary of the Voroshilov commission, to M.G. Gribanov at Vyshinsky's secretariat, no. KV-264s, 26 June 1944, attachment "Dokument o bezogorochnoi kapitulatsii Finlyandii," AVP RF, f. 0135, op. 28, papka 155,

d. 8, ll. 8–20. The cover letter of the below-mentioned draft treaty (21 July 1944) includes the original date (15 Oct 1943) of the Voroshilov commission's document on Finland's surrender.

137. News item about Veikko Helle's speech, *Helsingin Sanomat*, 28 Apr 1997; Mauno Koivisto to his father, 7 July 1944, in M. Koivisto, *Koulussa ja sodassa* (1998), 176.

138. The British envoy to Sweden V. Mallet's cable from Stockholm, no. 746, 1 July 1944, quoted in Evans, *Diplomatic Deceptions*, 64 (footnote).

139. Grafström's diary, 10 Sept 1943 (stupidity), 20 June 1944, 17 July 1944.

140. Maximilian Axelson's poem "Vandring i Wermlands Elfdal och finnskogar" (1852), quoted by T. Jansson, *Rikssprängningen som kom av sig: Finsk-svenska gemenskapar efter 1809* (2009), 264–65.

141. Ehrensvärd's diary, 23 and 26 June 1944. The Swedish *yverborenhet* is a neologism coined by Olof Rudbeck in *Atlantica* (4 vols., 1677–1702), based on the Greek myth of the Hyperboreans (lit. beyond Boreas, the God of the North Wind), who are mentioned by Herodotus. Rudbeck explained that these were Scandinavians. *Yverborenhet* refers to a notion of Greater Swedishness imbued with ancient beliefs. See D. King, *Drömmen om Atlantis: Olof Rudbecks jakt på en försvunnen värld* (2006).

142. The main martyr of this group was Olof Palme, who was killed by the Finnish Reds in the battle of Tampere in 1918. His name was inherited by his nephew and later Prime Minister, born in 1927.

143. The Soviet government's memo to Kerr, 29 Mar 1944, quoted in a cable from the United States Embassy in Moscow to the State Department, 31 Mar 1944, *FRUS*, 1944: I, 588.

144. Harriman to the Secretary of State, no. 2296, 27 June 1944, *FRUS*, 1944: III.

145. Grafström's diary, 14 July 1944 (on the meeting between Kollontay and Beck-Friis).

146. Kerr to Vyshinsky, 28 June 1944, containing Dekanozov's instructions, AVP RF, f. 0135, op. 28, papka 155, d. 3, l. 17.

147. Apunen and Wolff, *Pettureita ja patriootteja*, 364–79; Grafström's diary, 13 and 14 July 1944; Tanner's diary, 24 July 1944.

148. E. Roman, *Hungary and the Victor Powers, 1945–1950* (1996), 21, based on Ernö Gerö's notes from Moscow in early December 1944.

149. K. Novikov and P. Orlov to Vyshinsky and Dekanozov, 10 July 1944, AVP RF, f. 012, op. 5, papka 67, d. 67, ll. 78–84.

150. Voroshilov to Molotov, 22 July 1944, no. KV-302s, attachment copy of surrender terms for Finland, AVP RF, f. 012, op. 5, papka 67, d. 67, ll. 86–96.

151. Voroshilov visited Stalin's office six times in both May and June 1944, but after 29 June he next stopped only on 25 August, when Finland's peace terms were apparently set in stone.

152. Molotov's secretary Podtserov to Dekanozov, 25 Sept 1944, attached with O.V. Kuusinen's undated memo, "O fashistkom kharaktere shyutskorovskoi organizatsii v Finlandii (spravka)," AVP RF, f. 012, op. 5, papka 66, d. 201, ll. 5–13.

153. J.L. Runeberg, *The Tales of Ensign Stål*, trans. C.W. Stork (1960). Translation above is translator's own. Using Runeberg's poem "Kulnev" as his proof, Paasikivi demonstrated to Zhdanov, in fall 1944, that the poet was no

revanchist. Zhdanov: "I know it. It is a splendid poem." Paasikivi's diary, 27 Nov 1944.

154. H. Kochanski, *The Eagle Unbowed* (2014), 384–433; A.F. Noskova, "1944 god," in V.S. Khristoforov (ed.), *Velikaya Otechestvennaya voina: 1944 god* (2014); N. Davies, *Rising '44* (2003), esp. 274–75, 314–15; W. Materski's and V. S. Parsadanova's articles in A.D. Rotfeld and A.V. Torkunov (eds.) *White Spots—Black Spots: Difficult Matters in Polish–Russian Relations, 1918–2008* (2015), 271–316; Stalin's visitor logbook, 21 July 1944 (in attendance were seventeen Poles who would form the pro-Soviet government, PKWN).

155. Harriman to Hopkins, 10 Sept 1944, quoted in F. Logevall, *Embers of War* (2012), 57–58.

156. Gilbert, *Winston S. Churchill, Vol. VII,* 652 (n. 1); Polvinen, *Teheranista Jaltaan,* 11–12. Apunen and Wolff, *Pettureita ja patriootteja,* 395, point out that Kymijoki has historically served as a geopolitical boundary for Sweden; a Russian military presence there could spur the Swedes to seek support from the West.

157. "Treatment of Finland" memo accepted by the Advisory Committee on Postwar Foreign Policy (PWC, headed by Secretary of State Hull), 18 July 1944, no. PWC-160a, Notter File, no. 1453-5.

158. P.J. Hynninen's memo, 17 Aug 1944, UMA 110 B 3.

159. Recent research has gone into this issue in greater detail, see Apunen and Wolff, *Pettureita ja patriootteja*; and J. Suomi, *Mannerheim—Viimeinen kortti?* A very good description and analysis in Tuomo Polvinen, *Between East and West: Finland in International Politics, 1944–1947* (1986).

160. Ehrensvärd's diary, 29 Aug 1944.

161. Khristoforov, "Finlyandiya dolzhna . . ." 158. The researcher does not mention any observations possibly made about Hackzell's pro-German background.

162. Eavesdropping information hereafter from Khristoforov's two articles: "Finlyandiya dolzhna . . ." and "Za kulisami." In neither does the author directly mention what methods were used to procure the intelligence, the records of which are now held in the Central Archive of the Federal Security Service.

163. The other members of the Soviets' delegation were Voroshilov, Zhdanov, Dekanozov and Litvinov, General Shtemenko and Rear-Admiral A.P. Aleksandrov. The latter was in a gulag 1938–40, and again under arrest from November 1941 to January 1942. After that he was appointed Chief of Staff of the Lake Ladoga Flotilla, before joining the control commission and rising to the rank of Chief of Staff of the Baltic Fleet. He died in a plane crash in 1946 at the age of forty-six.

164. Warner's memo, 8 Sept 1944, quoted in Evans, *Diplomatic Deceptions,* 86.

165. Eden's memo to the War Cabinet, 24 Sept 1944, *DBPO* I: IX, doc. no. 2.

166. Khristoforov, "Za kulisami," 36–37. The Marshal's comment reached Soviet ears when they eavesdropped on Carl Enckell's conversation with Generals Enckell, Walden and Heinrichs.

167. Suomi, *Mannerheim—Viimeinen kortti?*, 277–78. The Swedish envoy to Moscow, Söderblom, heard about the matter in early October, suggesting that the Soviets intentionally leaked information about it to Sweden.

168. Khristoforov, "Finlyandiya dolzhna," 174, 185 (fn. 81).
169. F.M. Shepherd to Eden, 6 Feb 1945, *DBPO* I: IX, doc. no. 5.
170. Francesco Guicciardini, *Cose fiorentine*: "Dio amatore delle repubbliche."
171. Conversation between Stalin and Eden, 15 Oct 1944, quoted in Gilbert, *Winston S. Churchill, Vol. VII*, 1022 (n. 1). Stalin met Mikołajczyk on 3 and 9 Aug 1944, in the midst of the Warsaw Uprising and just after the one in Lwów, the Polish equivalent of Vyborg.
172. F.J. Harbutt, *Yalta 1945* (2010), 332. Churchill's comments were made in May and December 1944, respectively.
173. In relation to population size, Finland's total losses (2.4%) are, of course, much (four times) greater than those suffered by Australia (0.6%).
174. V. Smetana, "Concessions or Conviction?" in *Imposing, Maintaining and Tearing Down the Iron Curtain* (eds. M. Kramer and V. Smetana) (2014), 66; N. Naimark, *Russians in Germany* (1995); A. Applebaum, *Iron Curtain* (2012), 31. An example of the consequences of the Red Army's abuses: in February 1945 Hungary ended up repealing its abortion ban and expanding its provision of orphan homes.
175. Michael Jonas, *Wipert von Blücher und Finnland* (2009), 421, 434.
176. G.A. Gripenberg's diary, 25 June 1946. This was told by Minister Uuno Takki, who was present in Moscow.
177. Jukka Lindstedt, *Kuolemaan tuomitut: Kuolemanrangaistukset Suomessa toisen maailmansodan aikana* (1999), 572–75.
178. Zhdanov's notes, summer 1940, quoted in E. Zubkova, *Pribaltika i Kreml 1940–1953* (2008), 122. Russian quote: "so svoim chortami."
179. F.M. Shepherd to Eden, 6 Feb 1945, *DBPO* I: IX, doc. no. 5.

III The Coup Threat (1948)

1. The concept of two camps is often called the Zhdanov Doctrine, after a speech he gave at the Cominform in September 1947. The idea, however, appeared in Zhdanov's statement after he had paid a visit to Sochi, where the Master was holidaying. See Y. Gorlizki and O. Khlevniuk, *Cold Peace: Stalin and the Soviet Ruling Circle, 1945–1953* (2004), 38.
2. Decision of the VKP(B) Politburo, 14 Oct 1947, *Vostochnaya Evropa v dokumentakh rossiiskikh arkhivov*, I, doc. no. 245. Finland is not mentioned separately, but the treaty initiative was kick-started there as well.
3. T. Polvinen, *J.K. Paasikivi: Valtiomiehen elämäntyö*, 4, 1944–1948 (1999), 418–32.
4. Excerpt from Abramov's report, March 1947, RGASPI, f. 495, op. 269, d. 28 (Paasikivi's personal file), part 1, l. 68. Passing comment on the outgoing diplomat in 1948, not knowing about his assessment on him, Paasikivi noted: "Abramov is generally a pleasant man." Paasikivi's diary, 12 Jan 1948.
5. Gladwyn Jebb's memo to Orme Sargent, 13 Jan 1948, from the *rezident* in London to the Komitet Informatsii (KI), in S.N. Lebedev et al. (eds.), *Ocherki istorii Rossiiskoi vneshnei razvedki*, pt. 5 (2003), 534–37; the idea of a separate Western Germany and a separate peace was expressed in A.A. Smirnov's memo to Molotov, 12 Mar 1948, in *SSSR i germansky vopros 1941–1949*, III, doc. no. 142.

6. Molotov's report from London, 16 Dec 1947, and Molotov to Stalin, 6 Jan 1948, in *SSSR i germansky vopros 1941–1949*, III, doc. nos. 126, 131; Stalin's visitor logbook, 3 Jan 1948, in *Na priyome u Stalina* (2008); J. Haslam, *Russia's Cold War* (2011), 92, 104–06; N. Petrov, *Po stsenariyu Stalina* (2011), 55.

7. P. Ruggenthaler, *The Concept of Neutrality in Stalin's Foreign Policy, 1945–1953* (2015), 128–29, 135, based on Soviet sources; J. Hanhimäki, *Scandinavia and the United States* (1997); J. Aunesluoma, *Britain, Sweden and the Cold War, 1945–54* (2003).

8. Kees Roterbloem, *Partner in Crime: The Life and Times of Andrei Zhdanov, 1896–1948* (2004), 318.

9. Stalin's visitor logbook, 5 Jan 1948. Savonenkov was in only for 25 minutes, six politburo members arrived 25 minutes before him and left 15 minutes after. Meetings on Germany in the logbook for 3 and 6 Jan 1948.

10. Memcon of Molotov's meeting with Petru Groza and Anna Pauker, 2 Feb 1948; Memcon of Stalin's meeting with the Hungarian delegation, 17 Feb 1948, in *Vostochnaya Evropa* I, doc. nos. 256 and 258.

11. M. Djilas, *Conversations with Stalin* (1962), 154–55. Djilas was received in Stalin's office on 16 Jan 1948. Molotov's note on Poland, before 4 Jan 1945, *Vostochnaya Evropa v dokumentakh rossiiskikh arkhivov*, I, doc. no. 36.

12. Minutes of the CPSU Politburo, item no. 66 (op = *osobaya papka*, special file), Question of the Ministry of Foreign Affairs, 13 Jan 1948, Instructions for the USSR's Envoy to Finland, RGASPI, f. 17, op. 162, d. 39, ll. 8, 11, quoted in Ruggenthaler, *The Concept of Neutrality*, 136–37. My thanks to Ruggenthaler for kindly sharing the original text in Russian.

13. Polvinen, *J.K. Paasikivi*, 433–37.

14. On 23 Jan 1948, Savonenkov listed six themes to Paasikivi for the forthcoming discussions in Moscow, but the defense agreement was not one of them.

15. Paasikivi's copy of this work contains a great deal of marginalia and can be found in the Turku University Library.

16. Paasikivi's diary, 23, 26 and 28 Jan 1948.

17. V. Zorin to Stalin, 23 Mar 1951, APRF, f. 3, op. 66, d. 573, l. 87. Published in Finnish in *Varjo Suomen yllä: Stalinin salaiset kansiot*, ed. by T. Vihavainen, O. Manninen, K. Rentola and S. Zhuravlyov (2017), p. 417; Savonenkov's replacement was V.Z. Lebedev, who had served for six years as ambassador to Poland.

18. Östen Undén's diary, 29 Jan 1948.

19. A. Kolpakidi, *Entsiklopediya sekretnykh sluzhb Rossii* (2004), 701–02; K. Degtyarev and A. Kolpakidi, *Vneshnyaya razvedka SSSR* (2009), 333–35, 150. These works use Sakharovsky's official CV. It was also the source of information about him in *Veterany vneshney razvedki Rossii* (1995, 133–35), but this work does not mention his assignment in Finland. Diplomatic stamp card no. 22/48, Sakharovsky, Alexandre, councilor (*neuvos*), Archives of the Ministry of Foreign Affairs (UMA), Register of Diplomats. His passport was stamped on 27 Jan 1948; on that occasion Sakharovsky was, perhaps, leaving. Thanks to Sami Heino for finding the card.

20. In addition to the above-mentioned reference works, see J. Haslam, *Near and Distant Neighbours: A New History of Soviet Intelligence* (2015), 176–17; V. Kirpichenko, *Razvedka: litsa i lichnosty* (1998), 271–72; Vladimir Antonov,

'"Sakharovsky umel ustroit' protivniku 'sladkaya zhizn',", *Nezavisimoe voennoe obozrenie*, 4 Sept 2009.

21. V.S. Antonov and E.P. Sharapov, "Aleksandr Mikhailovich Saharovsky," *Ocherki istorii Rossiiskoi vneshnei razvedki*, pt. 5 (2003), 454–55.

22. P. Sudoplatov et al., *Special Tasks* (1994), 337–39. I would be inclined to believe that the Prague operation mentioned in the memoirs took place, but some details are false and others exaggerated, as is often the case, to inflate the influence of the intelligence officer.

23. Polvinen, *J.K. Paasikivi*, 438; Paasikivi's diary, 12 Jan 1948.

24. Polvinen, *J.K. Paasikivi*, 438–39; and Paasikivi's diary, 11 Jan 1948.

25. Paasikivi's diary, 12 Jan 1948. Kekkonen improved reporting about his contacts to the President only from fall 1948; Rentola, *Niin kylmää että polttaa*, 70.

26. In return for Soviet support in the presidential elections, the "fellow" required an Agrarian League interior minister, so that Finland's security service could also be deployed against the West. Vilkuna (from Moscow) to Kekkonen, 25 Feb 1956, Urho Kekkonen's Archives 1/25, quoted in Rentola, *Niin kylmää että polttaa*, 408–10, KGB memo (I. Serov) on Finnish Security Police to CPSU Central Committee, 15 May 1956, published in Finnish in *Varjo Suomen yllä* (2017), 455–56. President Kekkonen was not able or willing to produce the measures wanted by the KGB.

27. Additional details in Rentola, "1948: Which Way Finland?" *Jahrbuch für Historische Kommunismusforschung* (1998), 99–124; Rentola, "Vesna 1948 goda: Kakoi put' vyberet Finlyandii?" *Severnaya Evropa*, vol. 4 (Nauka 2003), 61–89.

28. Hertta Kuusinen to Olavi Paavolainen, Sept (?) 1953, in H. Kuusinen, *Hamlet ystäväni* (1999), 166. I am grateful to Mikko Majander for drawing my attention to this.

29. Stenogramma no. 21, Hertta Kuusinen's informative talk at the VKP(b) Central Committee on the situation in Finland, 10 Jan 1948, RGASPI, f. 17, op. 128, d. 1159, esp. pp. 15, 21.

30. Yrjö Leino's notes, 1950s, National Archives of Finland, Yrjö Leino Archives, file 6.

31. Shepherd to Bevin, 7 Nov 1945, in T. Insall and P. Salmon (eds.), *Documents on British Policy Overseas (DBPO)*, ser. I, vol. IX (2011), doc. no. 38.

32. Zhdanov to Stalin and Molotov (shared with Beria, Malenkov, Mikoyan, Vyshinsky and Dekanozov), 20 Nov 1945, AVP RF, f. 07, op. 10, papka 34, d. 460, ll. 4–17, on Leino, ll. 12–14.

33. Savonenkov's memcon with Inkeri Lehtinen and Ville Pessi, 31 Jan 1948, a copy, RGASPI, f. 17, op. 128, d. 605, pp. 12, 15ff; Savonenkov's memcon with Pessi, 12 Feb 1948, AVP RF, f. 0135, op. 38, papka 170A, d. 6, pp. 23–25 (remark on Leino).

34. Raoul Palmgren, "Isänmaa ei ole kuin nainen . . .," presentation at an event of the Academic Socialist Society), *Vapaa Sana*, 18 Mar 1948.

35. Peter Kenez, *Hungary from the Nazis to the Soviets* (2006), 223–36. F. Nagy escaped to Switzerland and then to the United States. Answering to Hertta Kuusinen's talk on 10 Jan, Leonid S. Baranov of the Soviet CP Central Committee International Dept. hoped that soon the Finnish communists and even their timid ally Prime Minister Pekkala would be feared like the Hungarian comrades. Wavering elements would then find their side.

36. For more details, see N.V. Petrov, "Stalin i organy NKVD-MGB v sovyetizatsii stran Tsentral'noi i Vostochnoi Evropy. 1945–1953 gg." Unpublished PhD thesis, University of Amsterdam (2008), which was the basis for the book: N. Petrov, *Po stsenariyu Stalina* (2011).

37. In May 1950, Sakharovsky reported about 66 arrests in Romania in one night. Among the detainees were the leader of the National Liberal Party and a leader of the left-wing of that party, until recently an ally of the Communists. The report classified as war criminals: former ministers, leaders of the war industry, high-ranking military officers and those with contacts with British and American intelligence services. After this, Sakharovsky turned his attention to the Romanian Communist leadership, where he saw too large a proportion of Jews. Ultimately, Romania's Communist leader, Gheorghe Gheorghiu-Dej, had him summoned away. T. Volokitina et al., *Moskva i Vostochnaya Evropa* (2008), 456, 569–70, 634.

38. O. Jussila, *Suomen tie 1944–1948* (1990), 50–53, 59–60. The career histories now available show that Iron Tooth and the councilor were the same man, A.N. Fyodorov (b. 1905). He was to become a pharmacist, when, in 1929, he became instead an official at the security police OGPU in Leningrad, in leadership posts since 1937. During the Winter War he supervised the Baltic Fleet, and after that in Leningrad Smersh. In September 1944 he was sent to Helsinki with the control commission, and was promoted to colonel in July 1945. N.V. Petrov, *Kto rukovodil organami gosbezopasnosti 1941–1954: Spravochnik* (2010), 868.

39. Yrjö Leino's hastily prepared memo, written in pencil, untitled, unsigned and incomplete, KA, Archive of the Ministry of Finance, Jh 2.

40. J. Martelius, "'Leinon vankien' pidätys ja luovutus Neuvostoliittoon," in M. Simola and J. Salovaara (eds.) *Turvallisuuspoliisi 75 vuotta 1919–1994* (1994), 164–69; and P. Kauppala, *Paluu vankileirien teille* (2011), 38–44.

41. Abakumov to Beria, ? May 1945 (day not visible), no. 720/A, picture of document in *Smersh: Istoricheskie ocherki i arkhivnye dokumenty* (2010), 143.

42. Sergey Fyodorovich Kozhevnikov (1904–61) was a vice chief of Smersh (responsible for surveillance of the Leningrad front) in Moscow, 1943–46, then in the same post at the successor organization, the 3rd Main Directorate of the Ministry of State Security (MGB). Alongside his Smersh role, Kozhevnikov was in the control commission, first briefly in Romania, and from September 1944 to July 1946 in Finland. Towards the end of his Finnish posting, he seems to have spent most of his time in Moscow. N.V. Petrov, *Kto rukovodil*, 471–72.

43. V.S. Khristoforov, *Organy gosbezopasnosti SSSR v 1941–1955 gg.* (2011), 312–13. There were 23 names on Abakumov's list dated 10 Apr 1945, but 20 in the report.

44. Kristoforov, *Organy* (2011), 301–03; D. Larsson and I. Palmklint (eds.), *Raoul Wallenberg: Redovisning av den svensk–ryska arbetsgruppen* (2000), 47–50.

45. Zorin's reports, 19–21 Feb 1948, quoted in G.P. Murashko, "Fevral'skii krizis 1948 g.," *Novaya i noveishaya istoriya*, 1998, no. 1, 57–59; Haslam, *Russia's Cold War*, 99–100; Petrov, "Stalin i organy NKVD-MGB," 209–11.

46. In the morning of 10 March 1948, Masaryk was found dead in his pajamas beneath the bathroom window of his apartment in the Foreign Ministry's

palace. In the 1990s former MGB officer Yelizaveta Parshina came forward. She had served as an illegal (a sleeper agent posing as a normal citizen) in Czechoslovakia from 1945 to 1953 and claimed to know who the murderer was: Captain Mikhail Bondarenko. She asserted that the hit had been ordered by the MGB's Prague representative, General Mikhail Belkin, a SMERSH vice chief as Kozhevnikov. Parshina's allegations have not been verified. The Prosecutor General's Office of the Russian Federation responded to the Czech request for information in 2003 by declaring that the documents relating to the matter were still state secrets. Vitaly Yaroshevsky, "Gospodin Stalin, mne ostaetsya tol'ko umeret . . .," *Novaya Gazeta*, 16 Dec 2011.

47. When he had escaped from preventive detention in 1941, Leino drifted towards Helsinki and took up the leadership of the SKP's fragile illegal networks. In a strife, his rival Aimo Rikka asked: "Who then would expel me?" Leino responded: "Me." After becoming a minister in early 1945, Leino was prepared to push Mannerheim to resign, but Zhdanov did not give him permission.

48. The Swedish Minister of Foreign Affairs Östen Undén's diary, 15 June 1950 (detailing Amelie Posse's account of Beneš's visit on 19 Aug 1949). The President died on 3 Sept 1949.

49. Vasil Kolarov's notes from his discussion with Stalin and Molotov, 10 Feb 1940, L. Gibianski (ed.), "Na poroge pervogo raskola v 'sotsialisticheskom lagere,'" *Istoricheski arkhiv*, 1997, no. 4. The original document is held at Bulgaria's Central State Archives in Sofia.

50. N.S. Khrushchev, *Vremya, lyudi, vlast* 2 (1999), 345–46; S.M. Miner, *Between Churchill and Stalin* (1988), 65. The doormat remark was made by Sir Orme Sargent criticizing the behavior of the British envoy.

51. Chen Jian, *Mao's China and the Cold War* (2001), 52–53; Jung Chang and Jon Halliday, *Mao: The Unknown Story* (2005), 360–70.

52. K. Jeffery, *MI6* (2010), 684. Among his British colleagues, Bosley was known as "the Ferret," but to Kekkonen he was, for some reason, "the Picture Merchant" (*Taulukauppias*). So stated Lieutenant-General Urpo Levo—the President's long-term adjutant—to the author.

53. British envoy Scott to Hankey, 2 Mar 1948, in *DBPO* I: IX, doc. no. 117.

54. Scott to Bevin, 27 Feb 1948; Etherington-Smith to Hankey, 28 Feb 1948; and Scott to Hankey, 2 Mar 1948, in *DBPO* I: IX, docs. nos. 115–17.

55. Hankey's remark, recorded in Scott to Bevin, 24 Nov 1947, in *DBPO* I: IX, doc. no. 102. In these issues, Paasikivi did not use Eero A. Wuori, who had close relations to Russians in London, but rather Yrjö Kallinen, Social Democratic Minister of Defense and a pacifist without any Eastern connections. The British also received accurate information from Sweden, so much so that the Foreign Office, in London, occasionally informed its representatives in Helsinki what was going on in the city where they were stationed. Bevin to Scott, 16 Dec 1947, in *DBPO* I: IX, doc. no. 104.

56. Etherington-Smith's remark (on Cold War) in Chiefs of Staff meeting, 28 Feb 1948; Robin Hankey's remark (on the Finns' character), 3 Mar 1948, quoted in H.P. Evans, *Diplomatic Deceptions* (2011), 256–57, 265.

57. Etherington-Smith to Hankey, 28 Feb 1948; Bevin to Scott (on the UN), 5 Mar 1948, in *DBPO* I: IX, docs. nos. 116 and 119.

58. Joint Intelligence Committee, Minutes of the 17th Meeting, 27 Feb 1948, The National Archives (TNA), Records of the Cabinet Office (CAB) 159/3.

59. Etherington-Smith to Hankey, 28 Feb 1948, in *DBPO* I: IX, doc. no. 116.

60. Lord Pakenham, quoted in J. Hanhimäki, *Scandinavia and the United States* (1997), 26–27. Although Chaplin's film went by a different name, it was seen as a retelling of the legend of Bluebeard. Indeed, the film's Finnish title was eponymous with the myth: *Ritari Siniparta* (The Knight Bluebeard).

61. Memcon, Andrei V. Zotov with Ville Pessi, 3 Mar 1948, a copy, RGASPI, f. 17, op. 128, d. 605, pp. 21–23.

62. Circular letter to the groups about tasks between 7 and 15 March, not dated, 4 or 5 March 1948, penciled No. 1, Kansan arkisto, SKP archives, Organization sector papers (Järj) Fb 4.

63. Paasikivi's diary, 4 and 5 Mar 1948; Warren's telegram, 6 Mar 1948, FRUS 1948: IV, pp. 770ff. Istomin's role as the Valpo supervisor was discovered in the 1950s espionage cases against former Red Valpo officials. Esko Vokkulainen's interrogation minutes, 15 June 1956, The Finnish Security Police archives (Supo), Personal file no. 5258a.

64. Yrjö Leino, *Kommunisti sisäministerinä* (printed in 1958, but distribution not allowed), 249–54.

65. Gromyko to Stalin about measures against Finland, 21 Nov 1949, with attachment no. 8, "Realization plan for the materials held by the Committee of Information about the illegal organization of Finnish reactionary elements," APRF, f. 3, op. 66, d. 640, pp. 51–54, 77–79.

66. Magill's report to the heads of military intelligence, 1 Feb 1948, quoted in Evans, *Diplomatic Deceptions*, 262. The same specious reasoning—that the general was perhaps untrustworthy and acting on Communists' instructions— was still prevalent in Etherington-Smith's remark included in Scott's report to Bevin, 9 Apr 1948, in *DBPO* I: IX, doc. no. 133.

67. Unless another source is mentioned, the quotations in this subsection originate from Yrjö Leino's notes (c. 1951–58), KA, Yrjö Leino's Archive, folders 4–6. Papers donated by Yrjö's son Olle Leino mostly lack titles and page numbers.

68. Hertta Kuusinen's farewell letter to Yrjö Leino, 22 Aug 1948 and the twelfth letter, in Olle Leino (ed.), *Vielä yksi kirje* (1990), 195, 168.

69. Yugoslavian Communist Milovan Djilas was struck by the same thought: "This was not that majestic Stalin of the photographs or the newsreels—with the stiff, deliberate gait and posture [...] He was of very small stature and ungainly build [...] He had quite a large paunch, and his hair was sparse [...] Not even his moustache was thick or firm [...] In Stalin's Politburo there was hardly anyone taller than himself." Djilas, *Conversations with Stalin*, 60–61, 108.

70. The occasion is described more tactfully in Leino's memoirs, *Kommunisti sisäministerinä* (1958), 142.

71. When Lithuania's Foreign Minister visited Moscow in 1940, Stalin escorted him along the Kremlin's corridors late one evening and commented: "Ivan the Terrible was in the habit of walking here." A few years later Stalin commissioned Soviet director Sergei Eisenstein to make a film about the notorious Russian ruler, see V. Zubok and C. Pleshakov, *Inside the Kremlin's Cold War* (1996), 16.

72. British memo of negotiations at the Kremlin, 18 Oct 1944, quoted in F.J. Harbutt, *Yalta 1945* (2010), xix–xx.

73. Paasikivi's diary, 14/15 Apr 1946. This was said by Leino in a government discussion about how to develop good relations with the Soviets.

74. Other SKP leaders thought that Leino still had connections and that he was perhaps in a position to clarify the advice received on Valpo-related matters. During the 1948 Treaty negotiations, the Soviets got their hands on Finnish government's materials. It is not proven that Leino handed them over, but he is the most likely candidate. His persistent links are also hinted at by his claim (see below) that an authority in Moscow tried to get him to take charge of the SKP in the aftermath of the 1948 Treaty.

75. "Can you really not see a difference in the way that someone like Urho Kaleva [Kekkonen] or some of our friends enjoy it [a drink]?" Hertta Kuusinen to Yrjö Leino, fifth letter, *Vielä yksi kirje*, 135. "Friend" was often used in high communist circles to mean "Soviet."

76. "To women too they [the gods] have given a gluttonous and voracious animal which, if denied its food in due season, becomes frenzied and can brook no delay ...," M. de Montaigne, *Essays*, III, 43, https://www.earlymoderntexts.com/assets/pdfs/montaigne1588book3.pdf (accessed 14 Dec 2022).

77. A.V. Zotov on meeting with Aili Mäkinen, 10 Mar 1948, a copy, RGASPI, f. 17, op. 128, d. 605, pp. 17–20.

78. SKP Circular to the groups (Ryhmille!), no. 3, Kansan Arkisto, SKP Järj Fb4.

79. The best account is in vol. 4 of the Paasikivi biography by Tuomo Polvinen (1997).

80. Molotov's meeting with Mauno Pekkala, 26 Mar 1948, interpreted and written down by Mikhail Kotov, AVP RF, f. 06, op. 10, papka 70, d. 986, pp. 8–11.

81. In fall 1947 the Soviet Union gave up on its aim of redefining in Eastern European treaties the potential attacker in more general terms, without explicit mention of Germany. From a political standpoint, labeling Germany as the attacker was more straightforward, both in the countries concerned and internationally. Moreover, by 1948, "Germany and its allies" also encapsulated the West, which was seen as forging an alliance with the western part of Germany.

82. A.I. Kolpakidi, *Entsiklopedia voennoy razvedki Rossii* (2004), 18; and A. Dienko, *Razvedka i kontrrazvedka v litsakh* (2002), 567.

83. J.L. Gaddis, *George F. Kennan: An American Life* (2011), 307.

84. Komitet Informatsii (P. Fedotov and K. Rodionov) to Stalin, Molotov, Vyshinsky and Zorin, 18 Mar 1948, in *Ocherki istorii Rossiiskoi vneshnei razvedki*, pt. 5, 541–42.

85. Documents from all these sources have been published in ibid.

86. See, e.g., Grafström's diary, 16–17 Mar and 13 Apr 1948.

87. Abramov to Zorin, 29 Mar 1948, quoted in M. Korobochkin, "Soviet Views on Sweden's Neutrality and Foreign Policy, 1945–50," in H. Carlbäck et al. (eds.), *Peaceful Coexistence?* (2010), 102–04. See also Rupasov and Samuelson, *Sovetsko-shvedskie otnosheniya* (2014), 90–98.

88. Chernyshev to Molotov, 25 May 1948, quoted and analyzed in Korobochkin, "Soviet Views on Sweden's Neutrality and Foreign Policy, 1945–50," 104–06.

89. Deputy Minister for Foreign Affairs A. Smirnov's memo to Molotov, 12 Mar 1948, in *SSSR i germansky vopros* III, doc. no. 142.

90. Memcon of Molotov's discussion with Ambassador Walter Bedell Smith, 4 May 1948, in *SSSR i germansky vopros* III, doc. no. 158.

91. On 5 Mar 1948 the United States National Security Council authorized the CIA to make clandestine arms deliveries to Italy, among other acts of interference, and George Kennan suggested banning the Communist Party in order to provoke a civil war. W.D. Miscamble, *George F. Kennan* (1992), 103.

92. Kostylev's cipher cable to Moscow, 24 Mar 1948, and Molotov's reply cable to Kostylev, 26 Mar 1948, quoted in E. Aga-Rossi and V. Zaslavsky, *Stalin and Togliatti* (2011), 254–56, the Italian original *Togliatti e Stalin* (1997), 239–41. The cables were first published in papers and articles by Mikhail Narinsky in 1995 and 1998; they come from the same part of the Russian Presidential Archives APRF (f. 3, op. 3) as the arrest plan paper for Finland quoted above.

93. See H.A. Richter, *Griechenland 1940–1950* (2012).

94. Paasikivi had read this maxim in Meinecke, *Die Idee der Staatsräson* (1925). Boccalini's original Italian: "... ma solamente al suo interesse, ch'è il vero Tiranno dell'anime de'Tiranni ..." (1677).

95. Rentola, *Niin kylmää että polttaa*, 45–46. The conversation in 1946 comes from Soviet records. Stalin's words at the 1948 dinner are from Leino's report at the SKDL board minutes, 13 Apr 1948, Kansan arkisto, SKDL Hall Cd1. In attendance on the hosts' side were the ten Politburo members, high-ranking diplomats and the leadership from different military branches. The Russified version of the interpreter's name was Ivan Petrovich Pakkonen. Stalin's dinner guest list, 7 Apr 1948, RGASPI, f. 558, op. 11, d. 389, s. 105.

96. Kollontay to Stalin, 8 Apr 1948, RGASPI, f. 558, op. 11.

97. Scott to Bevin, 9 Apr 1948, in *DBPO* I: IX, doc. no. 133; Paasikivi's truncated diary entry, 7 Apr 1948; and the attachment in Scott's letter to Bevin, 4 Apr 1948, in *DBPO* I: IX, doc. no. 140.

98. Scott to Hankey, 2 Mar 948; Scott to Bevin, 27 Feb 1948, in *DBPO* I: IX, doc. nos. 117, 115 ("Uncle Charles").

99. Bevin's remark, Cabinet meeting, 8 Apr 1948; Hankey's remark, Russia Committee meeting, 29 Apr 1948, quoted in Evans, *Diplomatic Deceptions*, 266–67.

100. Scott to Bevin, 5 Apr 1948 (with attachments) and 27 Apr 1948, in *DBPO* I: IX, docs. nos. 130, 137.

101. SKP Circular to the groups, nos. 5 and 6 (probably 13 or 14 Apr 1948), Kansan arkisto SKP Järj Fb4; speech by Tyyne Tuominen at a metalworkers' meeting at Vallila people's house in Helsinki, 11 Apr 1948, RGASPI, f. 17, op. 128, d. 600, pp. 107–15. She cited Czechoslovakia, where hundreds of thousands were on the move, but only shock troops acted.

102. SKP Circulars to the groups, no. 7, probably 17 Apr 1948; no. 8 (p. 3 missing); no. 9, possibly 28 April 1948 (quote), Kansan arkisto, SKP Järj Fb 4.

103. Journalist Drew Pearson heard this from Ambassador Sumner Welles, see Drew Pearson, *Diaries 1939–1959* (Tyler Abell ed.) (1974), 134, quoted in J. Lukacs, *The Legacy of the Second World War* (2010), 166. While this is a third- or fourth-hand source, I would be inclined to trust it, even if the phrasing should not be taken as verbatim.

104. Kolarov's aforementioned notes, 10 Feb 1948, *Istoricheski arkhiv*, 1997, no. 4, 101.

105. Haslam, *Russia's Cold War*, 104.

106. V. Dimitrov, *Stalin's Cold War* (2008), 176–77. The Bulgarian researcher's analysis is based on Kolarov's notes.

107. See E. Zubkova, *Poslevoennoe sovetskoe obshchestvo* (2006).

108. Haslam, *Russia's Cold War*, 94–95.

109. Alfred J. Rieber, *Stalin and the Struggle for Supremacy in Eurasia* (2015), 283 and 313.

110. SKP circular, no title, after 1 May 1948, RGASPI, f. 17, op. 128, d. 600, pp. 81–83 (first quote); SKP circular on the preconditions of election victory, marked by red pencil, no. 11 (second quote), SKP Järj Fb 4.

111. Zhdanov's report to Stalin, RGASPI, f. 77, op. 3, d. 88, final version pp. 49–55, draft to Stalin and Molotov, pp. 40–47. The report is not dated. In the final version the meeting is set on 13 April, but in the draft on 13 May. The latter seems to be correct. In a later report the meeting is set in May, Spravka to Suslov on the SKP, probably by Zhdanov's secretary and interpreter V.P. Teryoshkin, Aug 1948, RGASPI, f. 575, op. 1, d. 66, here p. 24. On 13 April, Pessi was present in the Diet session, and he took part in various meetings every day between 12 and 18 April. On the other hand, he was present in the Diet on 11 May, but absent on 13 and 14 May, and present again on 19 May. His participation in the SKP leadership meetings cannot be checked for this period, because all minutes of the highest bodies are lacking from 3 May for three weeks, probably to hide the preparations of the Moscow visit and the discussion about Pessi's report after his return.

112. Leino's notes, KA, Yrjö Leino's Archive, folder 6.

113. J. Rainer, *Imre Nagy: A Biography* (2009), 58; Beria's letter to Malenkov, 1 July 1953, doc. no. 1.3, in O.B. Mozokhin (ed.), *Politbiuro i delo Beria: Sbornik dokumentov* (2012).

114. Leino's notes, KA, Yrjö Leino's Archive, folder 6. The second sounding out of Leino by the Soviets was mentioned by the Minister of Internal Affairs, Sergei Kruglov, in July 1953 at a plenum of the Central Committee of the Communist Party of the Soviet Union (CPSU) as one of the recent sins of Beria. The case officer was the Helsinki *rezident* Mikhail Kotov. The CPSU CC minutes, *Der Fall Berija* (1993), 190–93.

115. Report from the British Embassy in Helsinki to the Foreign Office's Intelligence Research Department (IRD), "Analysis of Finnish Communist Party tactics and propaganda trends for the fortnight ending 1.6.1948," 2 June 1948, TNA, FO 1110/65. The report does not make clear whether Pekkala told his motives to the British directly, or to someone else, who passed the information.

116. Ibid.

117. Hertta Kuusinen to O.V. Kuusinen, 28 May 1948, Kansan arkisto, Hertta Kuusinen Papers.

118. Roterbloem, *Partner in Crime*, 325–30. Molotov was compelled to support his wife Polina's expulsion from the party in December 1948. He initially left his vote blank, but then retracted it and informed Stalin that he supported her removal. Polina Zhemchuzhina was subsequently arrested and sentenced to five years in a labor camp. She was released by Beria upon Stalin's death.

119. Gorlizki and Khlevniuk, *Cold Peace*, 38–43; A. Volynets, *Zhdanov* (2013), 561–85.

120. Gorlizki and Khlevniuk, *Cold Peace*, 79–89.

121. Kolpakidi and Sever, *Spetssluzhby rossiyskoy imperii unikalnaya entsiklopediya* (2010); a more recent compendium (Alekseyev, Kolpakidi and Kochik, *Entsiklopediya voennoi razvedki 1918–1945 gg.* [2012]), contains most of the same information, but does not mention the arrest.

122. Memoirs by Kalle Ranta, *Arpi korvassa ja sydämessä* (2000), 263. Ranta and Pakkanen served together as political officers during the Continuation War. Ranta knew that Fyodorov was a colonel in the KGB.

123. Petrov, *Kto rukovodil*, 868. Since Fyodorov's expulsion occurred during a period of de-Stalinization, it could well be connected to his actions as a SMERSH interrogator during the war.

124. Petrov, *Kto rukovodil*, 471–72.

125. Now there is an extensive biography by A.K. Sorokin, *"Prakticheskii rabotnik" Georgi Malenkov* (2021).

126. Colonel B.A. Lyudvigov's interrogation minutes, 8 July 1953, doc. no. 1.22 (p. 67); summary of the interrogations of B.A. Lyudvigov, P.A. Shariya and G.A. Ordyntsev (for the indictment), before 16 June 1954, doc. no. 1.165 (pp. 658–59); Beria's interrogation minutes, 10 July 1953, doc. no. 1.24 (p. 76), in *Politbiuro i delo Beria*.

127. W.D. Miscamble, *George F. Kennan and the Making of American Foreign Policy 1947–50* (1992).

128. The leaders of this tendency (Unto Varjonen, Väinö Leskinen and others) had been active in the Finnish Brothers-in-Arms Association, founded in August 1940 by the right wing, the military and the Social Democrats. It was abolished under Soviet pressure in February 1945. In the SDP this energetic young tendency allied with the old-style Tannerite wing to prevent any SDP alliance with the Communists.

129. M. Majander, *Pohjoismaa vai kansandemokratia?* (2004), 104.

130. Shepherd to Attlee, 19 Mar 1947, quoted in Evans, *Diplomatic Deceptions*, 223. The amount of troops was no exaggeration. In the first Soviet post-Winter War attack plan on Finland, written by hand in September 1940, 46 divisions were allotted to the project, added with many special units (of artillery, tanks etc.). Finland was able to mobilize 14 or 15 divisions.

131. A scholar of Imperial Russia has compared Finland's post-war position in its relations with the Soviet Union to Serbia's position in its relations with Austria-Hungary prior to the First World War. He qualifies this with a reminder that Finland's status adjustment required two wars and the fact that no significant ethnic Finnish minority was left under Soviet rule. D. Lieven, *Towards the Flame* (2015), 319.

132. The original Great Hate (*isoviha*) was the Russian occupation of Finland in 1709–21, during which countless atrocities were committed.

133. M. Flinckenberg-Glushkoff, *Pietarilainen polkuhevonen* (2013), 304–06. The memorialist's Finnish father had been killed in the war, and she lived with her mother in a larger family. The central figure was her grandfather, Deda-pappa, also called Kirill Butusoff. Granny Malja's brother, Max London, was one of Leino's prisoners arrested and abducted to the Soviet Union.

IV Pendulum Motions (1950–51)

1. "Spravka o reaktsionnoi deyatelnosti prezidenta Paasikivi," anon., handwritten date 5 Nov 1949, with attachments, RGASPI, f. 495, op. 269, d. 28 (1), ll. 39–59.
2. Paasikivi's diary, 20 Aug 1948.
3. V. Kuznetsov to Stalin, 10 Oct 1949, no. 2806-s, APRF, f. 3, op. 66, d. 640, ll. 42–44.
4. A. Gromyko to Stalin, no. 424 gi, 21 Nov 1949, APRF, f. 3, op. 66, d. 640, ll. 51–54. Distributed to Politburo members and Envoy Savonenkov.
5. Attachment no. 8 to Gromyko's letter to Stalin, 21 Nov 1949, APRF, f. 3, op. 66, d. 640, ll. 77–79.
6. Of course, the campaign was directed from the top. Molotov to Stalin, 11 Dec 1949, APRF, f. 3, op. 66, d. 640, l. 80. This was about an article by B. Leontyev, published in *Pravda* on 13 December.
7. V. Grigoryan to Stalin, 13 Aug 1949, attached with a message from Ville Pessi, not dated, but on 1 Aug 1949 (quote); Chiffer cable draft, Filippov [Stalin] to Pessi, APRF, f. 3, op. 66, d. 640, ll. 38–41.
8. V. Grigoryan to Stalin, 11 Oct 1949, attached with chiffer cable draft to Savonenkov (Helsinki), APRF, f. 3, op. 66, d. 640, ll. 49–50. The communists were able to prevent this kind of law, which should have passed by a 5/6 majority in the Parliament.
9. Excerpt from Abramov's report, March 1947, RGASPI, f. 495, op. 269, d. 28 (1), l. 68.
10. Paasikivi's diary, 9 Jan 1950.
11. Vyshinsky to Molotov, attached with a proposal to "Instance" (*Instantsiya*, meaning Stalin), 9 Feb 1950, RGASPI, f. 82, op. 2, d. 1340, ll. 1–3. As for the positions of those who should have remained former people, Vyshinsky mentioned Bruno Salmiala and Vilho Helanen of the pro-German IKL party, as well as four Social Democrats—Jorma Tuominen, Aarre Simonen, Unto Varjonen and Väinö Leskinen—who had been active in the Brothers-in-Arms Association. A much more comprehensive list can be found in Gromyko's memo, 15 Dec 1949, RGASPI, f. 82, op. 2, d. 1339, ll. 125–47. Both documents were still partially classified when the author saw them.
12. Vyshinsky's memo on a discussion with Reinhold Svento, 6 Mar 1950, APRF, 3, op. 66, d. 618, ll. 13–14.
13. Paasikivi's diary, 19 Mar 1950.
14. Envoy Savonenkov's cipher cable to Vyshinsky, nos. 6171 and 6159, 28 Feb 1950, RGASPI, f. 558 (Stalin), op. 11, d. 389, ll. 108–09.
15. Envoy Savonenkov's cipher cable to Vyshinsky, nos. 6823–6827, 6 Mar 1950, RGASPI, f. 558, op. 11, d. 389, ll. 111–15.
16. Outgoing cipher cable from the 3rd sector of the CPSU's foreign policy commission no. 104, 8 Mar 1950, Filippov to comrades Pessi and Kuusinen, RGASPI, f. 558, op. 11, d. 389, l. 116.
17. For a selection of Filippov's cables to China in 1950, see digitalarchive.wilsoncenter.org (accessed 16 Dec 2022).
18. Outgoing cipher cable of the 3rd sector of the CPSU's foreign policy commission no. 105, 8 Mar 1950, Filippov to Pessi, RGASPI, f. 558, op. 11, d. 389,

l. 118. Pessi's question was wired on 3 Mar 1950 (l. 110 in the same folder). On the SAK: Hertta Kuusinen to Stalin, 25 Apr 1950; Grigoryan to Stalin, 7 May 1950; draft cable from Filippov to Pessi, Kuusinen and Murto, RGASPI, f. 82, op. 2, d. 1344, ll. 51–57. Yrjö Murto was pushing for the Communists to detach themselves from the SAK, so Hertta Kuusinen requested that Stalin bring him into line. In Moscow, the matter was passed down for lower-ranking comrades.

19. Memcon Savonenkov—Gartz, 22 Mar 1950, APRF, f. 3, op. 66, d. 618, ll. 15–16.

20. J. Haslam, *Russia's Cold War* (2011), 119–28.

21. This Korean War connection was first introduced in Rentola, *Niin kylmää että polttaa* (1997), 120–46. It was then approved by the dean of Finnish twentieth-century historians, Tuomo Polvinen, in his biography, *J.K. Paasikivi*, vol. 5, 1948–56 (2003), 85.

22. Minister of Foreign Trade Menshikov to Molotov, 8 Apr, 13 Apr and 20 Apr 1950 (on the ten-year purchasing plan); Minister of Power Plants D. Zhimerin to Molotov, 19 Apr 1950; Memo on war reparations by A. Lavrentyev (Ministry of Foreign Trade), 17 Apr 1950, with statistical attachments, RGASPI, f. 82, op. 2, d. 1340, ll. 39–56, 72–98.

23. Minister of Shipbuilding V. Malyshev to Molotov, 18 Apr 1950, including attachment by deputy minister B. Chilikin about ship types, RGASPI, f. 82, op. 2, d. 1340, ll. 57–71.

24. A. Vasilevsky and S. Chemenko (General Staff) to Molotov, 21 Apr 1950, attached "Spravka po vooruzhennym silam Finlyandii," M. Zaharov, 21 Apr 1950, RGASPI, f. 82, op. 2, d. 1340, ll. 99–120.

25. Ehrensvärd's diary, 3 Oct 1946.

26. Memcon, G.M. Savonenkov–Åke Gartz, 12 May 1950, APRF, f. 3, op. 66, d. 618, ll. 17–18.

27. Molotov and Mikoyan to Stalin, 28 Apr 1950, RGASPI, f. 82, op. 2, d. 1340, ll. 138–44.

28. Kekkonen's memo, three parts, no title, no date (June 1950), Urho Kekkonen Archives 21/30, often quoted in Finnish scholarly literature; Memo by Gromyko and Sykiäinen (the interpreter) to comrade Stalin on a discussion with Finland's Prime Minister and Interior Minister Kekkonen, 13 June 1950, RGASPI, f. 558, op. 11, d. 389, ll. 120–25.

29. Gripenberg's diary, 29 Jun 1950, quoted by Polvinen, *J.K. Paasikivi*, vol. 5, 90. Savonenkov was the last Soviet official to assure Mannerheim (in 1946) that he would not be touched.

30. *Izvestia*, 15 June 1950.

31. Kekkonen's memo; Report by Toivo Kujala, SKP political section minutes, 16 June 1950, Kansan arkisto SKP Cd4.

32. Filippov to the Soviet ambassador to Prague and on to Gottwald, 27 Aug 1950, published in its entirety in N. V. Petrov, "Stalin i organy NKVD-MGB v sovyetizatsii stran Tsentral'noi i Vostochnoi Evropy. 1945–1953 gg." Unpublished PhD thesis, University of Amsterdam (2008), 192–93.

33. D. Volkogonov, *Sem vozhdei* (1995), 196; V. Zubok and C. Pleshakov, *Inside the Kremlin's Cold War* (1996), 64–71.

34. The conference was convened from 9 to 12 Jan 1951. Y. Gorlizki and O. Khlevniuk, *Cold Peace* (2004), 98–101; O. Khlevniuk, *Stalin* (2015), 297–98; M. Kramer, "Stalin, Soviet Policy and the Consolidation" (2009), 87–99; M. Kramer, "Stalin, the Split with Yugoslavia, and Soviet-East European Efforts to Reassert Control" (2014), 105–11. East Germans were not invited, but they did participate in the pilot training. P. Ruggenthaler, *Stalins großer Bluff* (2007), 34.

35. The chapter written by Vesa Tynkkynen and Petteri Jouko in the centenary history of the Finnish defense forces, *Suomen puolustusvoimat 100 vuotta*, eds. V. Tynkkynen and Mikko Karjalainen (2018), 142–44. On informed civilians see the discussion between Kekkonen and Paasikivi in the latter's diary, 9 Jan 1952.

36. V. Zorin to Molotov, 19 Apr 1951, including attached memo "O proiskah anglo-amerikantsev v Finlyandii," RGASPI, f. 82, op. 2, d. 1340, ll. 176–81.

37. A. Agosti, *Palmiro Togliatti* (1996), 384–88. Togliatti turned down Stalin's offer, certainly understanding that it would mean tighter control.

38. Pessi to dear comrade Stalin, 26 Apr 1951, and its Russian translation, on which Stalin made marginalia, RGASPI, f. 558, op. 11, d. 389, ll. 128–43; V. Grigoryan (CPSU's Foreign Policy Commission) to Stalin, 17 Apr 1951, attached with the revised draft instructions for the SKP, RGASPI, f. 82, op. 2, d. 1345, ll. 8–15; and Stalin's visitor logbook, 25 Apr 1951. Pessi had visited Stalin's office once, in October 1945, not as party leader but as a member of a larger cultural and political delegation.

39. K. Rentola, "Ikke blot for et par rublers skyld," in Morten Thing (ed.) *Guldet fra Moskva* (2001), and the attached statistics, pp. 291–92, based on RGANI fond 89 materials. The book is available in Russian as *Zoloto iz Moskvy* (2017).

40. Stalin's visitor logbook, 26 Apr 1951; Rudolf Sykiäinen, "Miksi ujostella?," *Karjalan Sanomat* (Petrozavodsk), 27 Dec 1995; SKP (V. Pessi) to the Central Committee of the CPSU(B) (invitation for O. Kuusinen), 20 Feb 1951; V. Grigoryan to Stalin, 3 Mar and 18 Apr 1951, attached a draft cable to the SKP, RGASPI, f. 82, op. 2, d. 1345, ll. 6–8, 24–26. Sykiäinen probably exaggerated, since Kuusinen had worked mainly in Moscow for years even while also being the head of the Karelian republic.

41. Lebedev was particularly active in spring 1948 in the Soviets' ideological campaign for the Eastern camp. He criticized the Polish Communists for appearing ashamed when they were forced to defend their policy of increased cooperation with the Soviet Union. The party had two dominant lines, neither of which was quite good enough for the Soviets. In Gomułka's group the spirit of Polish nobility (*shlyakhetskogo dukha*) and anti-Soviet mindset prevailed, while Minc's group of former emigrants was certainly pro-Moscow, but consisted predominantly of Jews. T. Volokitina et al., *Moskva i Vostochnaya Evropa* (2008), 57, 509–10.

42. Under the code name BLOK, Lebedev served the GRU at the Soviet Embassy in Belgrade, 1940–41. Alekseyev et al., *Entsiklopediya voennoi razvedki 1918–1945 gg.* (2012), 467.

43. Pessi and Hertta Kuusinen to the Central Committee of the CPSU(B), as an attachment in Grigoryan's letter to Stalin, 3 Jan 1951, the Russian translation

with Molotov's comments, 4 Feb 1951, RGASPI, f. 82, op. 2, d. 1344, ll. 97–111, note on page 106.

44. P. Ruggenthaler, *The Concept of Neutrality in Stalin's Foreign Policy* (2015), 197–227. It also gives a good overview of the state of research on this theme.

45. Paasikivi's diary, 21 Nov and 22 Dec 1951; Suomi, *Kuningastie*, 159–66.

46. Gromyko to Molotov (based on cipher cables from Helsinki), 9 Jan 1952; draft cable to Helsinki, hand-corrected by Molotov, and the Politburo's draft decision, RGASPI, f. 82, op. 2, d. 1340, ll. 183–85; Bo Petersson, *Med Moskvas ögon* (1994), 82–83.

47. Directive cable to Helsinki, approved by the Politburo, 15 Mar 1952, APRF, f. 3, op. 66, d. 627, ll. 77–78. Paasikivi probably did not become at all aware of the idea of the visit, which came from the writer Hella Wuolijoki.

48. Zorin to Lebedev, 9 Jan 1953, quoted in Nevakivi, *Miten Kekkonen pääsi valtaan* (1996), 75.

49. L.M. Ashworth, *A History of International Thought* (2014), 197.

50. Gripenberg's diary, 30 June–1 July 1950; a tidied version in Paasikivi's diary, 1 July 1950. The former quoted by Polvinen, *J.K. Paasikivi*, vol. 5, 90–91.

51. Ambassador Ingemar Hägglöf's presentation at the Journalists' Club in Stockholm, 25 Aug 1970, Archives of Sweden's Ministry of Foreign Affairs (UD), HP 1 Af: 290.

Bibliography

Archives

Arbetarrörelsens arkiv (ARAB), Stockholm
Swedish Labor Movement Archives
Per Albin Hansson's papers

Arkhiv Prezidenta Rossiiskoi Federatsii (APRF), Moscow (Archives of the President of the Russian Federation)
    fond 3   Resolutions of the Politburo and the Central Committee

Arkhiv vneshnei politiki Rossiiskoi Federatsii (AVP RF), Moscow (Archives of Foreign Policy of the Russian Federation)
    fond 06   Molotov's secretariat
    fond 07   Vyshinski's secretariat
    fond 012   Dekanozov's secretariat
    fond 0135   Referentura for Finland

Central State Archives of Bulgaria (TsDA), Sofia
    fond 146-B   Georgi Dimitrov's papers

Eduskunnan kirjasto, Helsinki (Library of the Diet)
    Microfilm Collection no. 181: Post-World War II Foreign Policy Planning: State Department Records of Harry A. Notter, 1939–1945 (Notter File), copy from the US National Archives RG 59 (State Department)

Kansallisarkisto (KA), Helsinki (National Archives of Finland)
    Etsivä keskuspoliisi / Valtiollinen poliisi (EK-Valpo, Detective Central Police / State Police)
    Valtiovarainministeriö (VM, Ministry of Finances)
    Suojelupoliisi (Supo, Security Police)
    Yrjö Leino

J.K. Paasikivi
War Archives
   Headquarters (Päämaja, PM)
      Foreign Office (Ulk 1)
   Small collection no. 1172

Kansan arkisto, Helsinki
   Suomen kommunistinen puolue (SKP, Communist Party of Finland)
   Organization Sector (Org)
   Political Section (Pol)

Krigsarkivet (KrA), Stockholm
   Swedish Military Archives
   Försvarsstaben, Underrättelseavdelningen (FST/Und)

Library of Congress (LOC), Washington D.C.
   D.A. Volkogonov

The National Archives of the United Kingdom (TNA), London
National Archives (US), Washington D.C.
   Office of Strategic Services (OSS)
   Records of the Cabinet Office (CAB)
   Foreign Office (FO)
   Special Operations Executive ((HS)
   War Office (WO)

Rossiiskii gosudarstvennyi arkhiv sotsial'no-politicheskoi istorii (RGASPI), Moscow (Russian State Archive of Social and Political History)
fond 17	Central Committee of the CPSU
fond 77	Zhdanov
fond 82	Molotov
fond 495	Comintern
fond 162	Politburo, CPSU
fond 558	Stalin

Ulkoasiainministeriön arkisto (UM), Helsinki (Finnish Foreign Ministry Archives)
   110 Sota 1941–44 (War 1941–44)
   Personal cards of foreign diplomats

Urho Kekkonen Archives, Orimattila
   Memoes

Tsentral'nyi Arkhiv Federal'noi Sluzhby Bezopasnosti (TsA FSB), Moscow (Central Archives of the Russian Federal Security Service)
   fond 3

Published Sources

Bayerlein, Bernhard H. *"Der Verräter, Stalin, bist Du!" Vom Ende der Linken Solidarität. Komintern und kommunistische Parteien im Zweiten Weltkrieg 1939– 1941.* Unter Mitarbeit von Natalja S. Lebedewa, Michail Narinski und Gleb Albert. Berlin: Aufbau, 2008.

Cadogan, Alexander. *The Diaries of Sir Alexander Cadogan 1938–1945*, ed. David Dilks. London: Cassell, 1971. (Cadogan's diary).

Dimitrov, Georgi. *Dnevnik (9 mart 1933–6 februari 1949)*. Sofia: Universitetsko izdatelstvo Sv. Kliment Okhridski, 1997. Compared with translations: *Tagebücher 1933–1943*, ed. B.H. Bayerlein (Berlin: Aufbau-Verlag, 2000); *Journal 1933–1949*, intr. Gaël Moullec (Paris: Belin, 2003); *The Diary of Georgi Dimitrov 1933–1949*, ed. Ivo Banac (New Haven, CT: Yale University Press, 2003). (Dimitrov's diary).

Documents diplomatiques français, 1939 (3 septembre–31 décembre); 1940, tome I (1er janvier–10 juillet). Paris: Ministère des Affaires Étrangères / Peter Lang, 2002 and 2004.

Documents on British Policy Overseas (DBPO). Series I, volume IX. The Nordic Countries: From War to Cold War, 1944–1951, ed. by Tony Insall and Patrick Salmon. London: Foreign and Commonwealth Office / Routledge, 2011.

Dokumenty vnešnei politiki (DVP). Moscow: Meždunarodnye otnošenija.
XXII: 2. *1939 god*. (1992).
XXIII: 1–2. *1940–22 iyunjy 1941* (1998).
XXIV. *22 iyunya 1941–1 yanvarjy 1942* (2000).

Ehrensvärd, Carl August. *Dagsboksanteckningar 1938–1957*, ed. Erik Norberg. Kungl. Samfundet för utgivande av handskrifter rörande Skandinaviens historia, Handlingar del 16, Stockholm, 1991. (Ehrensvärd's diary).

Der Fall Berija. Protokoll einer Abrechnung. Das Plenum des ZK der KPdSU, Juli 1953. Stenographischer Bericht. Ed. and trans. Viktor Knoll u. Lothar Kölm. Berlin: Aufbau, 1993.

Foreign Relations of the United States (FRUS): Diplomatic Papers. Washington: GPO.

Grafström, Sven. *Anteckningar 1939–1944 and A*, utg. genom Stig Ekman. Kungl. Samfundet för utgivande av handskrifter rörande Skandinaviens historia, Handlingar del 14–15, Stockholm, 1989. (Grafström's diary).

Grif sekretnosti snyat: Poteri vooruzhennyh sil SSSR v voinakh, boevykh deistviyakh i voennykh konfliktakh. Statisticheskoe issledovanie, ed. G.F. Krivosheyev et al. Moscow: Voennoe izdatelstvo, 1993.

Gripenberg, G.A. *Dagbok 1944*. Kungl. Samfundet för utgivande av handskrifter rörande Skandinaviens historia, Handlingar del 41, Stockholm. (Gripenberg's diary).

Katyn: Plenniki neob"yavlennoi voiny, ed. N.S. Lebedeva et al. Moscow: MFD, 1997.

Khristoforov, V.S. *SSSR i Finlyandiya: protivostoyanie 1941–44 gg*. Moskva 2018.

Krėvė-Mickevičius, Vincas. "Conversations with Molotov," *Lituanus: Lithuanian Quarterly* 11 (1965), no. 2, 7–27. http://www.lituanus.org/1965/65_2_02_KreveMickevicius.html.

Kuusinen, Hertta. *Hamlet ystäväni. Kirjeitä Olavi Paavolaiselle*, ed. by Marja-Leena Mikkola. Helsinki: Tammi, 1999.

Lubjanka: Stalin i NKVD–NKGB–GUKR "Smerš," 1939–mart 1946, ed. by V.N. Khaustov, V.P. Naumov and N.S. Plotnikova. Moscow: MFD, 2006.

Maiski, Ivan Mihailovich *Dnevnik diplomata: London 1934–1943*, 2: 1 (Nauchnoe nasledstvo, tom. 33), ed. by A.O. Chubarian. Moscow: Nauka, 2009. Compared with translation *The Maisky Diaries*, ed. by Gabriel Gorodetsky. New Haven, CT: Yale University Press, 2015.

Moskva-Berlin: Politika i diplomatija Kremlja 1920–1941, ed. by G.N. Sevostyanov, vol. 3: 1933–1941. Moscow: Nauka and Arhiv Prezidenta RF, 2011.

Murhenäytelmän vuorosanat: Talvisodan hallituksen keskustelut (Discussions in Finnish Government during the Winter War), ed. by Ohto Manninen and Kauko Rumpunen. Helsinki: Edita, 2003.

"Na poroge pervogo raskola v 'sotsialisticheskom lagere"', Vasil Kolarov's notes, discussion with Stalin and Molotov, 10 Feb 1948, ed. by L. Ya. Gibianski, *Istoricheski arkhiv*, 1997, no. 4.

Na prieme u Stalina: Tetradi (zhurnaly) zapisei lits, prinyatyh I.V. Stalina (1924–1953 gg.), ed. by A.A. Chernobayev et al. Moscow: Novyi Hronograf, 2008. (Stalin's guestbook).

Organy gosudarstvennyi bezopasnosti SSSR v Velikoi Otechestvennyi voine: Sbornik dokumentov, I: 2, ed. by V.P. Yampolskii ym. Moscow: FSK / Kniga i biznes, 1995.

J.K. Paasikiven päiväkirjat 1944–1956. I–II, ed. by Yrjö Blomstedt and Matti Klinge. WSOY 1985–1986. (Paasikivi's diary).

Politbiuro i delo Beria: Sbornik dokumentov, ed. by O.B. Mozohin. Moscow: Kuchkovo polje, 2012.

Pribaltika i geopolitika 1935–1945 gg. Rassekretnye dokumenty Služby Vnešnei Razvedki Rossiiskoi Federatsii, ed. by L.F. Sotskov. Moscow: Ripol, 2010.

Puna-armeija Stalinin tentissä, eds. Ohto Manninen and Oleg A. Rzheshevski. Helsinki: Edita, 1997.

Schönherz, Zoltán, Notes, Comintern 30 Dec 1939, published by Krisztián Ungváry, "Die Weisungen der Komintern nach dem Molotov–Ribbentrop-Pakt an die kommunistischen Parteien am 30. Dezember 1939—dies bisher unbekannten Aufzeichnungen con Zoltán Schönherz," *Jahrbuch für historische Kommunismusforschung* 2010. Berlin: Aufbau Verlag, 2010.

Sekrety Gitlera na stole u Stalina, Mart-ijun' 1941 g., ed. by V.K. Vinogradov et al. Moscow: FSB, SVR and Mosgorarhiv, 1995.

Shearer, David R. and Vladimir Khaustov, *Stalin and the Lubianka: A Documentary History of the Political Police and Security Organs in the Soviet Union, 1922–1953*. New Haven, CT: Yale University Press, 2015.

SSSR i germanski vopros, 1941–1949: Dokumenty iz Arkhiva vneshnei politiki Rossiiskoi Federatsii, eds. G.P. Kynin and J. Laufer, I–III. Moscow: Mezhdunarodnye otnosheniya, 1996, 2000, 2003.

Stalin, J.V. *Teokset*. 7. osa. 1925. Petroskoi: Karjalais-suomalaisen SNT:n Valtion kustannusliike, 1951.

Tanner, Väinö. Unohdetut päiväkirjat 1943–1944. Toim. Hannu Rautkallio and Lasse Lehtinen. Paasilinna, 2011. (Tanner's diary).

Tegeranskaya konferentsia rukovoditelei treh derzhav—SSSR, SShA i Velikobritanii (28 noyabrya–1 dekabrya 1943 g.). Sovetskij Soyuz na mezhdunarodnykh konferentsiakh perioda Velikoj Otechestvennoj vojny 1941–1945 gg. Sbornik dokumentov. Tom 2, ed. by A.A. Gromyko et al. Moscow, 1978.

TsK VKP(b) i natsional'nyi vopros, vol. 2, 1933–1945, eds. L.S. Gatagova, L.P. Kosheleva, L.A. Rogovaya, Dzh. Kadio. Moscow: Rosspen, 2009.

Tuntematon talvisota: Neuvostoliiton salaisen poliisin kansiot (Tuntematon), eds. T. Vihavainen and A. Saharov. Helsinki: Edita, 2009.

Varjo Suomen yllä: Stalinin salaiset kansiot, ed. by T. Vihavainen, O. Manninen, K. Rentola and S. Zhuravlyov. Jyväskylä: Docendo, 2017.

Venona Telegrams. Published by National Security Agency. www.nsa.gov.

Vernadski, V.I. *Dnevniki 1935–1941 v dvukh knigakh*, ed. V.P. Volkov, 2. Moscow: Nauka, 2006.

Vielä yksi kirje. Hertta Kuusisen dramaattinen elämä ja rakkaus Yrjö Leinoon, ed. by Olle Leino. Helsinki: WSOY, 1990.

Voennaya razvedka informiruyet: Dokumenty Razvedupravleniya Krasnoi Armii. Yanvar' 1939–iyun' 1941, ed. by V.A. Gavrilov. Moscow: Demokratiya 2008.

Vostochnaya Evropa v dokumentakh rossiiskikh arkhivov, I, 1944–1948 gg., ed. by T.V. Volokitina et al. Novosibirsk: Sibirskii hronograf, 1997.

Zimnyaya voina 1939–1940 gg.: Issledovanija, dokumenty, kommentarii (Zimnyaya), ed. A.N. Saharov, V.S. Khristoforov and T. Vihavainen. Moscow: Akademkniga, 2009.

Zimnyaya voina 1939–1940 gg. v dokumentakh NKVD, eds. S.K. Bernev and A.I. Rupasov. St Petersburg: "Lik" 2010.

Media

Numbers of *Die Kommunistische Internationale, Pravda, Social-Demokraten, Izvestija* and others.

Books and Articles

Aga-Rossi, Elena and Victor Zaslavsky. *Togliatti e Stalin: Il Pci e la politica estera staliniana negli archivi di Mosca*. Bologna: il Mulino, 1997.

Aga-Rossi, Elena and Victor Zaslavsky. *Stalin and Togliatti: Italy and the Origins of the Cold War*. Stanford University Press, 2011.

Agosti, Aldo. *Palmiro Togliatti*. Turin: UTET, 1996.

Agrell, Wilhelm. *Venona: Spåren från ett underrättelsekrig*. Lund: Historiska Media, 2003.

Aleksandrov-Agentov, A.M. *Ot Kollontai do Gorbacheva*. Moscow: Mezhdunarodnye otnosheniya, 1994.

Alekseyev, M.A., A.I. Kolpakidi and V.Ia. Kochik, *Entsiklopedija voennoi razvedki 1918–1945 gg.* Moscow: Kuchkovo polje and Assosiatsija "Voennaja kniga," 2012.

Androsova, Tatjana. "Kauppapolitiikka Suomen ja Neuvostoliiton suhteissa vuoden 1944 jälkeen." *Historiallinen aikakauskirja* 100 (2002): 7.

Applebaum, Anne. *Iron Curtain: The Crushing of Eastern Europe 1944–1956*. New York: Doubleday, 2012.

Apunen, Osmo and Corinna Wolff. *Pettureita ja patriootteja: Taistelu Suomen ulko-ja turvallisuuspolitiikan suunnasta 1938–1948*. Helsinki: SKS, 2009.

Armstrong, John A. *Ukrainian Nationalism 1939–1945*. New York: Columbia University Press, 1955.

Assarsson, Vilhelm. *I skuggan av Stalin*. Stockholm: Bonnier, 1963.

Aunesluoma, Juhana. *Britain, Sweden and the Cold War, 1945–54: Understanding Neutrality*. London: Palgrave Macmillan, 2003.

Beria, Sergo. *Moi otets Beria.* Moscow: Olma, 2002.

Boheman, Erik. *På vakt: Kabinettsekreterare under andra världskriget.* Stockholm: Norstedts, 1964.

Bohlen, Charles W. *Witness to History 1929–1969.* New York: Norton, 1973.

Bouverie, Tom. *Appeasing Hitler: Chamberlain, Churchill and the Road to War.* London 2019.

Bushueva, T.S. *Krasnaya armiya est' nechto besprimernoye v mirovoi istorii: Ocherki istorii sovetskoi voennoi politiki 1924 g.–22 ijunja 1941 g.* Moscow: IRI RAN, 2011.

Butler, Susan. *Roosevelt and Stalin: Portrait of a Partnership.* New York: Knopf, 2015.

Carleton, Gregory. *Sexual Revolution in Bolshevik Russia.* Pittsburgh: University of Pittsburgh Press, 2005.

Carley, M.J. *1939: The Alliance That Never Was and the Coming of World War II.* Chicago, IL: Ivan R. Dee, 1999.

Carlgren, Wilhelm. *Svensk utrikespolitik 1939–1945.* Stockholm: Allmänna Förlaget, 1973.

Carlsson, Erik. *Gustaf V och andra världskriget.* Lund: Historiska Media, 2006.

Carlton, David. *Churchill and the Soviet Union.* Manchester: Manchester University Press, 2000.

Chang, Jung and Jon Halliday. *Mao: The Unknown Story.* London: Jonathan Cape, 2005.

Chen Jian, *Mao's China and the Cold War.* Chapel Hill, NC: The University of North Carolina Press, 2001.

Chuev, Feliks. *Molotov: Poluderzhavnyi vlastelin.* Moscow: Olma Press, 1999.

Cohen, Stephen F. *Bukharin and the Bolshevik Revolution: A Political Biography, 1888–1938.* New York: Knopf, 1973.

Costigliola, Frank. *Roosevelt's Lost Alliances: How Personal Politics Helped Start the Cold War.* Princeton, NJ: Princeton University Press, 2012.

Davies, Norman. *Rising '44: The Battle for Warsaw.* London: Macmillan, 2003.

Degtyarev, K. and A. Kolpakidi, *Vneshnyaya razvedka SSSR.* Moscow: Jauza, Eksmo, 2009.

Dienko, Anatoli. *Razvedka i kontrrazvedka v litsakh.* Moscow: Russkii mir, 2002.

Dimitrov, Vesselin. *Stalin's Cold War: Soviet Foreign Policy, Democracy and Communism in Bulgaria, 1941–48.* London: Palgrave Macmillan, 2008.

Djilas, Milovan. *Conversations with Stalin.* New York: Harcourt, Brace and World, 1962.

Duroselle, J.B. *Politique étrangère de la France. L'Abime, 1939–1944.* Paris: Seuil, 1986.

Edelman, Robert. *Spartak Moscow: A History of the People's Team in the Workers' State.* Ithaca, NY, and London: Cornell University Press, 2009.

Evans, Helena P. *Diplomatic Deceptions: Anglo-Soviet Relations and the Fate of Finland 1944–1948.* Helsinki: SKS, 2011.

Flinckenberg-Glushkoff, Marianna. *Pietarilainen polkuhevonen: Lapsuus kolmen kulttuurin katveessa.* Helsinki: Tammi, 2013.

Folly, Martin H. *Churchill, Whitehall and the Soviet Union, 1940–45.* London: Macmillan, 2000.

Förster, Jürgen. "The German Military's Image of Russia," in *Russia: War, Peace and Diplomacy*. Essays in Honor of John Erickson, L. and M. Erickson. London: Weidenfeld and Nicolson, 2004.

Gaddis, J.L. *George F. Kennan: An American Life*. New York: Penguin Press, 2011.

Garthoff, Raymond L. *Soviet Leaders and Intelligence: Assessing the American Adversary during the Cold War*. Washington, DC: Georgetown University Press, 2015.

Gat, Azar. "Containment and Cold War before the Nuclear Age: The Phoney War as Allied Strategy According to Liddell Hart," *Northern European Overture to War, 1939–1941*, ed. by Michael H. Clemmesen and Marcus S. Faulkner. Leiden: Brill, 2013.

Genis, Vladimir. *Nevernye slugi rezhima: Pervye sovetskie nevozvrashchentsy (1920–1933)*, vol. 2. Moscow, 2012.

Gerrard, Craig. *The Foreign Office and Finland: Diplomatic Sideshow*. London: Frank Cass, 2005.

Gilbert, Martin. *Winston Churchill*, vol. VII, *Road to Victory*. London: Heinemann, 1986.

Gorlizki, Yoram and Oleg Khlevniuk, *Cold Peace: Stalin and the Soviet Ruling Circle, 1945–1953*. Oxford: Oxford University Press, 2004.

Gorodetsky, Gabriel. *Grand Delusion: Stalin and the German Invasion of Russia*. New Haven, CT: Yale University Press, 1999.

Hanhimäki, Jussi. *Scandinavia and the United States: An Insecure Friendship*. New York: Twayne, 1997.

Harbutt, Fraser J. *Yalta 1945: Europe and America at the Crossroads*. Cambridge: Cambridge University Press, 2010.

Haslam, Jonathan. *Russia's Cold War: From the October Revolution to the Fall of the Wall*. New Haven, CT, and London: Yale University Press, 2011.

Haslam, Jonathan. '"Humint" by Default and the Problem of Trust: Soviet Intelligence, 1917–1941," *Secret Intelligence in the European States System, 1918–1989*, eds. Karina Urbach and Jonathan Haslam. Stanford, CA: Stanford University Press, 2014.

Haslam, Jonathan. *Near and Distant Neighbours: A New History of Soviet Intelligence*. Oxford: Oxford University Press, 2015.

Haslam, Jonathan. *The Spectre of War: International Communism and the Origins of World War II*. Princeton, NJ: Princeton University Press, 2021.

Haynes, John Earl and Harvey Klehr. *Venona: Decoding Soviet Espionage in America*. New Haven, CT: Yale University Press, 1999.

Heiskanen, Raimo. *Saadun tiedon mukaan . . . Päämajan johtama tiedustelu 1939–1945*. Helsinki: Otava, 1989.

Jeffery, Keith. *MI6: The History of the Secret Intelligence Service, 1909–1949*. London: Bloomsbury, 2010.

Jokisipilä, Markku. *Aseveljiä vai liittolaisia?* Helsinki: SKS, 2004.

Jonas, Michael. *Wipert von Blücher und Finnland: Alternativpolitik und Diplomatie im "Dritten Reich"*. Helsinki, 2009.

Jussila, Osmo. *Terijoen hallitus*. WSOY, 1985.

Käkönen, U.A. *Sotilasasiamiehenä Moskovassa 1939*. Helsinki: Otava, 1966.

Kauppala, Pekka. *Paluu vankileirien teille: Suomesta Neuvostoliittoon luovutettujen kohtalo 1940–1955*. Helsinki: Gummerus, 2011.

Ken, Oleg and Aleksandr Rupasov and Lennart Samuelson. *Shvetsiya v politike Moskvy 1930–1950-e gody*. Moscow: Rosspen, 2005.

Ken, Oleg and Aleksandr Rupasov, *Zapadnoe prigranitš'je: Politbjuro TsK VKP(b) i otnošenija SSSR s zapadnymi sosednimi gosudarstvami, 1928–1934*. Moscow: Algoritm, 2014.

Kenez, Peter. *Hungary from the Nazis to the Soviets: The Establishment of the Communist Regime in Hungary, 1944–1948*. Cambridge: Cambridge University Press, 2006.

Ketola, Eino. *Kansalliseen kansanvaltaan: Suomen itsenäisyys, sosialidemokraatit ja Venäjän vallankumous 1917*. Helsinki: Tammi, 1987.

Khaustov, Vladimir and Lennart Samuelson. *Stalin, NKVD i repressii 1936–1938 gg*. Moscow: Rosspen, 2009.

Khlevniuk, Oleg V. *Master of the House: Stalin and His Inner Circle*. New Haven, CT: Yale University Press, 2009.

Khlevniuk, Oleg. *Hozyain: Stalin i utverzhdenie stalinskoi diktatury*. Moscow: Rosspen, 2009.

Khristoforov, V.S. *Organy gosbezopasnosti SSSR v 1941–1945 gg*. Moscow: Izd. GAU Mosky, 2011.

Khristoforov, V.S. "Finljandija dolžna dobit'sja mira, no sohranit' nezavisimost'," in: *Velikaya otetšestvennaja voina: 1944 god*, ed. V.S. Khristoforov. Moscow: Izd. GBU "TsGA Moskvy," 2014.

Khristoforov, V.S. "Za kulisami sovetsko-finljandskih peregovorov o peremirii. 1943–1944 gody." *Novaia i noveishaia istoria* 2015, no. 2.

Khristoforov, V.S. *SSSR—Finlandiya: Protivostoyanie 1941–1944 gg*. Helsinki: IRI RAN, 2018.

Khrushchev, N.S. *Vremya, lyudi, vlast': Vospominaniya*, 2. Moscow: Moskovski novosti, 1999.

Kilin, Juri. *Suurvallan rajamaa*. Rovaniemi: Societa Historiae Finlandiae, September 2001.

Kirpichenko, Vadim. *Razvedka: litsa i lichnosti*. Moscow: Geja, 1998.

Kochanski, Halik. *The Eagle Unbowed: Poland and the Poles in the Second World War*. London: Allen Lane, 2012.

Kolpakidi, A.I. *Entsiklopedija sekretnyh služb Rossii*. Moscow: Astrel: Transitkniga, 2004.

Korobochkin, Maxim. "Soviet Views on Sweden's Neutrality and Foreign Policy, 1945–50," in *Peaceful Coexistence? Soviet Union and Sweden in the Khrushchev Era*, ed. by H. Carlbäck, A. Komarov and K. Molin. Stockholm: Södertörn University, 2010.

Kotkin, Stephen. *Magnetic Mountain: Stalinism as a Civilization*. Berkeley, CA: University of California, 1995.

Kotkin, Stephen. *Stalin*. Vol. 1: *Paradoxes of Power, 1878–1928*. New York: Penguin Press, 2014.

Kotkin, Stephen. *Stalin*. Vol. 2: *Waiting for Hitler, 1929–1941*. New York: Penguin Press, 2017.

Kramer, Mark. "Stalin, Soviet Policy, and the Consolidation of a Communist Bloc in Eastern Europe, 1944–53," in Vladimir Tismaneanu (ed.), *Stalinism Revisited: The Establishment of Communist Regimes in East-Central Europe*. Budapest: CEU Press, 2009.

Kramer, Mark. "Stalin, the Split with Yugoslavia, and Soviet–East European Efforts to Reassert Control, 1948–1953," in Mark Karmer and Vit Smetana (eds.), *Imposing, Maintaining, and Tearing Open the Iron Curtain: The Cold War and East-Central Europe, 1945–1989*. The Harvard Cold War Book Series. Lanham, MD: Lexington Books, 2014.

Kronvall, Olof. Den bräckliga barriären: Finland i svensk säkerhetspolitik 1948–1962. Stockholm: Försvarshögkolan, 2003.

Kuznetsov, N.G. *Krutye povoroty: Iz zapisok admirala*, ed. R.V. Kuznetsova. Moscow: Molodaja gvardija, 1995.

Laaksonen, Lasse. *Todellisuus ja harhat*. Helsinki: SKS, 1998.

Larsson, D. and I. Palmklint (eds.), *Raoul Wallenberg: Redovisning av den svensk-ryska arbetsgruppen*. Stockholm: Utrikesdepartemet, 2000.

Lebedeva, N.S. 'Katynskoe prestuplenie', in A.V. Torkunov and A.D. Rotfeld (eds.), *Belye plyatna—chernye plyatna: Slozhnye voprosy v rossiisko-polskkih otnosheniyakh*. Moscow: Aspekt Press 2010.

Leino, Yrjö. *Kommunisti sisäministerinä*. Helsinki: Tammi, 1958.

Leskinen, Jari and Pekka Silvast. *Suljettu aika: Porkkala Neuvostoliiton sotilaallisena tukikohtana vuosina 1944–1956*. Helsinki: WSOY, 2001.

Lieven, Dominic. *Towards the Flame: Empire, War and the End of Tsarist Russia*. London: Allen Lane, 2015.

Logevall, Fredrik. *Embers of War: The Fall of an Empire and the Making of America's Vietnam*. New York: Random House, 2012.

Lorbeer, H.J. *Westmächte gegen die Sowjetunion 1939–1941*. Freiburg: Rombach, 1975.

Lukacs, John. *The Legacy of the Second World War*. New Haven, CT: Yale University Press, 2010.

Majander, Mikko. *Pohjoismaa vai kansandemokratia? Sosiaalidemokraatit, kommunistit ja Suomen kansainvälinen asema 1944–1951*. Helsinki: Suomalaisen kirjallisuuden seura, 2004.

Majander, Mikko. *Demokratiaa dollareilla*. Helsinki: Otava, 2007.

Manninen, Ohto. "Neuvostoliiton operatiiviset suunnitelmat 1939–1941 Suomen suunnalla," *Sotahistoriallinen Aikakauskirja*, 1992.

Manninen, Ohto. *Kerttu Nuorteva: Neuvostokaunotar vakoilujohtajana*. Helsinki: Edita, 2006.

Manninen, Ohto. *Miten Suomi valloitetaan: Puna–armeijan operaatiosuunnitelmat 1939–1944*. Helsinki: Edita, 2008.

Manninen, Ohto. "NKVD:n henkilökohtaiset kontaktit Moskovan rauhan taustalla," *Sotilasaikakauslehti*, 2014: 2, 50–52.

Manninen, Ohto and Raimo Salokangas, *Eljas Erkko: Vaikenematon valtiomahti*. Helsinki: WSOY, 2009.

Martelius, Juha. "Leinon vankien pidätys ja luovutus Neuvostoliittoon," in *Turvallisuuspoliisi 75 vuotta 1919–1994*, eds. Matti Simola and Jukka Salovaara. Helsinki: Sisäasiainministeriö, 1994.

Mastny, Vojtech. *Russia's Road to Cold War: Diplomacy, Warfare and the Politics of Communism, 1941–1945*. New York: Columbia University Press, 1979.

Mayers, David. *The Ambassadors and America's Soviet Policy*. New York: Oxford University Press, 1995.

Meinander, Henrik. *Suomi 1944: Sota, yhteiskunta, tunnemaisema*. Helsinki: Siltala, 2009.

Meltyukhov, M.I. *Upushchennyi shans Stalina: Sovetski Sojuz i bor'ba za Evropy: 1939–1941. Dokumenty, fakty, suzhdeniya*. Moscow, 2000.

Mikojan, Anastas. *Tak bylo*. Moscow, 2000.

Miscamble, Wilson D. *George F. Kennan and the Making of American Foreign Policy, 1947–1950*. Princeton, NJ: Princeton University Press, 1992.

Modin, Yuri (with Jean-Charles Deniaux and Agnieszka Ziarek). *My Five Cambridge Friends: Philby, Burgess, Maclean, Blunt, and Cairncross by their KGB Controller*. London: Headline Books, 1994.

Mononen, Toni. *Saadun tiedon muokkaajat: Päämajan tiedustelutoimisto viholliskuvan muodostajana 1939–1944*. Helsinki: Maanpuolustuskorkeakoulu, 2023.

Munch-Petersen, Thomas. *The Strategy of Phoney War: Britain, Sweden and the Iron Ore Question 1939–1940*. Stockholm: Militärhistoriska förlaget, 1981.

Murashko, G.P. "Fevral'skii krisiz 1948 g. v Tshehoslovakii i sovetskoe rukovodstvo. Po novym materialam rossiiskikh arkhivov." *Novaya i noveishaya istoriya* 1998, no. 3.

Murphy, David E. *What Stalin Knew: The Enigma of Barbarossa*. New Haven, CT, and London: Yale University Press, 2005.

Naimark, Norman M. *The Russians in Germany: A History of the Soviet Zone of Occupation, 1945–1949*. Cambridge, MA: The Belknap Press of Harvard University Press, 1995.

Naimark, Norman M. *Stalin and the Fate of Europe: The Postwar Struggle for Sovereignty*. Cambridge, MA: The Belknap Press of the Harvard University Press, 2019.

Nevakivi, Jukka. *Apu jota ei pyydetty*. Helsinki: Tammi, 1972, updated as *Apu jota ei annettu*. Helsinki: WSOY, 2000.

Nevakivi, Jukka. *Miten Kekkonen pääsi valtaan ja Suomi suomettui*. Helsinki: Otava, 1996.

Nevezhin, V.A. *Sindrom nastupatel'noi voiny: Sovetskaya propaganda v preddverii "svyashchennyh boev," 1939–1941 gg*. Moscow: Airo-XX 1997.

Norberg, Erik. "Det militära hotet. Försvarsattachéernas syn på krigsutbrottet 1939," in B. Hugemark (ed.), *Stormvarning. Sverige inför andra världskriget*. Norstedt: Probus, 1989.

Noskova, A.F. "1944 god: kompromissy i smena veh v sovetskoi politike na pol'skom napravlenii," in V.S. Khristoforov (ed.), *Velikaia Otečestvennaia voina. 1944 god:* Issledovanija. dokumenty, kommentarii. Moscow: Memorial, 2014.

Ocherki istorii Rossiiskoi vneshnei razvedki. Moscow: Mezhdunarodnye otnoshenia. Vol. 3: *1933–1941 gody*, ed. E.M. Primakov et al. (1997); Vol. 5: *1945–1965 gody*, ed. S.N. Lebedev et al. (2003).

Osborn, Patrick R. *Operation Pike: Britain versus the Soviet Union, 1939–1941*. Westport, CT: Greenwood Press, 2000.

Peltovuori, Risto. *Saksa ja Suomen talvisota*. Helsinki: Otava, 1975.

Petrov, N.V. "Stalin i organy NKVD-MGB v sovjetizatsii stran Tsentral'noi i Vostotšnoi Evropy. 1945-1953 gg." Unpublished dissertation, Amsterdamin yliopisto, 2008.

Petrov, N.V. *Po stsenariju Stalina: rol' organov NKVD–MGB SSSR v sovjetizatsii stran Tsentral'noi i Vostochnoi Evropy. 1945–1953 gg.* Moscow: Rosspen, 2011.

Petrov, N.V. *Kto rukovodil organami gosbezopasnosti 1941–1954: Spravochnik.* Moscow, 2010.

Polvinen, Tuomo. *Teheranista Jaltaan: Suomi kansainvälisessä politiikassa* 2: 1944. Helsinki: WSOY, 1980.

Polvinen, Tuomo. *J.K. Paasikivi: Valtiomiehen elämäntyö.* Helsinki: WSOY. Vol. 3: 1939–1944 (1995); Vol. 4: 1944–1948 (1997); Vol. 5: 1948–1956 (1999).

Pons, Silvio. *Stalin and the Inevitable War 1936–1941.* London: Frank Cass, 2002.

Pons, Silvio. *La rivoluzione globale: Storia del comunismo internazionale 1917–1991.* Turin: Einaudi, 2012.

Radzinski, Edvard. *Stalin.* Helsinki: WSOY, 1996.

Rainer, Janos. *Imre Nagy: A Biography.* London: I.B. Tauris, 2009.

Ranta, Kalle. *Arpi korvassa ja sydämessä: Muistelmia ja mietelmiä myrskyisän vuosisatamme historian pyörteissä tuhlatusta elämästä.* Helsinki: WSOY, 2000.

Rautkallio, Hannu. *Pohjoinen liitto: Wallenbergit ja Suomi.* Helsinki: Otava, 2021.

Rees, Laurence. *World War II Behind Closed Doors: Stalin, the Nazis and the West.* New York: Pantheon Books, 2008.

Rentola, Kimmo. *Niin kylmää että polttaa: Kommunistit, Kekkonen ja Kreml 1947–1958.* Helsinki: Otava, 1997.

Rentola, Kimmo. *Neuvostodiplomaatin loikkaus Helsingissä 1930.* Helsinki: Suojelupoliisi, 2007.

Rentola, Kimmo. "Intelligence and Stalin's Two Crucial Decisions in the Winter War, 1939–40." *The International History Review* 35: 4 (Oct. 2013).

Revolusjon, kjærlighet, diplomati: Aleksandra Kollontaj og Norden, ed. Yngvild Sørbye. Oslo: Unipub, 2008.

Richter, Heinz A. *Griechenland 1940–1950: Die Zeit der Bürgerkriege.* Mainz: Ruhpolding, 2012.

Rintala, Ohto. *Yhdysvallat ja Saksan koalition pienet maat: Suomen, Romanian ja Unkarin sodanjälkeinen asema Yhdysvaltain ulkoministeriön suunnittelupöydällä 1942–1945.* Politiikan ja talouden tutkimuksen laitoksen julkaisuja 15. Helsinki, 2014.

Roberts, Geoffrey. *Stalin's Wars: From World War to Cold War, 1939–1953.* New Haven, CT, and London: Yale University Press, 2006.

Roman, Eric. *Hungary and the Victor Powers, 1945–1950.* London: Macmillan, 1996.

Roterbloem, Kees. *Partner in Crime: The Life and Times of Andrei Zhdanov, 1896–1948.* Montreal and Kingston: McGill-Queens University Press, 2004.

Rowe, Lars. *Pechenganikel: Soviet Industry, Russian Pollution, and the Outside World.* PhD dissertation, University of Oslo, 2013.

Ruggenthaler, Peter. *Stalins großer Bluff: Die Geschichte der Stalin-Note in Dokumenten der sowjetischen Führung.* Munich: Oldenbourg, 2007.

Ruggenthaler, Peter. *The Concept of Neutrality in Stalin's Foreign Policy, 1945–1953.* New York: Lexington Books, 2015.

Rupasov, Aleksandr and Lennart Samuelson. *Sovetsko–shvedskie otnoshenia: Vtoraja polovina 1940-kh—nachalo 1960-kh gg.* Moscow: Rosspen, 2014.

Rzheshevski, O.A. *Stalin i Churchill. Vstrechi. Besedy. Diskussii. Dokumenty, kommentarii 1941–1945.* Moscow: Nauka, 2004.

Sebag Montefiore, Simon. *Stalin: The Court of the Red Tsar*. London: Weidenfeld and Nicolson, 2003.

Self, Robert. *Neville Chamberlain: A Biography*. London: Ashgate, 2006.

Semirjaga, M.I. "Neuvostoliittolais-suomalainen sota v. 1939–40," *Talvisota, Suomi ja Venäjä*, ed. T. Vihavainen. Helsinki: SHS, 1991.

Seppinen, Jukka. *Hitler, Stalin ja Suomi*. Helsinki: Minerva, 2009.

Sinitsyn, Jelisei. *Vaiettu totuus* (Otava 1995), in Russian *Rezident svidelstvuet*. Moscow: Geja, 1996.

Smetana, Vit. "Concessions or Conviction? Czechoslovakia's Road to the Cold War and the Soviet Bloc," in *Imposing, Maintaining and Tearing Down the Iron Curtain: The Cold War and East-Central Europe, 1945–1989*, eds. Mark Kramer and Vit Smetana. Lanham, MD: Lexington Books, 2014.

Sokolov, B.V. "The Soviet Policy towards the Baltic States in 1939–41," *Northern European Overture to War: From Memel to Barbarossa*, eds. Michael H. Clemmesen and Marcus S. Faulkner. Leiden: Brill, 2013.

Sorokin, A.K. *"Prakticheskii rabotnik" Georgi Malenkov*. Moscow: Sistema, 2021.

Steiner, Zara. *The Triumph of the Dark: European International History 1933–1939*. Oxford: Oxford University Press, 2011.

Sudoplatov, Pavel et al., *Special Tasks: The Memoirs of an Unwanted Witness, a Soviet Spymaster*. Boston, MA: Little, Brown, 1994.

Suomen puolustusvoimat 100 vuotta, ed. by Vesa Tynkkynen and Mikko Karjalainen. Helsinki: Edita, 2018.

Suomi, Juhani. *Kuningastie. Urho Kekkonen 1950–1956*. Helsinki: Otava, 1990.

Suomi, Juhani. *Mannerheim—Viimeinen kortti? Ylipäällikkö-presidentti*. Helsinki: Siltala, 2013.

Tala, Henrik. *Suomea pelastamassa*. Helsinki: Helsingin yliopisto, 2012.

Tamkin, Nicholas. *Britain, Turkey and the Soviet Union, 1940–45*. London: Palgrave Macmillan, 2009.

Tanner, Väinö. *Suomen tie rauhaan 1943–44*. Helsinki: Tammi, 1952.

Thing, Morten, ed. *Guldet fra Moskva. Finansieringen af de nordiske kommunistpartier 1917–1990*. Helsinki: Forum, 2001.

Thomas, Martin. "Imperial Defence or Diversionary Attack? Anglo-French Strategic Planning in the Near East, 1936-40," in Martin S. Alexander and William J. Philpott (eds.), *Anglo-French Defence Relations between the Wars*. London: Palgrave Macmillan, 2002.

Tributs, V.F. *Baltiitsy srazhayatsya*. Moscow: Voenizdat, 1985.

Tuomioja, Erkki. *Häivähdys punaista*. Helsinki: Tammi, 2006.

Turtola, Martti. *Risto Ryti: Elämä isänmaan puolesta*. Helsinki: Otava, 1994.

Van Dyke, Carl. *The Soviet Invasion of Finland 1939–40*. London: Frank Cass, 1997.

Velikaia Otechestvennaia bez grifa sekretnosti. Kniga poter'. Noveishje spravochnie izdanie. Moscow, 2009.

Veterany vneshnei razvedki Rossii, ed. by T.V. Samolis. Moscow: SVR Rossii, 1995.

Vihavainen, Timo. *Stalin ja suomalaiset*. Helsinki: Otava, 1998.

Visuri, Pekka. *Mannerheimin ja Rytin vaikeat valinnat*. Helsinki: Docendo, 2013.

Visuri, Pekka. *Paasikiven Suomi suurvaltojen puristuksessa 1944–1947*. Helsinki: Docendo, 2015.

Vladimirov, Viktor. *Kohti talvisotaa*. Helsinki: Otava, 1995.

Vlizkov, Andrei. "Lagernaja planida Aleksandra Starostina," *Molodezh Severa*, no. 45, 6.11.2003 www.mskomi.ru/arhiv/new078.htm

Volkogonov, D. *Sem vozhdei: Galereya liderov SSSR*, 1. Moscow: Novosti, 1995.

Volkogonov, D. *Stalin: Triumf i tragedija, Politicheskii portret*. Moscow: Novosti, 1989.

Volokitina, Tatiana, G. Murashko, A. Noskova and T. Pokivailova, *Moscow i Vostochnaia Evropa: Stanovlenie politicheskikh rezhimov sovetskogo tipa (1949– 1953): Ocherki istorii*. Moscow: ROSSPEN, 2008.

Volynets, Aleksei. *Zhdanov*. Moscow: Molodaja gvardija, 2013.

Voskresenskaja, Zoja. *Pod psevdonimom Irina*. Moscow: Sovremennik, 1997.

Wahlbäck, Krister. *Jättens andedräkt: Finlandsfrågan i svensk politik 1809–2009*. Stockholm: Atlantis, 2011.

Weinstein, Allen and Alexander Vassiliev, *The Haunted Wood: Soviet Espionage in America—The Stalin Era*. New York: Random House, 1999.

West, Nigel and Oleg Tsarev, *Crown Jewels: The British Secrets at the Heart of the KGB Archives*. New Haven, CT: Yale University Press, 1999.

Yerofeyev, Vladimir. *Diplomat: kniga vospominanii*. Moscow: Zebra E, 2005.

Zubkova, Elena. *Pribaltika i Kreml 1940–1953*. Moscow: RAN, 2008.

Zubkova, Elena. *Poslevoennoe sovetskoe obshchestvo: Politika i povsednevnost' 1945– 1953*. Moscow: Rosspen, 2006.

Zubok, Vladislav and Constantine Pleshakov. *Inside the Kremlin's Cold War: From Stalin to Khrushchev*. Cambridge, MA: Harvard University Press, 1996.

Index